Translating
World Affairs

by Ruth A. Roland

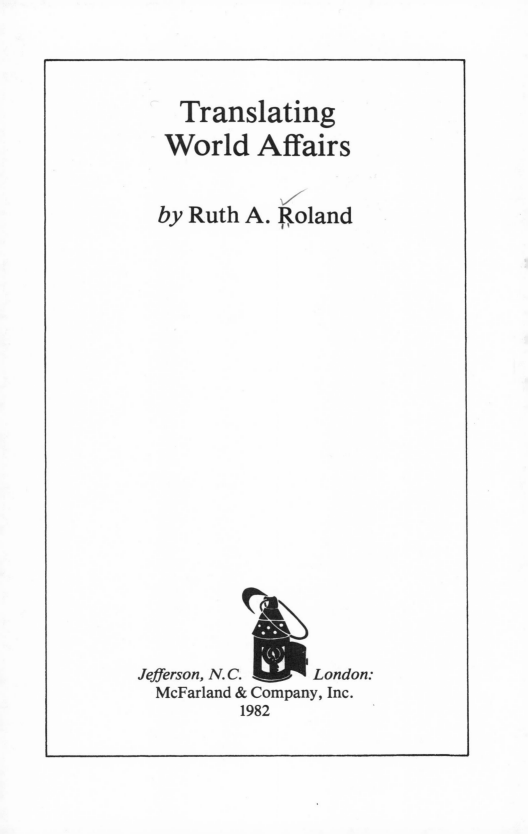

Jefferson, N.C.   *London:*
McFarland & Company, Inc.
1982

Library of Congress Cataloging in Publication Data

Roland, Ruth A., 1922—
Translating world affairs.

Bibliography: p.
Includes index.
1. International relations — Translating — History.
2. World politics — Translating.
3. Translating and interpreting — History.
I. Title.
JX1311.R74   327'.0141   82-6521   AACR2

ISBN 0-89950-047-1

Manufactured in the United States of America

McFarland & Company, Inc., Publishers
Box 611, Jefferson, North Carolina 28640

Table of Contents

"The question is," said Alice, whether you can make words mean different things."

"The question is," said Humpty, "which is to be master — that's all."

Lewis Carroll,
Through the Looking-glass

Foreword

Somewhere in the chronicles of political history there hides a "missing link." Library shelves overflow with accounts of bilateral and multilateral conferences, meetings with chiefs of state, as well as regular, ongoing political and economic contacts at the international level. Surely, thoughtful readers must often wonder about the practical, functional aspect of intercourse among nations, of which none is more basic than language.

According to both the *Bible* and much of the world's cultural mythology, at one time in the far-distant past, all human beings spoke a single tongue. (The story of the Tower of Babel may be found in Genesis 11:7-9.) But verifiable history does not recall such an idyllic period. In all ages, at all times, relatively few people, not excluding national leaders, have boasted true fluency in a tongue not their own. According to Plutarch, Cleopatra spoke so many languages that she was able to greet most foreign ambassadors in their own tongue, whether they were Arabs, Ethiopians, Hebrews, Medes, or Syrians, and Mithridates the Great is thought to have known more than twenty languages. But these persons were as exceptional then as they would be today.

This being the case, how have mutually incomprehensible humans maintained their ceaseless, intimate contact throughout the ages? We all know the answer. Bilingual or multilingual people, known as interpreters or translators, have been the intermediaries. Without their services, there could have been no "international relations." But how seldom are these invisible yet indispensable persons noted by the historians! When we read, for example, that Sir Percival Englishman was received at the Court of Siam in 1670, in all probability we are left to conjecture how Sir Percival communicated with the Siamese. Clearly, an interpreter was at work. But who was he? Siamese? English? Some other foreigner? Was he a courtier, a professional diplomat, a priest, a merchant?

Translators and interpreters have been largely ignored by historians for two reasons. First, there is often a total lack of historical documentation. People of power and influence in centuries past seldom considered a

v

mere interpreter's name to be worth recording. Secondly, most historians, confined to "important" events and to the limitations imposed by the desired size of their books, cannot be expected to include every intriguing tidbit they may uncover. But might it not be worth while to devote some special attention to these key individuals of political history? Such is the intent of this work, which is presented as a tribute to *both* translators and interpreters, although, for the sake of brevity, only the concept "translating" appears in the title.

A few disclaimers may be in order. This book is not a study in linguistics. Written not by a linguist but by a political scientist, it is intended for the general reader who may be curious about the work of translators and interpreters, or who may have an interest in international affairs or diplomatic history. But even within this restricted scope, it does not purport to be either comprehensive or definitive. No attempt has been made to cover every part of the world or to encompass within these pages every linguist who ever left his mark on earth. Military interpreters, for example, have been almost excluded except in the chapter on linguists of ancient days, when the boundary between military and civil functions was virtually nonexistent. To have done otherwise would have taken us too far afield and made the work unnecessarily cumbersome.

What we have tried to do is to paint a general view of the world in which the political linguist functions, and has functioned, throughout history. Where we have spied something of particular interest or significance, we have swooped down upon it and claimed it with enthusiasm. It is the author's hope that readers will be left with an enhanced understanding of this very special, too often unappreciated, career field, even—perhaps—that some talented young linguists may be enticed into it.

CHAPTER I

Translator or Interpreter?

I and Pangur Ban, my cat,
'Tis a like task we are at.
Hunting mice is his delight,
Hunting words I sit all night.
...
Practice every day has made
Pangur perfect in his trade.
I get wisdom day and night
Turning darkness into light.*

It should not surprise us too much to learn that the words "translator" and "interpreter," occasionally misused even by those who should know better, often confuse the layman. But these words do not mean the same thing and are not to be used interchangeably except in referring to someone who performs both functions, which would be a rare circumstance today.

Interpreters *orally* render one language into another, while translators deal with *written* material. But this bald statement leaves a host of questions unanswered. How do the two professions differ in the personal qualities demanded of each? Why can some persons perform beautifully in the one capacity but not in the other? Is there any difference in the status and income associated with each?

Regardless of whether the process be oral or written, the basic task is the conversion of thoughts or concepts expressed in a particular language into another tongue. Note that we do not speak of "words" being converted, but of "thoughts or concepts," and therein lies the key to the difficulties inherent in the process. Consider this: in one language of India, the word *kal* may mean either "yesterday" or "tomorrow," while the word *parson* may mean either "the day before yesterday" or "the day after tomorrow." Surely anyone concerned with that particular linguistic group would be well advised to anticipate a preoccupation with the

*Robin Flower, Poems and Translations, *London: Constable, 1931; used by permission.*

1

present and some lack of interest in either the past or the future. Yet in the United States, the average layman's idea of the art of translation is a simple-minded substitution of one word for another. Largely because of this mistaken evaluation, the profession has never, in this country, enjoyed the high level of respect it has commanded in Europe, and comparative salary scales have reflected the discrepancy in status. Linguists have even been told by ignorant superiors, "Don't try to understand. Just translate."

One way to appreciate what translators and interpreters are faced with is to note the distinction between the *phenotype* (overt dictionary meaning of a word) and the *cryptotype* (implication or unconscious meaning). "The totality of meaning is a joint product of cryptographical and phenotypical matters."[1]* It is the cryptographical meaning, obviously, which lies at the root of most semantic problems.

One need not be a genius to find a synonym for an English word in a foreign-language dictionary, but all too often this so-called "equivalent" is not precisely that. Missionaries working on the *Bible* had their ingenuity taxed to the utmost when they found that such Near Eastern creatures as sheep and donkeys were unknown in polar lands. Likewise, the lack of any true French equivalent for "trusteeship" caused the word to be rendered, in the early days of the United Nations, as "système de tutelle." But since "tutelle" carries no connotation of "trust," and the English "trusteeship" is in no way related to "tutelage," that solution was far from satisfactory. Perhaps the "chaos of nonequivalency" (as one linguist puts it) reached its height in China during World War II when much time had to be wasted in finding (or inventing) such fine distinctions as "spare parts," "separate spare parts," "repair spare parts," "replacement spare parts," and "component spare parts."[2]

Where true equivalents do not exist, it may be tempting to select the word or phrase which most appeals to us because of our cultural background. "Pet," for example, might be rendered as "domestic animal" in a tongue which lacks such a term (and some do), but this choice is far from conveying the emotional and cultural implications of the English word. Yet such poor substitutes are not unknown at the highest level of political linguistics. To a French reader, the phrase "un écart-type de deux" in a technical report is meaningless, as is the "système d'orientation recours," used in World Health Organizational documents as an equivalent of the English "referral system."[3] Most professionals agree that, where no true equivalent exists, a word or phrase should be allowed to stand without translation, as is frequently done, just for example, with the distinctively French *chez*.

See Chapter Notes, beginning on page 141.

A major pitfall for the language student and for the inexperienced translator is the "false friend" — a foreign word which looks so much like a word in one's own tongue that it is all too easy to assume it has a similar meaning. But *brutto* in Italian does not mean "brutal," nor does the French *joli* mean "jolly," despite the corruption of the pirates' ensign, the *joli rouge* (handsome red flag) to "jolly roger." Probably the all-time classic example of false friend disease, which appears only in closely-related languages, would be the translation of "l'anglais avec son sangfroid habituel" as "the Englishman with his usual bloody cold."

Nonequivalency has led to international misunderstanding upon a number of occasions. One of the better-known stories in the history of diplomacy involves the mistaken rendering of the French *demander*, which implies merely a polite request, as "demand," thereby giving offense to the other party. In a similar incident many years later, it has been suggested that the fate of Hiroshima may have been sealed by mistranslation in Washington of a Japanese word. After the Potsdam Conference of 1945, an ultimatum had been sent to Japan demanding its surrender. The reply from Tokyo contained the word *mokusatsu*, whose most accurate meaning would be "delay until discussion has taken place." But the translator rendered it as "ignore," a response ill-received in Washington.[4] And the author Vincent Sheean produced a minor flap in 1947, with his allegation of pro-Nazi sympathies in the British zone of occupied Germany. A pamphlet designed to explain the Nuremburg Trials to the German people had used the word *Menschlichkeit* for "humanity." Sheean said this was in error, the word meant "kindliness," a quality held in contempt by the Nazis. Thus, as Sheean saw it, to call the war criminals guilty of *Verbrechen gegen die Menschlichkeit* ("crimes against humanity") was to make them appear martyrs to their fellow Germans. The proper word, he felt, was *Menschheit*.[5]

Even in the U.S.–Iranian negotiations of 1980–1981 for the release of the hostages, the political differences had been aggravated by language misunderstandings, since four different tongues were involved from time to time: English, Farsi (Persian), and, for the Algerian mediators, Arabic and French. A common Persian noun, *ta'a hod*, which, according to Persian–English dictionaries can mean "guarantee," "commitment," or "understanding," became a particular source of contention during the final stages of the bargaining.[6] When Iranian Prime Minister Mohammed Ali Rajai informed reporters that the Ayatollah Khomeini had agreed to a proposal suggested by the Algerians, he used the word *ta'a hod*, which was then understood by some journalists to signify an "undertaking," but by others to mean a "guarantee." Later, Radio Teheran interpreted the word as "guarantee," but the translator in London rendered it as "undertaking." Obviously, the differences are profound.

One recurring problem in international relations is that of discrepant texts, or diverging translations, of treaties. Whenever an agreement is drawn in more than one language, the question must arise as to which text is to be considered the authoritative one in case of a semantic dispute. On this matter, international lawyers have not always agreed. One school of thought holds that any ambiguity should redound to the disadvantage of the party responsible for it, who ought to have been more careful in their phraseology. Others believe that all versions of a text should be considered equal by all parties concerned *unless there is included in the treaty a stipulation to the contrary.* This last phrase is important, for most treaties since World War I have specified which text is to be the authoritative one, in the hope that this might forestall such annoying situations as the following examples.

In 1919, a dispute arose over discrepancies in the English and French versions of Article 21 of the League of Nations Covenant, the latter of which appeared to change the meaning of the Monroe Doctrine. In the French version, the Doctrine had been subordinated to the Covenant by a statement that the former was "not to be considered as incompatible with any one of the provisions of the present pact," while the American version subordinated the Covenant to the Doctrine by specifying that the latter was "not affected by the engagements of the Covenant."[7] A more recent incident occurred in 1954, when the United States and the Soviet Union were concluding a mutual security treaty in English and Russian. Charles Bohlen, then American ambassador to Moscow, who knew Russian well, scrutinized the two texts line for line and discovered that, while the English version prohibited both countries from "entering" an alliance of which the other was not a member, the Russian word meant "participating in," rather than "entering." Thus, according to the American version, the United States could remain in NATO, since she was already in it, not "entering," but the Russian text would have compelled her to quit it.[8] The reader is also referred to the appalling examples of textual conflict discussed in Chapter IV, the Chinese–Portuguese Treaty over Macao and the French–Chinese Treaty of 1860.

Even the United Nations Charter itself is not free of textual divergence. While the English version of Article 33 contains the phrase, "...is likely to endanger the maintenance of international peace and security," the French and Spanish texts read "is susceptible to threaten," rather than "is likely to endanger"—not exactly the same thing. The Russian and Chinese texts likewise diverge, with the former reading "could threaten" (i.e., might possibly threaten), which is far less emphatic than either the French, Spanish or English versions, and with the Chinese reading "suffices to endanger." Thus, while the English version suggests a definite degree of *probability*, the other languages, to varying degrees, merely consider the *possibility*.[9] In the touchy world of international relations, this sort of imprecision is by no means as trivial as one might think.

No matter what rules may be formulated, in the final analysis the dilemma can be resolved only by the most experienced and knowledgeable translators. In no organization is a problematical text scrutinized by a single person. The original translator's rendition may be examined by a number of revisors, by the chief of the translating service, and, in some cases, by a board of experts whose word will be final.

Until about the time of World War I, translating and interpreting were usually performed by the same person. The general assumption was that anyone who could speak two or more languages ought to be able to perform in either capacity, and too many people still cling to this delusion. But sixty or more years ago, even the most "difficult" subject matter had been relatively simple. As science and technology advanced, as business, politics and the professions became ever more complex, a strange phenomenon was increasingly noted. Skilled linguists who could translate written material with ease were found to suffer from mental or vocal blockage when called upon to function orally. According to Jean Herbert, one of the more accomplished interpreters of modern times, whose opinion on this matter is surely authoritative: "The work of the translator and that of the interpreter are mentally different and can hardly be combined. Rare indeed are people who can do both satisfactorily."[10]

Clearly, something beyond a mere feeling for words, certain intangible personal qualities, determine whether aspirants should direct themselves toward translating or toward interpreting. Since World War II, these qualities have been well identified, and much has been written about them. Applicants for linguistic positions today are evaluated as much on the basis of their psychological characteristics as their language skills.

Translation of written materials is a slower process than interpreting. Even if the completed assignment be required within a few minutes, the translator still has time for reflection and rephrasing which the interpreter does not have. An oral linguist must do his work simultaneously and he must be right the *first* time, which involves picking exactly the right word or phrase, not one which "will do." (André Vishinsky, at the United Nations, used to speak at the rate of 300 words per minute. Of course, few talk that fast, but the interpreter never knows when he may be called upon to service someone who does.) A translator, on the other hand, is permitted to begin with words which "will do," and later, after he has had a chance to ponder, to replace them with a better choice. Clearly, then, an interpreter must be quick witted, which—to correct a common misconception—is not at all the same thing as being "more intelligent."

Since oral work is considered more demanding mentally and emotionally than written work, interpreters are the élite of the profession, usually earning appreciably more than translators.[11] This is particularly true of those working at high-level conferences or at sessions of international organizations.

Yet, there is another side to the story. An interpreter has the advantage of being right on the spot, assisted by the speaker's tone and gestures, which may sometimes be more significant than his words. Translation, on the other hand, is continually frustrating. The translator may see how the text might be improved but cannot implement the improvement, being, after all, only a subordinate. Moreover, the revisors, or senior translators found in most large translating departments who are charged with checking and perfecting the work of their underlings, frequently seem to feel it necessary to earn their keep by altering more than is warranted. To add to the translator's irritations, the work must often be done from documents sloppily or ambiguously written, or couched in highly technical jargon. Texts are often "syntheses of parts, contributed in different languages.... Yet the translation of all these texts ... must be able to withstand the fire of critics in all languages."[12]

Written translation falls into either of two categories—literary or "technical"—and the difficulties involved in each instance are quite dissimilar, demanding different skills. The first commandment for the "technical" translator, whether working in engineering, medicine, economics, law, the military or politics, is *absolute accuracy*. With this type of material there is no room for flights of fancy. Thus, the technical translator must boast a thorough familiarity with his subject. Ethical nonliterary translators (or interpreters, for that matter) never accept assignments in a field with which they are insufficiently acquainted, and this point of honor goes far beyond a mere knowledge of technical words and phrases. It is possible for a person who knows nothing about medicine to sit down and memorize a dictionary of medical terminology, something which serious, career-minded secretaries and librarians often do. But this alone would not suffice to make one feel secure in a career as a medical translator, for the background knowledge and experience would be lacking. As Lord Bertrand Russell put it, "No one can understand the word 'cheese' unless he has a non-linguistic acquaintance with cheese."[13]

This being the case, a great many translators hold at least one degree in their area of expertise. Multinational corporations seldom hire professional translators as such, but use employees of their organizations who happen to be skilled in the language required, and they may even subsidize language instruction for their employees. To rely on an "outsider" could conceivably jeopardize a sizeable investment. Another reason why "insiders" might be preferred is the matter of confidentiality, although all reputable linguists are the soul of discretion, never revealing any secrets to an unauthorized person. (Hence the traditional use of the sphynx as the insignia for the interpreters' corps in national armies.)

But few public organizations of an international character are able to be so selective. The texts their translators must deal with are varied in the extreme, yet it would be far too expensive to hire a translator who was an expert in each and every specialty. Translators for such agencies must, therefore, become specialists in many different fields — perhaps law, economics, politics, and sociology. A few years ago, a text on mosquito ovaries for the Malaria Division of the World Health Organization had to be translated by a gynecologist, because no one with a degree in biology or entomology happened to be on the staff. The inevitable result of spreading the expertise too thin has been to encourage vagueness and imprecision in translations, in the hope of making no gross error.

Are skilled translators who lack the requisite background forever barred from fields that are of interest to them? By no means, provided they are willing to work hard to overcome their deficiencies. One such man desired a post as translator for a consortium of British firms manufacturing machinery for sale to the Soviet Union. Among the specified duties was the proper labelling of machine parts in Russian, with instructions for their installation and use. Although the man's knowledge of Russian was virtually perfect, in matters technical he was an ignoramus. But by first memorizing lists of terms for machine parts in both languages and then arranging for visits to factories where he could observe the equipment in operation, he found it possible to survive on the job until experience had perfected his skill.[14]

Had the said translator been less conscientious or less capable, he might have produced some such horror as this rendition (from the original French) of instructions for the installation of new desks at the United Nations, here given in the official English version:

> Turn the B tube of a number of turns corresponding about to 2 lb. for instance; for a typewriting machine of 34 lb., weight about, turn the tube of 17 teeth. To unbend the spring: engage the spindle into a hole, turn the tube, take out a click, take off the second spindle, take out the second click, and brake the tube by hand.[15]

Quite another thing is literary translation, which will not concern us beyond a few explanatory words in this chapter solely to contrast technical and literary work. In a sense, as its practitioners seldom neglect to remind us, literary translating is more difficult and demanding than technical work because of its very imprecision. For the literary translator, to achieve total fidelity to the original would be the kiss of death. Rather, the problem to be solved is that of *reasonable* fidelity vs. creative license. Some linguists maintain that "from the point of view of art-form, translation can never be successful. If you are true to the original, you will in fact be unfaithful to it [i.e., in spirit] and if you make free with the original, you will not produce a translation."[16]

As an illustration of the type of work that ravages the very soul of the original, Jacques Barzun has cited the Czech version of John Dos Passos' *Three Soldiers*, one of the earliest American novels to be generously peppered with profanity. Encountering a man who had read the Czech version, Dos Passos received the following critique: "Well, it has some very powerful passages, but then, every once in a while, it says, 'Goodness gracious, captain!'"[17]

In the translation of poetry, Ezra Pound rated poetic genius higher than expertise in the foreign tongue. Although doctrinaire linguists will defend to the death the dogma that one must not attempt to translate (professionally) from or into a language one cannot speak, Pound proved the contrary. His renditions of Chinese poetry are regarded by authorities as among the world's finest, yet he had only a reading knowledge of Chinese. His fascination with the language was in its ideograms; he had very little interest in its spoken forms.

The story of Ezra Pound and his Chinese poetry holds a message whose significance will become more evident as we compare the work of translators and interpreters. It is a mistake to assume that one cannot have a thorough mastery of a language in written form without being able to speak it, or, conversely, that fluency in speaking necessarily guarantees expertise in the written word. Widespread failure to recognize this truth has been responsible for the hiring of many inept translators. For instance, a few years ago, automobiles with the well-known "body by Fisher" were being advertised in French-speaking Belgium under this slogan: "Corpses by Fisher."[18] Another monumental goof by an American auto corporation was General Motors' treatment of its Chevy Nova. The manufacturers had forgotten that "no va," in Spanish, means "It doesn't go," and sales didn't go so well in Latin America until the car's name was changed to "Caribe."[19] There is little doubt that these two masterpieces were the work of those who spoke both languages with the verve of a magpie.

Since style is quite as crucial as content in literary translating, it should not be difficult to understand why linguists regard this kind as a creative art, and technical translating as a science or functional tool. The ultimate example of the latter—a far cry from poetic self-expression—

would doubtless be the use of *damen*, *damas*, *signoras*, etc., on the door of the ladies' room.

Scandinavian lands draw the sharpest distinction between literary and technical translators by requiring those who wish to do public, or governmental, work to be licensed as "state authorized" or "sworn" translators. In Sweden, all notaries public must pass an examination in French, English and German, while Finland, which has followed the practice only since 1968, stresses English, French and Russian. The Swedish test, administered nationwide, is a full-day ordeal, encompassing general, legal and scientific material. Although the use of dictionaries is permitted, only about 10 percent of the Swedish applicants succeed on the first try (they may try three times), while in Finland the average of success is one in three.[20]

It is an unhappy fact that most literary translators have looked down their noses at what they have regarded as a lesser breed. Some even refuse to acknowledge as "real" translators those who labor outside the field of creative literature. But such an attitude is not appropriate. Even if a technical translator be not a particularly brilliant writer, he must be both broadly cultured and the master of at least one technical field, an accomplishment that many of the *literati* cannot boast. Also frequently overlooked is the awesome responsibility resting upon technical translators' shoulders, a burden from which their literary counterparts are largely free. At worst, a technical translator may be sued if some calamity occurs because of inaccurate work.

As elicited during a poll of professionals, we find the following definition of the ideal technical, or nonliterary, translator. "A good translator above all should know ... what he does not know, and where he can fill the gaps. He must surround himself with a veritable intellectual fortress of dictionaries, books, journals."[21] Qualities agreed upon by all include a virtually encyclopedic knowledge coupled with a willingness to continue learning throughout life, sensitivity to the context of the material one is working with, and the ability to achieve a nice balance between fidelity and (yes, even in technical work!) a high standard of literacy.

Technical translators do not feel free to omit words or phrases they would not personally choose, and they may never improve upon the original by correcting errors, ambiguities or inconsistencies, for to do this would violate the "style" of the original. (Where literary material is concerned, some editors — but not all — insist that improvement upon the original is the mark of a fine translator.)[22]

Our brief discussion of the art of translating would be incomplete without some mention of computer translation. Most people who have any interest in languages are aware that this technique is available today.* But they may be uncertain of its reliability or of the degree to which it has been perfected. Professional translators are, of course, most concerned with the possibility of machines' putting them out of business in the foreseeable future. At the moment, this seems unlikely.

Machine translating, invented by a British scholar, A. Donald Booth, and an official of the Rockefeller Foundation, Warren Weaver, was a by-product of World War II advances in the science of cryptography. Dr. Norbert Wiener of the Massachusetts Institute of Technology and a world authority on artificial intelligence, harbored some doubts as to the feasibility of translations by machine because of the culturally and emotionally "loaded" nature of language—doubts which have proven to be well founded. Nevertheless, during the 1950's, Professor Wiener's own institution, M.I.T., worked at developing the new technique, while another group did likewise at Georgetown University. By 1954, researchers had succeeded in translating 60 sentences from Russian to English, working with only six grammatical rules and using approximately 250 words.[23] The first textbook in machine translation was published shortly thereafter.[24] By that time, the Georgetown system, SERNA, had translated 100,000 words of a text which it had never "seen" before, and *Pravda*, the Moscow newspaper, was being rendered in "rough but comprehensible" English.[25] Since then, progress on the machines has continued to be gratifying—but only up to a point.

The most serious defect of machines when put to this purpose is their incurable "literal-mindedness," which permits them to do really good work only when the prose is of the imbecilic type, quite free of abstract or subjective content. Attempts to translate material which cannot be rendered literally, word-for-word, have produced some ludicrous results, most evident in the translation of ethnic proverbs or idioms. Two of the best-known computer boners are these:

> In English: "Out of sight, out of mind"
> To Russian: "Invisible insanity"
>
> In English: "The spirit is willing, but the flesh is weak"
> To Russian: "The whiskey is all right, but the meat has gone bad."[26]

Compare this with the product of human translators, who, almost instantly, came up with the precise English equivalents for two Russian proverbs:

There are even several competing small, reasonably priced computers for tourists, which supply foreign equivalents for crucial words and phrases, though, in 1982, they were not yet accounted very sophisticated.

In Russian: "You can't change the hump on a hunchback"
To English: "You can't change the spots on a leopard"

In Russian: "He ran away from the wolf only to meet the bear"
To English: "He leaped from the frying pan into the fire."[27]

If we examine, even in the most rudimentary fashion, how translating machines do their work, it should be no mystery why mishaps
readily occur. "Garbage in, garbage out" applies as emphatically to
machine translating as to any other kind of computer operation. Even if
it ever becomes possible for machines to do a perfect job of translating any kind of material, this will not put the human translators out of
work, for every machine operation must be preceded by a careful
analysis of the text to be read, and the final product must then be scrupu-
lously checked.

First comes a "lexical scan," since the machine can read a text only
after it has been broken down into its grammatical components (words)
and every possible dictionary meaning for each word has been determined. Next, each sentence will be parsed (analyzed as to grammatical
terminology), and this must be done in as many different ways as it might
be possible to interpret the sentence. Here are a couple of examples of
texts which cause translators to tear their hair: "We saw the Grand
Canyon flying to Los Angeles" and "We would like to receive a list of
your employees broken down by sex"—to which some wit responded,
"We have none broken down by sex, but we have a number who drink
too much."

Clearly, the ready availability of lexical dictionaries would be most
helpful in speeding up the work, especially in technical fields blessed with
a jargon all their own. And, indeed, most of the work on machine translation to date has centered around the compilation of such dictionaries,
whose information will be found within three distinct codes: the part of
speech (noun, verb, etc.), syntax (word order in the sentence), and
semantic features (the various meanings of words). When the text is fed
into the computer, the dictionary first checks its codes and then the
machine carries out such other programs as may be called for.

Since we shall be primarily concerned with political-legal translation,
which is exceptionally difficult because of the abundance of archaic terms,
it might be of interest to point out that one researcher, referring to legal
terminology as a "world unto itself," has identified no less than nine
separate categories of law. They are: interior (domestic); foreign affairs;
civil and penal; financial; economic, labor and social administrative;
post, transport and communication; and "special areas," such as,
perhaps, refugee problems or space law. Carrying the breakdown still
further, "foreign affairs" would encompass its own terminological

categories: consular law, law of international organizations, law of public international administration, and the principles of international law.[28] *Every single one* of these has its own special jargon which must be translated (be it by human or by machine) with 100 percent accuracy. Moreover, most legal texts are a kind of stew concocted by many different chefs, and the translator must follow the rule of taking the oldest, or original text as the authoritative one. So important is legal and administrative terminology in today's world that there now exist a number of institutions devoted solely to research in this field.*

To date, even the most ardent champions of machine translation have been compelled to admit that, except in the compilation of dictionaries of terminology, computers have not done a truly satisfactory job. A 1966 report based on a Russian–English project of the Foreign Technical Division at Wright–Patterson Air Force Base revealed 7,573 errors in 200 pages of text, or approximately 38 errors per page.[29] Specifically, words and phrases were omitted, wrong words and unnecessary words were used (as, for instance, to "cope up" with something rather than to "cope" with it), the word order (syntax) was sometimes bad, and there was occasional "poor judgment" as to which Russian words should be retained without translation.

While the machines have undergone considerable improvement since that report, they are not yet error-free and, aside from the obvious objections to inaccurate translation, errors are expensive. The cost of machine translation does vary somewhat according to the system used, but all are more expensive than the conventional method, simply because the output must be carefully checked and corrected by human translators. The temptation to compare the process with that of automatic dishwashers is irresistible: in both cases, the work almost has to be done twice.

A pioneer in machine translating, Victor Yngve, pinpoints the central problem as the need for a machine that can "understand" what it is translating. He admits that this will be difficult to achieve; nevertheless, "Some of us are pressing forward undaunted."[30]

Interpreters, as we have said, are nearly always ranked higher and paid better than their silent counterparts. Every quality characterizing the highest-level translator must be present in the interpreter, plus many more. Being able to participate in meetings without appearing intrusive,

Two of them are the International Institute for Legal and Administrative Terminology, in Berlin, and the World Information Center for Legal, Economic and Administrative Terminology, in Munich. The former researches comparative political institutions and the designations by which they are known in different lands, publishing the results in glossaries. (See Hans Schwartz, "Legal and Administrative Language," Babel 23 [1977], 19.)

knowing how to dress for all occasions, possessing a digestive system tolerant of queer foods eaten at odd hours — these are just a few of the seldom-noted attributes that are assets, if not downright requirements, for the professional interpreter.[31] Most imperative is the need for mental agility, and a quality perhaps best defined by the modern slang word, "unflappability," or coolness under pressure. What we mean by this can perhaps be demonstrated through a story told by Lord Strang, formerly of the British Foreign Office.

An applicant for a higher post in Cairo was undergoing examination. Asked how he would request his servant, in Arabic, to "Come here," he correctly replied, "Ta alâ kina." But the examiner then demanded to know how, if the servant were standing beside him, he would ask him to go away. Being uncertain of the proper phrase, the man, with scarcely a moment's hesitation, replied, "I would move away from him and then say, "Ta alâ kina.""[32] *That* is unflappability! And no matter how skilled and knowledgeable a linguist may be, if he cannot think fast on his feet, or if he becomes rattled under fire, he will never succeed as an interpreter, although he might well make a fine translator.

According to one British diplomat of long experience, one of the six most important elements in conference diplomacy is having reliable secretaries and interpreters. Yet, only a few years ago, a former chief of the Geneva United Nations Interpretation Section estimated that there were not more than 500 "fully qualified"* conference interpreters in the world.[33] He had in mind, of course, the cream of the profession. But in this career, being less than the cream simply will not do. If one does not expect to qualify, ultimately, for the élite, one would be well advised to enter another profession.

Most Western linguists believe it best to interpret *into* one's mother tongue whenever possible. (The U.N.'s simultaneous interpreters and those working for most other international organizations and conferences work only into their native tongue.) Ordinarily, therefore, an American would render a German speech in English, while his German counterpart on the other side of the table would convert the American's speech into German. Since emergency situations do arise, however, the most able conference interpreters are sometimes called upon to interpret *both* ways, an experience few of them eagerly anticipate.

Jean Herbert, who interpreted for many of the European conferences of 1919, recalls a session lasting a month, at which he was the sole interpreter, working six days a week in French, English and German. At

---

*As of 1975, the Association of Conference Interpreters had a roster of 900 qualified members; by "qualified" is meant mastery of three languages and at least 200 days of working experience.

one point, he momentarily fell asleep on his feet, but apparently continued to talk without anyone noticing the incident.[34] And A.H. Birse was the only interpreter present at the conversations in 1943 between Churchill and Stalin, working both sides of the table, occasionally for as long as seven hours at a time.[35] (Two hours is generally regarded as the limit before fatigue sets in and proficiency begins to decline.)

Interestingly, the Russians believe that interpreting *from* one's mother tongue is sometimes preferable to the reverse, an opinion which seems to reflect an underlying philosophy different from that of most peoples. Certainly, whichever activity the interpreter is engaged in, he will turn out the most polished product in the language in which he feels most at home. Is, therefore, the mental operation of "decanting" one's own thoughts the most important aspect of interpreting, or is the rendering of another's thoughts into a perfect version in one's own language more significant? Do we detect at least a suggestion, here, that the Russians are more concerned that others understand *their* message "loud and clear" than that they understand the others'?

As we shall see, Latin was the common diplomatic tongue of Europe from the end of the Roman Empire to the Reformation, thereafter being gradually supplanted by French. Because, in their heyday, Latin and French were the languages of all cultured people, with fluency in either or both deemed essential for the professional diplomat, interpreters were often not really needed.* Yet they were frequently employed for prestige reasons, or to allow the diplomats more time in which to think. (Consecutive interpreting still serves the same purpose in the Security Council of the U.N. During this style of interpretation, the negotiator's mind is left free to concentrate on the matter at hand, instead of having to concern itself with verbal expression.) In such cases, the linguist would formerly sit or stand beside his "principal" (the word applied to the person for whom one is interpreting), and provide a whispered commentary, sentence by sentence. It was a boring, laborious procedure.

At about the time of World War I, the rise of the two great English-speaking powers to world eminence offered the first real challenge to the primacy of the French language since the 16th century. Because it soon became apparent that to make French the *sole* official language at the Versailles Conferences would be unacceptable, delegates were permitted to choose either French or English, and were provided with interpreters who immediately rendered remarks from the one language into the other. This was the system known as *consecutive interpreting*.

The most serious flaw in the consecutive technique is the amount of time consumed, at least three minutes of interpreting being required for

European contacts with the Orient were another story; see Chapter IV.

every five minutes of the original speech. Until the élite of the profession had perfected their art, frequent pauses were necessary to give the interpreter time to catch up. But, as linguists came to rely more and more on phenomenal memories bolstered by a few notes, the pauses became fewer and farther between. André Kaminker, one of the most eminent interpreters of this century (and father of French film actress Simone Signoret) could read a page from a phone directory and repeat all the names in proper order.[36]

Because their concern should be with ideas rather than with words, most professionals frown on the use of shorthand. Notetaking has become an art in itself, with amazingly complicated rules, stressing key concepts and their linkage, through such devices as abbreviation, negation, accentuation, verticalism and *décalage* (a "staircase" format for the association of ideas).[37] Indeed, the uninitiated might be pardoned for confusing a page from a conference interpreter's note pad with a mystery writer's preliminary plot, or a choreographer's diagrammatic scheme. Despite all this, the ideal to be striven for remains the U.N. interpreter who flawlessly repeated an hour-long speech after jotting only one word on his pad!

Between the two great wars, a new, speedier technique appeared, that of *simultaneous interpreting*. Its rudimentary origin was in the practice of employing "whisperers" *(chuchoteurs)* who murmured a continuing running commentary audible only to a few people sitting close together. Some improvement was attained by the "hushaphone," or Filene-Finlay Speech Translator, a hand microphone known irreverently as *la bidule* ("the spittoon"). Into it the interpreter whispered his words, which were then relayed, electronically amplified, to the earphones of his auditors. This primitive form of simultaneous interpreting, barely audible in only two languages, was the brainchild of Edward A. Filene, of the Boston department story family, and a British scientist, Professor Gordon-Finlay. First tested at the International Labor Organization (ILO) in 1926, it was used only at the opening of the conference, during discussions on the director's report, and whenever the conferees found themselves pressed for time.

One interpreter would sit in an "orchestra pit," just below the speaker's rostrum, carefully whispering into the "hushaphone" in an almost vain attempt to avoid drowning out his colleague, who was doing likewise. Another interpreter sat with the president and director, rendering their words from one official language (French or English) into the other. Unlike the arrangement at the Nuremburg War Crimes Trials nearly twenty years later, or at the U.N. and other present-day organizations that use the system, headsets at the ILO were reserved for conferees and for the press. The general public in attendance had none, which meant that they often found it difficult to follow the proceedings.[38]

Since satisfaction with early "simultaneous" was less than overwhelming, a number of technical improvements were introduced before it was tried again by the ILO in 1928–1929, once more at Mr. Filene's expense. A few of the problems presented by this crude technique from the infancy of simultaneous interpreting may be deduced from the instructions given by the ILO to its interpreters.[39]

Those on the platform were warned to face the audience, speak clearly, and make an effort to use complete sentences, so that little editing would be necessary for the ILO's *Provisional Record*. They were told that, during plenary sessions, interpreting might be done either from the platform directly or through the "hushaphone," and that speeches should be summarized to some extent, bringing out the salient points. It would be permissible, in some cases, for a speech delivered in a language other than French or English to be interpreted on the platform by linguists of both tongues, or for one interpretation to be made on the platform and the other through the "hushaphone." The division of work was to be determined by the chief interpreter, who was also charged with ascertaining that an interpretation by phone had been concluded before the next speaker addressed the meeting. Interpreters were further admonished to learn from the clerk of the conference which persons were to speak, to try to obtain texts of the speeches in advance, and, where possible, to prepare preliminary summaries. An effort was made to keep the same interpreters assigned to each committee throughout its proceedings, but they might be required also to assist in the translation of urgent documents.

Because a saving of nearly seven hours' working time could be effected by the use of the "hushaphone," the League Assembly at Geneva later adopted it. But it remained, by all accounts, a stressful, nerve-wracking experience for interpreter and auditor alike. Remarkable improvements in the technique following World War II have now made it the method of choice at nearly all important international conferences, at least during the plenary sessions.

Leon Dostert, a colonel in the United States Army and chief interpreter at the Nuremburg War Crimes Trials of 1946–1949, pioneered in the development of the modern system, in collaboration with International Business Machines, who offered the free use of their equipment at Nuremburg. It is difficult to imagine how, without the benefit of efficient language services, anything could have been accomplished in Germany, for the linguistic burden attendant upon the trials was truly awesome.

At the outset, the principle had been laid down that, to ensure each defendant a fair trial, he must be given, prior to the beginning of the trial, a copy of the indictment and of all relevant documents, translated into a language familiar to him, and his preliminary examination by the prosecution must be conducted in his own tongue.[40] These strictures were implemented by the Rules of Procedure adopted at Nuremburg, which provided that the defendants were to receive copies of relevant documents in their own language 30 days before the trial began, and that all documents must be translated into German.[41] Into the hands of the commissioners of the Tribunal poured over 38,000 affidavits signed by some 155,000 people, all of which had to be translated into any number of languages (German, French, English and Russian being the official tongues), and oral testimony was presented by more than 250 people.[42] Every bit of material read aloud or spoken in open court at Nuremburg was rendered simultaneously into the four official tongues.

At every seat in the room, including the prisoners' dock and the galleries for press and visitors, were a telephone headset and a small dial numbered from one to five. By dialing the proper number, the listener could either hear the original speech in the language of the speaker, or an instantaneous rendering into one of the other four languages by one of 12 interpreters seated in a glass booth at the end of the room. By pressing a button, an interpreter could flash a light which would warn speakers that they should slow down in order to enable him to catch up. (It needs to be remembered that many of those testifying did so under great emotional stress.) Essentially, this is the same arrangement used in the General Assembly Hall of the United Nations today.

At Nuremburg, some remained skeptical as to the practicality of simultaneous interpretation. A number of experienced consecutive interpreters feared that the anonymity of the booth would not only downgrade their status but destroy their "style." Journalists, too, expressed some misgivings lest inaccurate interpreting result in miscarriages of justice. One of them suggested, only half-facetiously, that the phrase "freimachung des Rheins" might be conceived as referring to early Nazi plans for reoccupation of the Rhineland, whereas it meant nothing worse than the clearing of the Rhine River for navigational puposes.

In all likelihood, some minor errors were made, although none of the accused ever complained of inaccurate translating or interpreting. (For one thing, there were plenty of German linguists on hand to catch any mistakes.) If consecutive interpreting had been used, the trials would assuredly have taken much longer than the two-and-a-half years (October 1946–April 1949) they did take, and the system worked well enough to make a favorable impression on most observers, whether linguists or laymen. Yet it is worth noting that the simultaneous method was ruled impractical for Nuremburg's counterpart in Tokyo, the International

Military Tribunal for the Far East. The miserable failure of an attempt to interpret simultaneously into Japanese for the benefit of some visitors of that nationality to the U.N. led to a decision not to try it at the Tokyo Tribunal.[43]

Both Charter[44] and Tribunal rules required all documents to be translated into English and Japanese at least 24 hours before being offered as evidence. The head of the prosecution's Language Section having estimated that each single page would require eight man hours of work, a rule was adopted that no document for the prosecution might be translated until it had been certified as essential by the Chief of the Trial, after which it would be reproduced in English and Japanese, 250 copies each.[45]

Because every person examined orally reduced the speed of the trial to one-fifth of its normal pace (and there were 419 witnesses!), the court found it necessary to require the Japanese among them to submit their testimony in advance in the form of affidavits, some 779 of which were then deciphered by a very large corps of interpreters. The Tokyo trials, which lasted through 818 sessions from April 29, 1946, to April 16, 1948, produced 50,000 pages of translated documents.[46] But even with all the care taken, discrepancies and ambiguities were so many that the Tribunal was soon forced to establish a Language Arbitration Board. Composed of three members, one appointed by the 11-judge Tribunal, one by the prosecution and one by the defense, its decision was to be final in case of disputed testimony or translations.

In 1946, it having been well-determined that meeting time could be cut in half by using the simultaneous method of interpreting, Colonel Dostert was invited to bring his paraphernalia to the United Nations for a tryout. Despite the Nuremburg success, a battle of heroic proportions now began boiling up among the language specialists at the U.N. Once more, many highly qualified interpreters, convinced that the consecutive method was the more accurate and that the other would be the downfall of the profession, refused to cooperate in the experiment. Since new blood had to be brought in, it was fortunate that the U.N. was able to secure the services of the legendary André Kaminker, who trained most of the original simultaneous interpreters both there and, later, at the Council of Europe.[47]

The General Assembly of the U.N. has had simultaneous interpretation since 1947, and the Security Council since 1950, although consecutive interpreting may also be used in the latter if the speaker does not waive his right to it. Why so? Apparently to provide a welcome respite during which Council members who do not need to hear that particular speech may confer or visit the restroom.

Some of the warnings advanced by devotees of the consecutive technique have proven to be at least partially valid. For one thing, the interpreter is now on much less intimate terms with his principal than under the old system, often working with him for some time before ever setting eyes on him. Both delegates and interpreters may find such anonymity discomfiting. Moreover, since the interpreter has now become only a disembodied voice, the voice is all-important. It had always been essential that an interpreter not allow his tone to betray his personal feelings on an issue, but it is now more difficult to strike the necessary balance between disinterestedness and an impression of boredom. Also, over the years, it has been discovered that interpreters who had originally been trained in the consecutive method are likely to do well when they turn to simultaneous interpreting, but the reverse is not always true, possibly because the consecutive-trained have learned to process information in their minds more efficiently. In one experiment, some persons being trained as simultaneous interpreters were asked to listen to recordings of French prose and to simultaneously interpret the material into English. Other trainees were required merely to listen, but not to interpret. After each passage, both groups were tested for recall and comprehension of the material, and the test scores were found to be lower for those called upon to interpret simultaneously while listening.[48]

A Chinese–English interpreter, Colonel Robert B. Ekvall, insists that, while the simultaneous method may work well enough if the languages are not too dissimilar, the product will range from the awkward to the grotesque when they are very different. His opinion would appear to be confirmed by the story of the Tokyo War Crimes Tribunal, as related above. All in all, Colonel Ekvall still believes that "for highest accuracy, consecutive interpreting is necessary."[49]

Regardless of which method is used, the procedure always encompasses three distinct steps: *understanding* correctly, *converting* accurately, and *delivering* with style. Some of the more common problems include the necessity of obtaining a copy of the text far enough in advance, finding word equivalents, "storing" (mentally) the material for exactly as long as necessary and no longer, and—possibly the Black Curse of the interpreter's existence—dealing with his principal's double negatives. (Some speakers tend to use a number of negatives in the same long, complex sentence. Do these ultimately add up to a positive or a negative statement?) A former chief of the U.N. Translation Division recommends that, if hopelessly lost in the underbrush, the interpreter try to remember the speaker's *usual* stance on questions of that sort and hope for the best![59]

To *understand* well, the interpreter must enjoy perfect hearing and must sit or stand close enough to the speaker to avoid missing any words. Despite popular belief, the anonymous person who may be observed in newspaper photographs standing like a shadow just behind the distinguished foreign visitor is more often an interpreter than a bodyguard.

To *deliver* well, the interpreter must have a fine voice and be an accomplished public speaker. (It doesn't hurt if he's even a bit of an actor.) Unless he can perform well in his own language, he is not likely to do so in any other. But beyond this, the interpreter should be merely an "echo" of his principal. He must reflect the principal's mood and style, even to the use of the same *variety* of language.[51] An interpreter never says, "Mr. François Mitterand believes...." Rather, he enters Mr. Mitterand's skin, and says, "*I* believe...." The late Eleanor Roosevelt once told a story that illustrates the point perfectly. According to her, when former New York Major Fiorello H. LaGuardia, making a speech at the U.N., reached for a glass of water, all five interpreters "working" him did likewise![52]

Thus, if the principal sounds devious, so must the interpreter. If the principal speaks in an ambiguous, equivocating manner, on no account may the interpreter clarify his remarks, for ambiguity is a powerful weapon in world politics, often being used deliberately to gain time or to confound the opposition. If the principal is hostile, the interpreter's manner should reflect that hostility. (It has been said that, in the early, prefeminist days at the U.N., a frequently heard objection to female interpreters was the incongruity of some male delegate's bellicose words emerging in a mild feminine voice.)

Americans, in their naiveté of happier times, seldom understood these subtleties. During the infancy of the U.N., after each polemical speech by a Russian delegate, the switchboard would light up with furious callers demanding that the interpreter be fired, because they saw him as obviously pro-communist. The poor scapegoat's only offense, of course, had been to faithfully echo the words, style and manner of the delegate whose speech he had been interpreting—precisely what he was being paid to do. Only one divergence from the original speech is permissible, and, in fact, mandatory. All "fat" and redundancy should be cut from it, so that the "echo" will require only about 75 percent of the time needed for the original.

But the veritable heart and soul of the interpreting process is the *conversion* step, which must be performed mentally in seconds, before delivery can be made. Not only must the interpreter be well-versed in the subject matter of the meeting, but he must be so intimately acquainted with the culture of the principal's homeland that clichés, proverbs, idioms, nuances of meaning and stories gleaned from the national literature, do not go over his head, and so that no offense will be *unintentionally* given or taken.

An American agronomist sent to Egypt to teach modern methods of agriculture inquired of a farmer, through his interpreter, how good a crop he was expecting. Much to the American's astonishment, the farmer flew into a rage. A greatly embarrassed interpreter explained that, since only God knows the future, anyone who tries to foretell it is a lunatic, and that, therefore, the farmer considered himself insulted.[53] In a conference situation, a good interpreter would have altered his principal's remarks in such a way as to remove the offense, since it had clearly not been intended.

Another example of cultural ignorance is surely the widely-circulated story of Hitler's "rug-chewing." Many Americans of the 1930s and 1940s actually believed that the Chancellor, in his tantrums, would kneel on the floor and nibble at the rug. This tale arose only because there is, in the German language, an idiom, "to chew the rug," which means, simply, "to rant and rave." Those unfamiliar with this fact took the phrase literally, and those who knew better, but who were delighted to perpetuate a tale reflecting unfavorably on Hitler, never bothered to correct them.

Finally, we might consider the Japanese expression, "It isn't tea," which means precisely the same thing as (take your choice) "It's not cricket," "It's not according to Hoyle," or "It's not kosher." The full significance of this idiom can be appreciated only by one acquainted with the intricate rules governing the formal tea ceremony, the *cha-no-yu*.

To sum up the matter of conversion difficulties, it has been said that even the most experienced interpreter feels terror in his heart when he hears these eight small words: "In my country, we have an old saying...."

Some professional linguists feel the ideal interpreter would be a living encyclopedia. And research has disclosed that true bilinguals possess, to a greater degree than monolinguals, a trait psychologists call "cognitive flexibility," which means that they tend to be creative, looking at problems from various points of view, perhaps because their exposure to diverse cultures has taught them that there is always more than one way to attack a problem.[54]

History records many instances of mental virtuosity on the part of interpreters. We might begin with Charles Alison, Oriental secretary and interpreter to Lord Canning, British ambassador to Turkey during the 19th century. Canning had become increasingly irritated by the Turkish habit of executing apostates from Islam, but his protests never elicited more than the reply, "It is written in the *Holy Koran*." The learned Secretary Alison, boldly declaring, "It is **not** written in the *Holy Koran*," was able to prove, to the satisfaction of the Turks themselves, that the said injunction came only from the lesser *Book of Traditions*, thereby removing from it the status of divine sanction. At another time, offended by an Ottoman dignitary's custom of falling to his knees to call down Allah's curses upon the infidels, Alison himself got down on *his* knees, and, in colorful and fluent Turkish, begged Allah to teach the Muslim dogs a lesson.[55]

And what about the great Paul Joseph Mantoux, French interpreter at a disarmament conference of the League of Nations? Sir John Simon, the British delegate, had concluded his speech with a quotation from Shelley, just the sort of thing interpreters most dread. But Mantoux, without a moment's hesitation, "rendered the Shelley quotation in French verse, reaching a peak which will never be surpassed in the history of the art [of interpreting]."[56]

Richard W. Brislin, in an intriguing analysis of the considerable power wielded by interpreters over their principals, has identified four distinct kinds of power.[57] All of them demonstrate but a single truth: the principal could not function without the interpreter, and he who is truly needed holds the whip hand. Examples of such powers as exercised by interpreters will be cited abundantly in later chapters, but for the moment, one or two will suffice, demonstrating the power of a skilled interpreter to rescue a naive client from the consequences of his own ignorance.

In A.D. 1394, the founder of the Ming Dynasty of China had begun diplomatic relations with the Mongol, Tamerlane. From the latter came a letter of submission to the emperor's authority, couched in the most obsequious terms. But it is improbable, according to one scholar, that such words ever came from Tamerlane, who was not a servile type, and who, in any case, being a Muslim, would not have acceded to an infidel emperor's claim to supremacy.[58] In all likelihood, a translator had altered the wording in the interests of prudence.

Much more recently, a newly appointed American ambassador had arrived in Belgrade to confer with Marshal Tito at a time when the Yugoslav dictator was not at all popular in the United States. And what did this well-meaning neophyte do but blithely invite Tito to come to this country to explain his views! Knowing that any such invitation, particularly to a communist leader, would embarrass the United States greatly if it had not first been cleared by the president and Department of State, the horrified interpreter took it upon himself to alter his superior's remarks to a mere "hope that some day, after he had turned over the reins of government," Tito might make such a visit.[59] According to Brislin's pattern of interpreters' powers, the aforementioned linguist would have been exercising "legitimate" power, this being based on his conviction that his own superior knowledge of protocol or of cultural differences justified his intervening, without permission, in order to keep his superior from making a disastrous mistake.

Top-ranking interpreters, well aware of their own worth, oft-times venture liberties which lesser employees would not dare. One such was Oleg Troyanovsky, Russian English-language interpreter for Khrushchev and Molotov and, since January, 1977, Soviet ambassador to the United Nations. At a meeting of the Conference of Foreign Ministers in Moscow, for which he was interpreting, Troyanovsky reprimanded Britain's Aneurin Bevin for telling a good-natured joke about Lenin — even though Molotov had laughed heartily at the story![60] Troyanovsky had also been known to omit some of Khrushchev's frequent references to God (an unthinking habit typical of the Russian peasantry), which the interpreter deemed inappropriate for a communist leader.

Then, there was the battle won by a League of Nations interpreter against Sir Austen Chamberlain, a man overly proud of his fluency in French. Chamberlain had accused the interpreter of having distorted his statement, but the interpreter was able to satisfy the League Council that the implications of *his* version were more to the point than what Sir Austen believed appropriate.[61]

André Kaminker, the subject of more stories than possibly any other interpreter of modern times, had been, at the U.N., rendering (into French) a speech of Mr. Molotov's. The hour was late, everyone was eager to leave, but Mr. Molotov kept right on talking. When his turn came to interpret, Mr. Kaminker summed up the entire oration in these words: "M. Molotov dit 'non'" ("Mr. Molotov says 'no'").[62] And when a speaker once complained to Kaminker that "That is not exactly what I said," the interpreter replied, "No, sir, but it is what you ought to have said."[63]

Even the English-language interpreter for Adolf Hitler, whenever anyone at a conference became excited and talked too fast, did not hesitate to intervene and restore order by reminding the participants that he could process only so many words at a time. In fact, the room in which Hitler, Mussolini, Chamberlain and Daladier conferred in 1939 came to be dubbed "the school-room," because one of the conferees had jokingly remarked that the interpreter (Dr. Paul Schmidt) resembled a school-master trying to curb unruly pupils.[64]

But perhaps the most sublime example of a liberty-taking interpreter (although, in this case, with the connivance of his principal) was the occasion of a visit by Ferenc Molnár to President Calvin Coolidge in 1927.[65] Accompanying the non-English-speaking author and playwright as his interpreter was Count László Széchenyi, Hungarian minister to the United States and husband of Gladys Vanderbilt. When the President inquired of Molnár regarding Hungary's economic situation, a subject of which the writer knew nothing, the latter and the Count hastily conspired to "put one over on" Coolidge. In Hungarian, Molnár related a sad story about an aged actress, a tale which he adjudged particularly suitable for the purpose because "Hungary's economic situation is probably sad and because the sadness of the story will enable both of us to look properly serious." Széchenyi then interpreted "Molnár's economic views" at some

length, culminating in a request that the United States grant Hungary
a loan.

Of course, interpreters do make mistakes, which in time become a
part of the profession's legendary lore. During a U.N. discussion on aid
to underdeveloped countries, an American delegate stressed the relationship between public health and the availability of privies. But the interpreter rendering the speech into French, knowing not what a "privy" was,
interpreted it as "private law." Appalled, his partner in the booth slipped
him a note with two letters hastily scribbled on it — "W.C." — (the
ubiquitous European "water closet"). Glancing at it, the recipient scribbled back, "You run along. I'll be all right."[66] Authorities on interpreting
have recommended that a companion who has specialized knowledge or
information should not hesitate to pass a note to the working interpreter,
but it seems that the possibility of a breakdown in communication between colleagues was not foreseen.

Boners are not, however, always the fault of the interpreter. One
laborer in the vineyards of the U.N., trying to render the words of an
English-speaking native of India into Spanish, misinterpreted something
which sounded like "kay-jeez" as "cages." It had been intended as "kgs.,"
the abbreviation for "kilograms." There was also the Russian delegate,
speaking English, who nonplussed his interpreters by stressing a wrong
word, so that his "What's on the road ahead?" came out as "What's on
the road, a head?"[67]

The trouble with errors in interpretation is that, given the wrong circumstance, they could provoke an "international incident," or at least
give the diplomats a rather hard time for a while. One of history's earliest
examples of such an occurrence was the severe reprimand given the interpreter for England's ambassador to Moscow in 1588, who had caused a
mini-crisis by omitting the czar's honorific titles when the envoy addressed him.[68] Something of the same kind happened at the surrender
negotiations between Japan and the United States on August 19, 1945,
when the Japanese were horrified to discover that the document opened
with these words: "I, Hirohito, Emperor of Japan...," using the word for
"I" rather than the customary imperial "We." General Douglas MacArthur's chief interpreter, Colonel Sidney Mashbir, changed the "I" to
"We" with the approval of his chief, who commented, "I have no desire
whatever to debase [Hirohito] in the eyes of his people."[69]

During President Nixon's administration, while personal
negotiations were going on between the President and Emperor Hirohito,
the Emperor, at one point, responded to a question with "I'll think about
it." The interpreter should have made it clear to Mr. Nixon that this answer translated as a "no"; since this was not done, the result was a misunderstanding which produced some resentment.[70] Oriental people do

not like to say anything which might give offense, a fact well known to any "old Asia hand" who has ever tried to get an interpreter to repeat anything which he considered rude. (A Japanese scholar once wrote an article on "Sixteen Ways to Avoid Saying 'No' in Japanese.")[71]

Far worse things happened when President Carter visited Poland in December, 1977, and the free-lance contract interpreter supplied by the State Department turned the visit into a worldwide joke. Among his errors, the interpreter (an American) put such words as these into Mr. Carter's mouth: "When I abandoned the United States," rather than "When I left the United States," "Your lusts for the future" instead of "Your desires for the future," and "Our nation was woven," which should have been "Our nation was founded." Reportedly, although most Poles laughed the matter off, some government officials, including First Secretary of the Party Edward Gierek, were rather annoyed, and the American was soon replaced by a Pole who had worked for the United States Embassy in Warsaw.[72]

One's first reaction, probably, would be to marvel that such an inept linguist should have been assigned to a high-level mission. Even to those ignorant of Polish, it would seem that the words which the interpreter stumbled over were so elementary that even a person with less-than-native fluency should have been able to select the correct ones. This was not a situation calling for familiarity with obscure Polish proverbs.

But there is more to this story than appears on the surface. High-level political interpreters are not expected to do their work blind. The invariable practice is to furnish them, as far in advance as possible, copies of their principal's speech and any other relevant documents, so that they may be well-prepared for their duties. When such materials are not forthcoming within a reasonable time before the interpreter is called upon to perform, he feels that he has a legitimate grievance.

According to the man involved in the Warsaw fiasco, he had been given no copy of the President's remarks until a half-hour *after* the plane had landed and Mr. Carter had finished moving through the reception line. As if this were not enough, the interpreter had been forced to work in the open air under the most adverse weather conditions, standing in cold, freezing rain for two hours, until he was, in his own words, "thoroughly frozen and soaked to the marrow of my bones."[73]

Moreover, the author has been told by persons well informed on this incident, that the interpreter's true field of expertise was not Polish, but Russian, and that certain turns of phrase which would have been quite correct in Russian were inappropriate in Polish. One cannot help wondering why, in the entire city of Washington (or even, in the air age, the entire United States) there could have been found no suitable interpreter whose *primary* language was Polish!

We may hope that the unlucky man consoled himself with the thought that the interpreter does not live who has not made a number of "goofs" at some point in his career. How must it feel to suddenly realize that you have been repeating your principal's speech — or part of it — *in his own language*? This misadventure, so we have been informed, has happened at one time or another to nearly every interpreter.

CHAPTER II

The Linguist of
Ancient and Medieval Days

As anthropologists know, even the most primitive of peoples maintained an intertribal communication which must be deemed an elementary form of diplomacy. But since not all tribes spoke the same language, it is certain that some of the emissaries were bilingual. Although sign language and message sticks were commonly used, at least one authority believes that the sticks, representing merely the envoy's accreditation, were meaningless except in conjunction with an oral message.[1] If we pursue this custom into early historical times, we find that King Murshilish II, brother of Shubbiluliuma I, the "Hittite Bismarck," so feared lest messages to other states be inaccurately delivered that he required his messenger to commit the text to memory, with the written version to be the authoritative one in case of any discrepancy.[2]

Although references to interpreters abound in the *Bible*, in historical accounts of the ancient Near East, and in the literature of Greece and Rome, it is regrettable that the names of specific persons are seldom mentioned. Among the Biblical sources, we may note that, when Joseph's famine-stricken brothers came to him to plead for grain after he had become governor of Egypt, while conferring among themselves "they knew not that Joseph understood them, for he spoke unto them by an interpreter" (Genesis 42:23). In a strikingly antifeminist section of *Esther*, the Persian King, Ahasuerus, commanded Queen Vashti to appear before him, but when she refused to come, the King, persuaded that to permit such defiance would be to set a bad example for all wives, "sent letters into all the King's provinces, into every province according to the writing thereof and to every people after their language, that every man should bear rule in his own house; and that it should be published according to the language of every people" (Esther 1:22). Later, convinced by Haman that the Jews should be destroyed, Ahasuerus summoned his secretaries, and "there was written, according to all that Haman had commanded, unto the King's lieutenants and to the governors that were over every province, and to the rulers of every people of every province [letters] according to the writing thereof, and to every people after their language" (Esther 3:12). The Book of *Ezra* relates how, "in the days of Artaxerxes wrote Bishlam, Mithredath, Tabeel and the rest of their companions, unto Artaxerxes, King of Persia; and the writing of the letter was in the Syrian tongue, and interpreted in the Syrian tongue" (Ezra 4:7). Finally, in the Book of *Daniel* is the story of Nebuchadnezzar and his attempt to force the Jewish people to worship a golden image. A herald was sent forth, proclaiming, "To you it is commanded, O peoples, nations and languages, that at what time ye hear the sound of the cornet, flute, harp, sackbut, psaltery, dulcimer and all kinds of music, ye fall down and worship the golden image" (Daniel 3:4). In each of the cases cited, some kind of interpreter was plainly required.

Linguists of olden times interpreted for both maritime and land-based merchants, for the military and for migrant labor. Many of the "scribes" so frequently mentioned in historical accounts were, in fact, translators or interpreters,[3] as public notaries in Scandinavia, today, are required to be.

The choice of a linguistic career in those days seems, quite often, to have been mere happenstance. If, for example, a man had been raised in a bilingual home by parents of different nationalities, he could easily have turned such an asset to financial advantage. One who did exactly that was the Greek–Persian interpreter, whose mother had been a Lycian and his father a Persian, engaged by Alexander the Great during his invasion of Persia.[4] Or consider the shipwrecked, half-starved native of India who had been dragged before Ptolemy VII by an Egyptian coast-guardsman. Although the Indian spoke not a word of Greek (the language of the Ptolemies), he had something that the Egyptians badly wanted—knowledge of the route to India. Since he, for his part, desired only to be returned to his native land, it came to pass that, after several weeks of intensive tutoring in Greek, the Indian was able to promise that he would accept the travelling companionship of an Egyptian if allowed to return home.[5]

But it was not uncommon for young men to be especially selected and trained for the profession of interpreter. Egypt having evolved into a society of occupational castes by 1500 B.C., the Pharaoh Psamtik II (594–588 B.C.) created the nucleus of a brand-new interpreters' caste when he sent "a considerable number" of Egyptian boys to Greece for the specific purpose of learning the language.[6] Since Egypt at that time swarmed with Greeks (mostly merchants), a ready supply of bilinguals was a necessity.

Alexander the Great and Quintus Sertorius (c. 123–72 B.C.) likewise produced their own linguists. Having probably a greater need of language services than any other figure of the ancient world, the Macedonian ruler "drafted" 30,000 Persian boys to be taught Greek, according to Plutarch's *Lives*, and Sertorius, the Roman statesman and military genius who dominated Spain for eight years, decreed that children of noble birth, recruited from all over the land, would undergo instruction in Latin and Greek.[7]

Despite a preference for noble trainees in some cases, it is likely that the majority of ancient interpreters were of lowerclass birth. Often "they were freedmen or slaves, and the language which they interpreted, especially into Greek or Latin, was their own vernacular."[8] Since those fortunate enough to learn a second language by birth or by subsidy were spared the expense of training for another livelihood, small wonder that the occupation proved attractive to many! Linguists were conceded a certain status (often that of the diplomat) and working conditions were, in general, more than satisfactory for the times.

Yet the profession was not without its hazards. Again according to Plutarch's *Lives* ("Themistocles"), upon one occasion, the people demanded, and were granted, the death of the Greek interpreter at the Persian Embassy in Athens, who had dared to "make use of the Greek language to voice the demands of the barbarians."* Equally vicious was the behavior of the Roman Emperor, Caracalla. A man notorious for his cruelty toward friends and relatives and for his congeniality toward foreigners, Caracalla had granted Roman citizenship to nearly all the inhabitants of the Roman Empire.[9] But his motives become suspect when we learn that it was his custom to suborn emissaries from the outlying regions, urging them to invade Italy and to capture Rome in the event of his assassination. Since only the interpreters were present at these interviews, Caracalla would then conceal his treachery by having them put to death.[10]

Nevertheless, the abuse of persons having diplomatic status was not in accord with usual practice. We know this from the fate of Antimachus, who had pleaded for the execution of Menelaus and Odysseus, the ambassadors charged with persuading the Trojans to restore Helen of Troy to Greece. Antimachus's proposal had so shocked the public sensibility that later, when his sons fell into the hands of King Agamemnon, they were beheaded in retaliation for their father's outrageous suggestion.[11] A group of Spartan nobles even offered their own lives in recompense after some envoys from the Persian King, Darius, had been slain in Sparta.[12] Instances of mistreatment of ambassadors and interpreters were exceptional, which is why history records them. Even among primitive men, the messenger's person had been sacred and inviolable.[13]

*The Persians had demanded a gift of earth and water as a token of submission.

For diplomatic purposes, the Sumerian tongue and its successor, Akkadian,[14] were the most widely-used languages of the ancient Near East, which means that the significant political documents of the day were inscribed in those tongues. We hear, for example, of a peace treaty of approximately 2,600 B.C. between two Mesopotamian city-states, carved in Sumerian on a stone pillar. Since the dispute had been mediated by a third party (one Mesilim), whose tongue was not Sumerian, an interpreter must have been involved in the negotiations. And a translator surely prepared the message found in Akkadian on one of the Tell-el-Amarna tablets, from King Shubbiluliuma I (1375–1335 B.C.) to Egyptian Pharaoh Amenophis I (1370–1350 B.C.), congratulating him on his accession to the throne. Finally, in Egyptian on the walls of Rameses II's mortuary temple but in Akkadian in the original draft, is a treaty concluding a long period of struggle between the two great powers and establishing the respective boundaries between the realms of the Pharaoh and Hittite King Hattushilish III (1275–1250 B.C.). Engraved on a piece of silver for transmission to Rameses, the Egyptian version of the treaty differed slightly from the Hittite version, apparently for the purpose of soothing Egyptian feelings. Such ancient agreements were drawn in the two or more languages of the parties concerned, exactly as they are today, which necessitated the services of a translator.[15]

From the 9th to the 7th century B.C., the dominant power of the Near East was the authoritarian, imperialistic and often cruel Assyrian. Strangely, the mighty efforts of these warlike people to raise their own tongue to preeminence came to naught. For a competitor had arisen—Aramaic.[16] By the 9th century, state documents were commonly being inscribed in both Assyrian and Aramaic, a fact verified by a piece of sculpture from that period depicting the recording of a treasury inventory after a conquest. Two scribes are taking down a list of items from dictation, one working in Aramaic with a pen on papyrus, the other in Assyrian with a stylus on a clay tablet.[17]

From the time of Persia's Cyrus the Great (Cyrus II, c. 600 B.C.–530 B.C.), although the Aramaic tongue was in general use for diplomacy and for the royal decrees of the Persian Empire, bilingualism had become as common as in the Sumerian Empire.* But the Persians had frequently to deal with lands whose tongues were unfamiliar to them. Artaxerxes I (464–504 B.C.) found it necessary to dispatch a bilingual messenger,

*Sometimes even trilingualism: inscriptions on a monolith at the enclosure wall of Darius's capital at Persepolis dating from about 513 B.C. are in three languages: Persian, Akkadian and Elamite (another Semitic tongue). (See Olmstead, History of the Persian Empire, p. 175.)

Artaphernes, to Sparta, to complain that the Spartan delegations to his Court could not be understood, and to request that better interpreters be provided henceforth. This Persian message was prepared in Aramaic, written in Assyrian script, and then translated into Greek. Darius, too, in "shaking down" a foreign noble for the gift of 100 sheep for his daughter, employed an interpreter who rendered the demand in Elamite.[18]

In antiquity, when the dividing line between the civil and military spheres of government could scarcely be detected, military interpreting was simply one aspect of political interpreting. It is known that Cyrus the Younger* employed linguists in his army, for Herodotus and Xenophon speak of them. In the ranks of the Persian Army were 10,000 Greeks, led by Xenophon, who had been hired by Cyrus to assist him in his effort to overthrow his brother, King Artaxerxes. A bilingual army demands bilingual announcements, and before the Battle of Cunaxa,† Pategyas, a Persian member of Cyrus's personal staff, galloped up to shout, in two languages, that the enemy was approaching (described in Xenophon's *Works*). At another time, Cyrus sent his personal interpreter, Pigres, to order a feigned attack by the Greek mercenaries in order to impress a female visitor, and when attacking Babylon, he directed men who could speak Assyrian to warn the population that all who did not remain inside their homes would be slain (see Xenophon's *Cyropaedia*).

Indeed, Cyrus was not famed for his compassion. Herodotus (in his *History of the Greek and Persian War*) reveals how the wealthy Croesus, king of Lydia, had fallen into the Persian's hands at the capture of Sardis. Poor Croesus, condemned to incineration on a pyre, began to utter some cryptic remarks, incomprehensible except for one word, which sounded like "Solon." When interpreters of the Lydian language were brought to the scene, Cyrus learned that his captive had been trying to tell him how he had once been honored by a visit from the great sage, Solon. The ploy worked, for an awed Cyrus spared his prisoner's life.

In early Greek diplomacy, which had become a highly polished art as early as 600 B.C., the diplomat's voice and style of delivery had been considered so crucial to the success of the mission that he was almost invariably an actor, professional orator or stage entertainer.[19] Aeschines declared it to be the height of ignominy for both the envoy and his state if he stumbled over his tongue, while Plutarch put in a good word for the interpreter by admonishing rulers who were not practiced speakers that

---

Persian Achaeminid prince, 424–401 B.C., second son of Darius II and brother of Artaxerxes II, king of Persia at the end of the Peloponnesian War.

†*The decisive contest, 401 B.C., which Cyrus had been on the verge of winning until fatally wounded.*

they should always be accompanied on diplomatic missions by someone who *was*.[20] Demosthenes, that most accomplished of orators, had served as Theban consul *(proxenos)* in Athens. In his *De Falsa Legatione*, he reveals the importance which his countrymen attached to "mere words":

> If [Aeschines] has purposely deceived you for money while holding office as ambassador, do not let him off, do not listen to the suggestion that he is not to be put on trial for "mere words." For what are we to bring any ambassador to justice, if not for his words? Ambassadors have control, not over warships and military positions ... but over words and opportunities. If an ambassador has not wasted the opportunities of the state, he is no wrong-doer; if he has wasted them, he has done wrong.... Where the political system is based on speeches, how can it be safely administered if the speeches are false?[21]

There was good reason for the stress on oratory. Unlike modern envoys, Greek diplomatic representatives were not just messenger boys, but advocates, actually arguing before the assembly of the city-state to which they had been accredited.[22] Besides Demosthenes were Prodicus, Hippias and Pytho of Byzantium, the latter twice commissioned an envoy of Philip of Macedonia, among those Greeks whose powers of expression were widely heralded.

Like the Persians, the Greeks were constrained to rely upon bilinguals when coping with armies of varied nationalities. During the retreat of Xenophon's "ten thousand," the presence of skilled interpreters averted total disaster upon at least two occasions.

At one point, according to Xenophon's *Works*, some natives of the countryside had been harassing the Greek retreat. Interpreters who spoke the language of these people (the Macrones) had been sent to parley with them. At first, the Macrones objected that the Greeks were invading their homeland, but after the latter had given their word of honor that they were only passing through on their way to the sea, and the pledge had been sealed by an exchange of lances, the Greeks were allowed to continue in peace. Later, when Xenophon's forces reached the boundaries of the land of the Mossynoicoi ("wigwam dwellers"), an interpreter named Timesitheus had been sent to inquire whether the Greeks might expect to pass as friends or enemies. The Mossynoicoi had replied that they would not be allowed to pass at all, since a people relying upon fortifications as the Greeks did were obviously up to no good! But Timesitheus, with all the aplomb of a modern diplomat, pointed out the advantage of an alliance with the Greeks by reminding the Mossynoicoi of nearby tribes hostile to them. Following this exchange, Xenophon and the Mossynoicoi chieftain conferred, with Timesitheus interpreting. The happy outcome was an alliance, the Mossynoicoi supplying the Greeks ships and guides.

Two years after the assassination of Philip of Macedon, who had organized the League of Corinth to liberate the Greek cities then under Persian rule, Philip's son Alexander crossed the Hellespont and defeated the Persian Army. Darius fled the field, abandoning his mother, wife and children to the mercies of the Macedonian, who treated his captives with magnanimity. Someone less kindly disposed had misinformed the prisoners that Darius had been killed, and there was much weeping and wailing until Alexander sent Mithrenes, an interpreter skilled in Persian, to reassure them.[23]

Like most army commanders of his day, the Macedonian king claimed for his service numerous foreign (Asian) mercenaries, whom he could address only through interpreters. During a campaign, his beloved horse, Bucephalus, had been stolen by a member of one of these minority groups, the Mardians. Overcome by grief, Alexander sent an interpreter to warn the Mardians that, if Bucephalus were not returned forthwith, all of them might expect to die. The horse soon reappeared, laden with gifts.[24]

By 236 B.C., having subjugated Asia Minor, Persia, Egypt and Babylonia, Alexander set his sights on India, which proved to be the worst mistake of his career. But his misadventures in that land, some of them involving interpreters, remain a source of amusement to history buffs. As a man of intellectual tastes — after all, his tutor had been Aristotle — Alexander wished to learn more about the strange Hindu religion. Unfortunately, he could only rely upon three interpreters to transmit the Brahmin priest's words to him. This state of affairs did not please the priest, who, observing that the interpreters "knew languages but no philosophy," declared that to attempt to expound his doctrine through such a filter would be like expecting water which flows through mud to remain pure.[25] Nor was that the end of Alexander's difficulties with the Brahmins. At another time, he was puzzled to observe some priests stamping their feet on the ground as soon as he appeared. Inquiring through his interpreter as to the meaning of such odd behavior, he was told that, although he had been able to conquer a great part of the earth, upon his death he would possess only as much of it as would be required to hold his body — which portion the priests were marking out with their feet![26]

By approximately 30 B.C., Latin had become the official language of the Roman Empire. Two examples of diplomatic use of the tongue might be the interpreting of the audience of King Tiridates of Armenia before Emperor Nero, and the use of carefully "security-cleared" linguists at a top-secret conference between Sulla and Bocchus, king of Mauretania. The names of Roman interpreters, like most others of the ancient world, were all too seldom recorded, but we do learn of one Publicius Menander, a freedman who was so gifted that Roman envoys setting out for Greece always tried to retain him.[27]

That the Romans employed military interpreters quite as frequently as did the other ancients seems clear from Julius Caesar's comment (in his *Gallic War*) on dispensing with "the usual interpreters," a remark which certainly implies their customary presence. Nevertheless, only twice does Caesar directly refer to the use of interpreters, namely,

> The best course appeared to be to send [to negotiate with the German Ariovistus, who had invaded Gaul] Valerius Procillus.... He was a highly accomplished and extremely brave young man, his loyalty was beyond question, [and] he could speak Gallic, which, after long practice, Ariovistus now speaks fluently.

> Disturbed by these developments, Quintus Titurius sent his interpreter to Ambiorix ... to ask for quarter for himself and his men....

We also know, from Plutarch's *Lives,* that Mark Antony (82–30 B.C.), in his expedition to Parthia (now Syria) retained Alexander of Antioch, his friend and an interpreter of Parthian, to ascertain which route would be safest for Antony to follow. And by no means to be overlooked are the services of Flavius Josephus (c. A.D. 37/48–100), the distinguished Jewish priest, scholar and historian, whom Roman military power had so strongly impressed when he had gone on a mission to Rome in A.D. 64. Josephus was back in Jerusalem during the siege six years later, serving as intermediary and interpreter between his fellow Jews and the Roman General, Titus Flavius Vespasianus,[28] probably with Greek as the medium of expression. While Titus made every effort to persuade the Jews to save themselves by surrendering the city peacefully, Josephus supported his countrymen's position only with reluctance, and he later accepted Roman citizenship. But the Jews remained adamant, and Titus destroyed the city at great cost in human life.

Ultimately, Latin was to become both the universal idiom of international relations and Rome's own tool for achieving political and cultural hegemony. But the triumph of this newly admired tongue aroused the most bitter jealousy among proponents of the Greek language, Europe's more ancient medium of culture. It is true that many Greeks, ethnocentric though they were, found themselves grudgingly impressed by the strength and conciseness of Latin, having noted that fewer words were required to render a speech from Greek into Latin than vice versa.* Yet Greek continued to be taught in Roman schools, was often

*Amusingly, the same argument has been advanced today in favor of English over

used in the Senate, and even remained the political language of the eastern part of the Roman Empire after Latin had been decreed the official tongue. Some time prior to the second century B.C., the Secretariat of the Roman Senate had instituted the practice of translating senatorial decrees affecting the eastern portion of the Empire into Greek, and archaeologists have discovered thousands of Greek translations of official Roman documents and communications. Says one scholar,

> Knowledge of Greek, which even the elder Cato found it profitable to learn, was essential to every Italian who aspired to play a part in public life, even to many whose ambition was only to make money.... Cultured Romans could speak Greek more fluently and write it with greater accuracy than most Englishmen of the same class can write or speak French, for it was the only foreign language which they were required in boyhood to learn and they learned it in intercourse with the Greeks.[30]

In fact, a Latin slang word, *graeculus* ("Greek-imitating"), arose to denote the fad among noble Romans for each home to harbor its resident Greek teacher, philosopher and companion. Examples of Roman fluency in Greek are numerous. One Publius Crassus could converse in five Greek dialects, the father of the Gracchi addressed the citizens of Rhodes in perfect Greek, and Pontius Pilate spoke Greek in his negotiations with the Hebrews.[31] Cicero, who held office in Asia, spoke Greek and wrote a history of his consulship in that language. Yet apparently he spoke the tongue more easily than he wrote it, for in a letter to an acquaintance, he says, "I desire you would see that I have a writer sent to me who understands Greek, as I lose much time in transcribing my lectures" (from the collected *Letters*).

In fact, the very considerable rivalry which developed between these two great tongues presaged the more recent competition between French and English. Cicero's paternal grandfather was said to have commented that a man who knew Greek well was generally a knave,[32] and Cato the Elder (Marcus Porcius Cato, 234–149 B.C.), an antihellene despite his bilingualism,[33] while serving in Greece as a military tribune, chose to address the Athenians through an interpreter because "he despised people who admired only Greek"[34]—in other words, he wanted to put them in their place. Tiberius Nero Caesar, also fluent in Greek, adamantly refused to speak it in the Senate. Once, when some Senators had oc-

---

French: a comparison of phone bills indicates that the same conversation can be conducted more economically in English. However, English is much the more difficult to learn. (See Franklin Roudybush, Diplomatic Language, *Basle: SATZ Repro AG, 1972, pp. 11-12.)*

casion to use the word *emblema*, Nero sarcastically demanded to know whether a Latin equivalent could not be found, and at another time, he forbade a Greek soldier to present his testimony in his mother tongue.[35]

There is no question but that the presence or absence of an interpreter could carry political implications. Often, as Valerius Maximus affirms in his *Memorable Deeds and Sayings*,[36] Roman state policy dictated the use of an interpreter even when unnecessary, as an assertion of superiority, a means of "showing the flag." Shortly before the Battle of Zama,* Hannibal and Scipio Africanus had conferred, accompanied only by their respective interpreters. Since both knew Greek and Hannibal spoke Latin, they could easily have conversed without any intermediaries, but according to Livy's *History of Rome* declined to do so as a matter of national pride. We might also cite the Roman general, Aemilius Paulus, who had informed ten Macedonian chieftains in Latin of the Senate's directives, followed by an interpretation into Greek by one C.N. Octavius.[37] Yet, after the Battle of Pydna in which Perseus had been taken prisoner, Livy says, Paulus addressed *him* directly, without interposing an interpreter. The difference seems to lie in the fact that Perseus, last king of the Macedonians, had held the mighty arms of Rome at bay for three years (in the Third Macedonian War, 171-168 B.C.), thereby winning the respect of Paulus.

Let us now turn our attention to the most peculiar language difficulties of Cathage. To many historians, the "mercenary revolt" of 241-237 B.C. had been a purely economic affair. Because Cathage had been unable to pay its hired soldiers for some time, a day came when they poured into the city in a terrifying horde, demanding their money. Attempts to disperse them had only added fuel to the fire, igniting a full-scale uprising in which horrible cruelties were perpetrated on both sides. But there is much more to this tale than a simple demand for back pay.

The Cathaginians had experienced particularly sticky communications problems with their mercenary armies, which spoke a potpourri of tongues — Lybian, Iberian, Celtic, Liberian, Italian, Greek and more — plus, of course, Punic (Cathaginian). No one person could address an army *en masse*. Whenever a commander needed to make a speech (which was often, for the use of written notices was hardly possible before the invention of printing), his words had to be relayed four or five times through interpreters, who were usually officers belonging to the various linguistic groups. But because the Cathaginian Army was far from innocent of political factions, even when these

---

In 202 B.C.; the Romans under Scipio Africanus defeated the Carthaginians under Hannibal at a site called Naraggara, in modern Tunisia: the last and decisive battle of the Second Punic War.

amateur linguists correctly understood the message they were to interpret, they frequently had motives to misinterpret. So often had this been happening that, by 240 B.C., mistrust and disaffection among the rank and file had reached alarming proportions.

To Gesco, a government emissary, was entrusted the task of restoring discipline. Summoning the men to huge mass meetings served by interpreters, he did his best to clarify misunderstandings and to lay down the law. Unfortunately, two popular rabble-rousers—Mathos, a Lybian, and Spendius, a Campanian slave—soon thwarted his best efforts. Few among the throng could (or would?) comprehend the words of Gesco's interpreters, but the violent invectives of this troublesome duo — probably delivered in vulgarized Punic—were understood by all, and up would go the cry "Throw!", a code word for the stoning of anyone, other than Mathos or Spendius, who tried to speak.[38] Eventually, Hamilcar Barca, Hannibal's father, put together an army of several thousand pure Carthaginians, which quelled the uprising. After the two demagogues were captured, Spendius was crucified and Mathos made to run the gauntlet through the streets of Carthage until he died.[39]

Another crisis involving the use of language occurred during the Second Punic War (218–220 B.C.), when the Carthaginians were waging war in Sicily under the leadership of Hanno the Great. But Hanno happened also to be the leader of an aristocratic, pro-Roman faction in Carthage. His opposition to the policy of foreign conquest pursued by Hamilcar Barca and his son Hannibal in the interests of the commercial classes had annoyed many Carthaginians, among them Suniaton, the most influential citizen of Carthage. Dispatching letters in Greek to Dionysius, tyrant of Syracuse, Suniaton treacherously warned him of the approach of Hanno's army, but the messages were intercepted and Suniaton was convicted of treason. In order that no one might henceforth communicate with the enemy except through the official interpreters, the Carthaginian Senate decreed that citizens of Carthage might no longer learn Greek.[40]

Officially, Rome "fell" in A.D. 476, when the German, Odoacer, deposed Romulus Augustulus. But the eastern portion of the Empire, whose capital was Byzantium (later Constantinople and now Istanbul), survived for another thousand years. Indeed, Byzantium's rulers regarded themselves as the legitimate heirs of the Roman Empire, a pretension that Rome declined to honor. After A.D. 800, Charlemagne's claim to imperial primacy conflicted with Byzantine ambition, and in 1054 a definite schism occurred, which was marked by the excommunication of Pope Leo IX and the Greek Patriarch, Michael Cerularius, each by the other.* Nor did the sacking of Byzantium in A.D. 1204 by the chivalrous knights of the Fourth Crusade do much to improve relations between the two halves of the Christian world.

A revival of the old linguistic competition between Western Latin and Eastern Greek constituted an important symbol of this mutual hostility. Although, as we have indicated, Latin had been the "official" tongue throughout the Roman Empire, in fact the policy had been "only perfunctorily and superficially imposed"[41] in the Greek-speaking areas. Emperor Constantine, however, had resolved to further the cause of Latin. After making Byzantium his capital in A.D. 330, he required the use of that tongue for all public purposes (including prayers by his soldiers!), and he himself addressed the Council of Nicaea (A.D. 325) in Latin, after which his words were interpreted into Greek.[42]

The street population of Byzantium was almost incredibly polyglot, as attested by a 12-century writer, one Tzetzes, who spoke of parleying with his fellow citizens in Russian, Italian, Arabic and Hebrew.[43] For commercial purposes, the city remained bilingual in Latin and Greek until after the death of Justinian I (A.D. 565). Although most public inscriptions were in Greek, certain early emperors, such as Theodosius I (378-395) and Theodosius II (408-450) had caused bilingual inscriptions to be carved in public places.[44] The last-named rulers had in fact founded a university in which "chairs" were established for 16 Greek-language and four Latin-language professors, and Emperor Arcadius (395–408) granted the two languages equal status in the law courts of Byzantium.[45] Coins usually bore Latin legends, but the highest officials used seals *(bullae)* characterized by a Latin inscription on one side and Greek on the other. Perhaps the boundary line between the two tongues is best exemplified by the greeting given Emperor Leo I in A.D. 473 when he attended a performance in the Hippodrome. He was saluted in Greek by the spectators, but in Latin by his Imperial Guard.[46]

The chief instrument for the perpetuation of the Latin tongue in Byzantium had, in fact, been the Roman army, but by the close of the 7th century, army commands were being given in Greek, and at the end of another two hundred years, Latin had been superseded even for legislative purposes.[47] As early as the 5th century, Pope Gregory I, on a visit to Byzantium, had encountered great difficulty in finding an interpreter well-versed in Latin, and from the time of Constantine Porphyrogenitus (905-959), "at best a few Latin words were still preserved in the old formulas of ceremonies and games, and in the manual of military commands. But the words were usually written in Greek letters, and so pronounced as to be unrecognizable."[48] When the said Porphyrogenitus conferred

Actually, the Latin excommunication was effected by the papal legate, one Humbert.

with Liutprand,* he found it necessary to do so through an interpreter, who observed that "every time Constantine undertakes to interpret a Latin word himself he betrays his ignorance."[49]

The psychological resistance to Latin by then so evident in the Greek-speaking areas of the East is confirmed by Emperor Michael III's denunciation of that language as "a barbarous and Scythian tongue," and the comment of Michael Choniates, metropolitan of Athens, that "asses would sooner perceive the sound of the lyre and dung beetles perfume than the Latins apprehend the harmony and grace of the Greek language."[50]

By the 12th century, thousands of foreigners (most of them merchants) were resident in Byzantium, permitted extensive trading privileges and exempted from most taxes. The largest number were Italian — from Venice, Genoa and Pisa particularly — although persons from all corners of the globe, even including an occasional black African, were to be seen. A Pisan, Leo Tuscus, served as official interpreter to the Byzantine government during the reign of the Regent Andronicus (c. A.D. 1142). Of necessity, a number of interpreters was also attached to the Imperial Guard, the Hetairea, since it was composed almost entirely of foreigners — Turks to 998, after which Basil II began recruiting Varangians (Vikings).[51]

Thus it may be seen that Byzantium was a most cosmopolitan city. But cosmopolitanism as an ideal did not infect the proletariat of the city. In general, by the 12th century, the court and the rural aristocracy remained somewhat pro-Latin, but both the official bureaucracy and the urban working classes were thoroughly steeped in Greek culture. Seething with hatred for the "Latins" (the Italians most of all), the populace rose up in 1182 and massacred several hundred, also selling 4000 into slavery to the Turks. Not only did this tragedy lead to a total breakdown in communication between East and West, but it aroused in the Italians a determination to place Latin rulers on the throne of Byzantium, an ambition which was one of the causes of the Fourth Crusade.[52] Pope Lucius III (1181–1185) did write to Leo Tuscus, the official interpreter, to learn the details of the atrocity, but when no satisfactory explanation was forthcoming, relations between the two branches of Christendom remained in a state of suspension for the next ten years.[53]

The Byzantine Empire boasted a complex, highly efficient, two-level bureaucracy, which, like its Chinese counterpart, existed primarily for

---

*Often, Liudprand(us). Born A.D. 920, of a wealthy Lombard diplomatic family, he became a priest, a secretary, an emissary of Berengar I to Byzantium and, in 961, bishop of Cremona. Fluent in Latin, Greek and German, in his three books — Antapodosis, Gesta Ottonis and Legatio — Liutprand displays a remarkable bilingual style of writing, part Latin and part Greek.

the conduct of relations with "barbarians"—in this case, non-Greeks. For centuries, the government maintained "barbarian academies," at which civil servants were required to attend lectures on foreign peoples. The academies were also the source of interpreters and guides for visitors from abroad.[54]

Although most civil servants never reached the exalted level of the Sacred Hierarchy, the top rung on the bureaucratic ladder, among those privileged few could be found the Logothete of the Drome, or foreign minister, one of whose duties was to supervise the Office for Barbarians. A corps of interpreters, "including every level of linguistic skill and ability," was a subsection of that office. Some of the linguists went on to better things and attained a fairly high status, such as that of Protospather, or the Eleventh Rank, just below the Patrician.[55]

An international incident of a linguistic nature is recorded from the reign of Isaac Angelus (Isaac II, 1155-1204). Frederick Barbarossa, on his way to the Holy Land in the Third Crusade, elected a land route through Thrace rather than the more customary sea route. Probably quaking with fear, Isaac wrote a threatening letter to Frederick, but the German seems to have taken offense mainly because of an error made by his translator, who had interpreted Isaac's family name, Angelus, to mean that he had been so presumptuous as to style himself "Isaac the Angel."[56] On the other hand, the Fourth Crusade provides us with an example of a delicate diplomatic mission entrusted to an interpreter. As Boniface of Montserrat approached Byzantium with several thousand men, Alexius III (d. 1211) dispatched Nicholas Roux—an Italian despite his name—to reproach the Crusader for menacing a Christian city.[57]

Intimately involved in the religious rivalry between East and West, the Greek language was to be carried far beyond the borders of the Byzantine Empire, extending Latin–Greek competition into Eastern Europe. During the 9th century, Michael III of Byzantium sent two Thessalonians, Constantine (then known as Cyril) and his brother Methodius, to the Slavic state of Moravia (Czechoslovakia), where their missionary efforts were to be supported by the Byzantine Government. The brothers' attempts to translate Eastern Church liturgy into a Slavic dialect culminated in Old Church Slavonic, destined to become the channel through which Eastern Europeans received the culture of the Greek-speaking world.[58]

However, since Latin missionaries from Austria had already been at work in Moravia, competition between the Eastern and Western rites and between the Latin and Slavonic tongues soon became intense. Insisting that only Hebrew, Greek and Latin were acceptable for use in the Mass, the German priests denounced Constantine-Cyril for his promotion of Slavonic, whereupon Cyril ridiculed this "three-language heresy" by citing St. Paul's First Epistle to the Corinthians. The relevant passage reads:

> For if the trumpet give an uncertain sound, who shall prepare himself to the battle? So likewise ye, except ye utter by the tongue words easy to be understood, how shall it be known what is spoken? For you shall speak into the air. There are, it may be, so many kinds of voices in the world, and none of them is without signification. Therefore if I know not the meaning of the voice, I shall be unto him that speaketh a barbarian, and he that speaketh shall be a barbarian unto me [1 Corinthians 14:8-11].

But the conflict was not quite as clear and straightforward as it might seem. Two Roman Catholic Popes, Nicholas I (d. 867) and Hadrian II (867–872), more alarmed at the independent stance adopted by the Bishops of Salzburg than by the activities of the Greek missionaries, chose to support the latter. Hadrian actually named Methodius to be "archbishop and papal legate to the Slavonic nations."[59]

In 865, the Khan Presiam converted to Christianity, becoming Boris I of Bulgaria, and making his the first feudal Slavic state to enter into community with Christian Europe. Bulgaria's earliest written literature consisted of translations from Greek into old Bulgarian, utilizing the "cyrillic" characters. Under Czar Simeon I (893–927) the son of Boris I, such literature (mostly of a religious nature) flourished through writers who were brilliant translators. The courts of the Bulgarian princes employed many bilinguals who recorded the instructions of the ruler and the oral communications of foreign emissaries. The translators of the written materials, often monks from the monasteries, were well-educated, but the oral communicators (interpreters, or *tlumaches*) tended to be common men, tradesmen who had grown up in a border region.[60] By contrast with the present day, translators in that time and place were accorded a higher status than interpreters, because they were nearly always more learned.

Bulgaria fell subject to the Byzantine Empire between 971 and 1187, and after the destruction of Moravia by the Magyars in the early 10th century, the Bulgarians became the transmission channel for the Slavonic tongue, written in cyrillic characters. It is believed that the earliest rites of the Russian Orthodox Church were conducted in Old Church Slavonic, introduced from Bulgaria.[61] Not surprisingly, translation was a thriving business in the Eastern Europe of the 9th and 10th centuries, and the *Russian Primary Chronicle* records the assembly of many scribes by Prince Yaroslav of Kiev, in 1037, to translate books from Greek into Slavonic.[62]

The final chapter on Byzantine culture is written with the capture of

Byzantium by the Ottoman Sultan Mohammed II, in 1453. In the frontier region first overrun by the Turks, Greek ceased to be the official
language of the bureaucracy in the Muslim year 81 (dating from the
Hegira—or A.D. 703 by the Christian calendar). Tradition has it that a
Greek clerk, finding insufficient ink in an inkwell, urinated into it to in-
crease the supply. The outraged ruler, Abd Al-Malik ibn-Marwân, then
ordained that the official language was to be changed to Arabic, telling
the Greek functionaries, "Seek your livelihood in any other profession
than this, for God has cut it off from you."[63]

Nevertheless, under the Turks, a portion of the old scribal classes
continued to be a part of the Muslim civil service.[64] Known as *iaziti*,
these scribes were usually bilingual (or polylingual) Christians, with a
knowledge of perhaps Greek, Turkish and Rascian.* Actually, this was
nothing new. Christian scribes had long been employed by Muslim
rulers—whether Seljuks, Mamelukes or Ottomans—and Greek was the
first language of Turkish diplomacy with the West. But Mohammed II
probably utilized the *raia* (Christians) more than any other ruler. We
know the names of at least two of his bilingual secretaries—Thomas
Katavolenos and Panagiotes Nicousios, the latter having been, at one
time, a grand dragoman (chief translator).[65] Greeks who served in such
capacity never renounced their Christian heritage, and the Turks did not
insist upon their doing so because their services were too valuable.

Thousands of Greeks, however, preferred not to live under Turkish
rule at all, and the Ottoman conquest set off a true diaspora. Long before
1453, some Greeks had been living in Western Europe and teaching their
language there—Manuel Chrysoloros, for example, who had been con-
ducting classes in various Italian cities and later in Germany, from about
1366.[66] Since such pre-conquest Greeks had paved their way, it was not
too difficult for others to follow, and Byzantine culture soon appeared in
all corners of Europe—in such cities as Lyon, Toledo, London,
Budapest, Vienna and Odessa—introduced by highly cultivated men and
women. To these émigrés belongs the credit for saving many ancient
books that otherwise would have been lost forever. One Janus Lascaris
entered Italy with a library of approximately 200 volumes, eighty of
which proved to be unknown to the librarians of Western Europe.[67] The
diaspora played no small role in the Renaissance, which was well under
way at about this time.

City-state governments frequently employed the refugees as interpreters or translators, and some names have been recorded. "Scribe"
(which in this case can only mean "translator") Michael Markokephalites,
for one, appears on documents drawn up at the Council of Trent (1545–

*A Serbian (Yugoslav) language of some importance in Ottoman Turkey.

1563).[68] Italy proved to be the main beneficiary of the diaspora, all of the sizeable Italian cities harboring Greek "ghettoes," of which the largest was that in Venice, attaining at one time a population of about 10,000. Among the better-known expatriate interpreter-translators of Italy were Marcus Musurus, a professor at the University of Padua and mentor to Erasmus, and Theodore Paleologus, Venetian interpreter and envoy to the Turkish sultan, who, at his death in 1532, was honored by burial in the Church of San Giorgio.[69] A number of Greeks, as we shall see, also entered the service of the Norman kings of Sicily, at whose court Greek was one of the official languages.

These expatriate Greeks did all within their power to subvert the Muslim government at Byzantium. Using a Greek church in Naples at their headquarters, agents having a knowledge of Turkish transmitted to the Spanish "information on the position of the Greek fleet, rebellions of the Pashas, and especially Turkish plans for future military action," while a network of spies and saboteurs operated from Constantinople to Cairo and Alexandria.[70] In 1790, Empress Catherine of Russia, whose dream was to drive the Turks from Constantinople, received a delegation of Greeks in St. Petersburg, who petitioned her in these words: "It is under your auspices that we hope to deliver from the hands of the barbaric Moslems an Empire which they have usurped, to free the descendants of Athens and Lacaedemon from the tyrannical yoke of ignorant savages."[71] Delighted, Catherine armed a fleet of ships purchased by some wealthy Greeks — and the Turks blew them out of the water. But Christian Greek "resistant forces" *(klephts)*, who persisted for centuries in the mountains of southern Macedonia, were to play an important part in the 1821 uprising against Turkey.[72]

We should expect the language problems of the Crusaders to have manifested themselves on two levels — among the multinational Christians themselves, and between the Christians and the Muslims. Europeans had not been entirely unacquainted with the Islamic world before the Crusades began. For about 300 years following Mohammed's death, it is true, militant Islam had made the Mediterranean virtually its own, and, by mutual consent, the two ideologies (which is what they really were) avoided each other except on the purely diplomatic level, such as the reception of an Arab delegation in 692 by Pepin of France. Of course, an occasional daring European ventured into Muslim territory on his own. In the middle of the 8th century, St. Willibald, accompanied by several other Englishmen, stopped off in Syria on his way to the Holy Land, where all were arrested by the Muslim authorities. But the Caliph's Spanish interpreter was able to convince him that they meant no harm and they were released.[73]

By the 10th and 11th centuries (the First Crusade began in 1096), Europeans, particularly Jewish merchants from southern France, had begun venturing into Muslim waters, and it was not rare for Christian and Muslim sailors to be serving on the same ships.[74] A 9th-century Arabic scholar, Ibn Khurradadbhbeh, had written about these men, trading back and forth between East and West, and speaking "Arabic, Persian, Greek, Frankish, Spanish and Slavonic."[75] The Jews had commonly served as teachers of the Arabic tongue long before the coming of Islam, and, as we shall see, they continued in that capacity long after its advent. Relations between Hebrews and Arabs had always been close. Zayd Ibn-Thábit, the Prophet's secretary, is said to have known Hebrew well, and the Jews of Medina employed Hebrew script in their Arabic correspondence with Mohammed.[76]

Just how difficult a time the Crusaders had, linguistically speaking, is subject to debate. On the one hand, as Fulcher of Chartres lamented, "Whoever heard of such a mixture of languages in one army? There were present Franks, Frisians, Gauls, Allabroges, Lotharingians, Alemanni, Bavarians, Normans, Italians, Dacians, Apulians, Iberians, Bretons, Greeks and Romanians. If any Breton or Teuton wished to question me, I could neither reply nor understand."[77] Having been there, he should know. On the other hand, it has been asserted that "the use of interpreters was so widespread that intercourse between people who did not speak the same language presented no difficulties."[78] We do know that the Crusaders had the practice of identifying themselves as such to their brothers-in-arms by making the sign of the cross with their fingers.

Despite the polyglot makeup of the armies, French served as the original *lingua franca* throughout the 200-some years of crusading, for French barons, whose countrymen were in the majority, had led the First Crusade, and the Latin Kingdom of Jerusalem, under Baldwin, was "French in body, soul and mind."[79] If any proof of French domination were needed, the fact that the Arabic word for "European" has ever since been *Ferenghi* ("Frank") should suffice.

Scarcely more information is available on the question of European intercourse with the Arabs than on the manner in which the Crusaders communicated with each other. Historians know that most of the Franks spoke some Arabic and a few were fluent, among them Richard the Lionhearted's man, Bernard, who was assigned to intelligence duties.[80] But for administrative purposes, the Europeans relied heavily upon Arabic secretaries and bilingual scribes, some of them Europeans who had long lived in the East. Two Crusaders recall that, after they had been captured by the Muslims (whom they call "Saracens"), "there were certain people who knew the Saracen and French tongues, and they put the Saracen speech into French for Count Peter [of Brittany]."[81] The "certain people" will forever remain unidentified, but the result of that particular encounter was the restoration of Damietta to the Saracens.

Strange as it seems to the modern mind, Christians and Muslims continued trading with each other throughout the years of hostility, and treaties (usually in Latin and Arabic), such as the one between Frederick II of Sicily and Abu Zakariya of Tunis, were not unusual.

No people—not even the French—have been more proud of their language than the Arabs, and the tongue has, in fact, been widely admired by others. The historian, Leopold Ranke, considered it second only to Latin as the most important language in world history.[82] To the Arabs, it is the "tongue of the angels" *(lisan al-mala 'ikah)*, for two reasons. When Adam was expelled from Paradise, so goes the Muslim legend, he was ordered to cease speaking the Tongue of the Angels and to speak Syriac (Aramaic) instead. Only later, after he had repented, was he allowed to resume the use of Arabic.[83] And it was in that language that God chose to make his most important revelations, to the Prophet Mohammed.

Like the Greeks, the Arabs have a long tradition of respect for eloquence, and the holy *Koran* itself, which word means "recitation" or "discourse," had been intended to be declaimed orally. For a long time, Muslims opposed the translation of their sacred book into any other language, not, as is commonly supposed, for reasons of fanatical exclusivity (after all, Islam is a missionary faith!), but because they believed that to use any other tongue than the one chosen by God as His instrument would be sacrilegious. The Western World's first translation of the *Koran* was that done by Peter of Cluny in 1141, and the first English translation, from the French, appeared in 1649.[84]

The transmission of culture during the Crusades and in the centuries following was a two-way street. From such missionaries as St. Francis of Assisi, André de Longjumeau,* and St. John of Damascus, a Syrian who spoke Aramaic, Greek and Hebrew and who was employed by the Umayyad Caliph of Damascus, Christian and Greek thought entered Islam.[85] The most interesting and controversial of the medieval missionaries to the East was, however, Ramon Lull.

A Catalan, Lull had learned Arabic from a Moorish slave whom he had purchased for that specific purpose. An intellectual who traveled widely, visiting the Pope, he wrote an incredible number of books, 488 of which have been traced.[86] In 1311-1312, Lull appeared before the Council of Vienna, which had been called to consider the work of the Knights

---

St. Francis accompanied the Crusaders of Innocent III to Damietta in 1219 and preached to the Muslim ruler, Nasir-al-Din Muhammad; de Longjumeau was a Dominican friar who had previously served Louis IX as emissary to the Tartars.

Templar, and there presented a proposal for the founding of Oriental language schools to train missionaries to the Islamic lands.[87] The Council's decision was to establish five chairs — in Rome, Bologna, Paris, Oxford and Salamanca — for instruction in Arabic, Hebrew and Chaldean. The professors were to be appointed by national monarchs and (in the case of the Roman school) by the Pope. Despite ample warning, Lull himself persisted in preaching to the Moors of Spain, where, in 1316, he was stoned to death.[88]

Arabic culture entered Europe primarily through two centers, Spain and Sicily. The Muslims had subjugated Spain in the early 8th century and bilingualism had, at first, been common in both everyday life and in literature. Musa Ibn Nusair, one of the two generals responsible for the Spanish conquest, had set the tone for future policy by minting coins in Toledo in 714, bearing both his name in Latin and the Islamic Confession of Faith in Arabic.[89] In time, however, so arabized did the cultivated citizens of Toledo become that one of their number bemoaned the almost total disappearance of Latin.[90]

Toledo was destined to become one of the world's great centers for translation. For a hundred years, a school for linguists founded by Dominico Gundisolvi attracted scholars from all over Europe. Most of the translator-instructors were Jews, who were generally fluent in Arabic, Hebrew, Spanish and occasionally Latin. In 1250, this institution became the first School of Oriental Studies in Europe, for the purpose of training missionaries to the Muslims *and* the Jews.[91] But since the translation work at Toledo was mostly either philosophic or scientific in nature, we need not dwell upon it.

Of more interest to us are the administrative language practices of the Muslim and Norman rulers of Sicily. From 902 until 1091, while the island was in Muslim hands as a dependency of the Tunisian Aghlabids and later the Fatimids, Sicily boasted many famous linguists, such as Musa ben Asbagh, Ibn-Rahiq, and Ibn Al-Birr. Arabic was, of course, the court language, but the polyglot population of Palermo, the capital, was a wild mixture of races from East and West.[92]

Early Norman adventurers, returning from the Crusades, entered the service of Guaimar IV of Salerno, established themselves firmly in southern Italy at the expense of the Byzantines and, in 1059, the Pope conferred upon their leader, Roger Guiscard, the title of Duke of Apulia, Calabria and Sicily. With the flexibility so characteristic of Normans everywhere, those of Sicily established a remarkable quadrilingual administration, in which Arabic, Greek, Latin and Norman French were all official court languages.[93] Of the five principal men of the court of Roger II (1111–1154), who himself spoke both Greek and Arabic, two were Arabs and the other three were Greeks. Roger's Grand Vizier from 1125,

George of Antioch, was an Arabic-speaking Orthodox Greek (Roger preferred that tongue for diplomatic correspondence), but many of the Arabs remained in the lower reaches of the bureaucracy.[94] On a day-to-day, practical level, "Muslim emirs, Greek logothetes, Norman justiciars and ecclesiastical dignitaries worked side by side in the curia regis" (king's council).[95] Even after the German emperor, Henry VI, wrote *finis* to the Norman period by conquering Sicily in 1194, this type of administration persisted for some time, and not until the early 14th century did Arabic become extinct in Sicily.[96] It is doubtful if anything quite like the Norman arrangement has ever been seen, before or since, in the annals of public administration.

As one might expect, the multilingual nature of the Palermo Court attracted some of the most accomplished linguists from all over Europe. Under Frederick II (1272–1337), particularly, a number of Christian and Jewish translators were at work at Palermo, rendering Arabic texts (some of which were, themselves, translations from the Greek!) into Latin. The Englishman, Michael Scott, was a connecting link between the Sicilian Court and the great translation center which had sprung up in Toledo, where he had worked between 1217 and 1220. Besides Scott, other bi- or multi-lingual secretaries to Frederick II included Jacob and Yahuda Cohen, Giovanni and Mosè of Palermo.[97]

Language was, in fact, among the many interests that attracted Frederick's restless, inquiring mind. Fond of "scientific" experimentation, he commanded that a number of children be raised from birth in total silence and isolation, in order to find out what language they would ultimately speak![98] Nothing came of it, as they all died young, for reasons which would be no mystery to a modern psychologist.

As we follow the story of the language professions up to the Renaissance period, we shall see that their characteristics remain remarkably constant until well into modern times. In post-medieval to pre-19th-century Europe, as in the Middle Ages and the world of antiquity, for the most part no distinction was drawn between interpreters and translators, the practitioners of the art were frequently conceded diplomatic status but were not always subjects of the rulers whom they served, and the profession often proved to be a springboard to a more exalted position. Probably the most notable changes, evolving slowly and gradually over the centuries, were a greater recognition accorded the linguist's services, manifest in an increasing tendency to record his name, and in his improved bodily security (meaning there was less likelihood of his being penalized for an unwelcome message). The specialties of literary and "technical" translating increasingly diverge, until by the 19th century they are well on their way to becoming two separate professions. Finally, with the rise of modern nation-states and the development of their administrative apparatus come a greater awareness of the linguist's place within this scheme, and the desirability of subjecting him both to systematic training and to more stringent selection procedures. Only with the establishment of national foreign offices and of numerous inter-governmental organizations has the interpreting-translating profession reached maturity.

CHAPTER III

Europe and the
New World — To 1919

Europe

We have seen how bilingual Greek scholars, steeped in Byzantine diplomatic lore, had relocated to the four corners of Europe and, in the greatest numbers, to Venice. From them the Venetians had learned the art of diplomacy, had transmitted what they had learned to the other Italian city-states, and thence to the capitals of Europe. The word "byzantine," signifying the ultimate in deviousness and duplicity, has ever since been applied to Italian city-state diplomacy. The association is valid in the most literal sense, for European diplomacy, as an art, *is* of Byzantine origin.

No governments of antiquity had maintained resident diplomats in foreign lands, but had appointed them *ad hoc,* for special missions as needed. True diplomacy, of the modern type, had begun only with the custom of assigning permanent representatives to other nations. Although the Vatican had introduced such a resident mission (the Apocrisarius) to Byzantium as early as A.D. 453, the first true state mission is considered to have been that sent by the Duke of Milan to Cosimo dei Medici in 1450.[1] Until about a hundred years later, these emissaries had been known not as "ambassadors" but as "resident orators," a title which is significant. For linguistic ability, not social status, had been the first requirement of the early diplomat. Barbers, chemists and merchants had frequently served in such capacity, until the Vatican had begun to insist that these careers be reserved for the nobility.

One of the more usual entrées to ambassadorial status from the late medieval period had been the post of courier, and the names of nearly 300 of these men have been recorded.[2] Serving as messenger was the best way to pick up a number of languages beyond the one or two with which one might have started out. John Spritewell, courier to Elizabeth I, whose primary sphere of operation had been the Channel–Western

Europe route, could speak French, Spanish, Dutch and German, as well as English. Unfortunately, many of these persons were eccentric, or unstable, depending upon one's point of view. The career being a glamorous and ofttimes dangerous one, it had tended to attract men of unconventional type. Some of them, drinking to excess, had blabbed state secrets while in their cups, or they had overslept and, quite literally, missed the boat.[3]

Gradually, all European nations had developed messenger services which are still very much in use. The corps of King's Foreign Messengers in Britain, as distinct from the internal service, had been founded in 1772, with 16 messengers. Their numbers, and the frequency of journeys abroad, had varied from year to year. In 1802, for example, there had been 26 foreign journeys and 12 years later, 80 but the number of messengers had declined from a high of 20 in 1824 to only six by 1914. All applicants had been required to be not over 35 years of age and competent in foreign languages. Several of them had lost their lives in the line of duty, and one Andrew Basilico had distinguished himself by *eating* his dispatch when captured by the French in 1782.[4]

Because, in premodern times, it had actually been considered undesirable for an ambassador to be a subject of the king who employed him, there had grown up over the years a sizeable circle of professional diplomats who, meandering about Europe, had served various monarchs in turn. Many of them had been Italian, probably because modern diplomacy had been born in the Vatican and in the surrounding city-states during the Renaissance. One Franz Paul von Lisola, of Italian origin but French-educated and a citizen of Spain, had held diplomatic posts for at least seven different European governments.[5] Among Italians employed as ambassadors by the English court in the 13th century had been Sir Nicolin de Flisco, Antonio di Passano and Andrea de Portinari, while Henry VIII, three centuries later, also had an Italian representing him in the Netherlands.[6] William III had often chosen Dutchmen, French Huguenots or Swiss, while Louis XIV had used a German in Sweden and an Italian and a German in Italy.[7] Such men, as well as their bi- or multilingual secretaries, could obviously have constituted "security risks" if they had worked successively for two monarchs who were mutually hostile. In time, as the governments of Europe had become more sensitive to this possibility, diplomats would be required to be citizens of the state which they represented. (However, in the interest of economy, consulates are still often manned by a citizen of the nation in which the post is located.)

Medieval and Renaissance diplomats had frequently debated the question of which languages should be mastered by the professional envoy. For approximately twenty years at the very end of the 16th century and the beginning of the 17th, a large number of books on the art of government and international relations had appeared in print. On only one point are all the authors in accord: *Latin was indispensable.* Nearly every ambassador could speak it to some extent, and a few had been considered true classical scholars—Diego Sarmiento de Acuña, Count of Gondomar, for example—who had won the admiration of the British monarch, James I, for his fluency in Latin.[8]

The dominant role sustained by this ancient "dead" tongue for so many centuries following the collapse of the Roman Empire may be attributed to two circumstances: the importance of the Vatican and of ecclesiastical envoys in early diplomacy, and the later influence of the Holy Roman Emperors, whose ambition it had been to revive the glories of ancient Rome. Latin fell from favor only after the rise of powerful nation-states intent upon promoting their vernaculars which, in a number of cases, had evolved from the original Roman tongue.

By 1500, expertise in Latin had become much less common than in earlier centuries. Other tongues were coming to the fore as potential idioms of diplomacy, but for a long time no single one enjoyed preëminence. The author of one of the best manuals on diplomatic method ever written, François de Callières, had recommended fluency in German, Italian and Spanish, as well as Latin.[9] An earlier writer, Ottaviano Maggi, would have added to those tongues Turkish, Greek and French, while Alberico Gentili had simply advocated the mastery of at least three languages besides Latin, including that of the country to which one had been accredited.[10]

Despite the fact that Italian, during the second half of the 16th century, had probably been the best-known modern language in Europe, preferred by the English, Spanish and Austrian courts, and "the only modern language other than their own which most educated Frenchmen were willing to learn,"[11] it was not destined to supplant Latin as the language of diplomacy. German was little used except for communications with other Germanic states,* and as for English, during the entire Renaissance period one could have said of it what has more recently been said of another European tongue, "nobody knows Dutch except the Dutch." Thanks to the status of the French monarchy, the language of France had begun to make headway, yet many central European courtiers could not speak it, and even the English were well on the way to forgetting it. Says Mattingly, "Among Edward VI's ambassadors to French-speaking courts, Heynes, Bonner, Paget, Morison and Thirlby were all too deficient in French to use it for negotiation, and after making heavy weather in Latin, Paget and Thirlby were fain to try Italian."[12] Nine English diplomats of

---

Nor did all German rulers favor German; many preferred Latin, French or Italian.

the 17th century were said to have been noted for their fluency in French, eight others for Latin, four for Spanish, three for Italian, and one each for Portuguese and Dutch, but a German bilingual was a rare creature.[13]

History's most fascinating institutionalization of the profession of translator-interpreter was to take place in Ottoman Turkey. For some 300 years, the *dragoman* remained the key figure in diplomatic relations between Eastern and Western Europe. By the 16th century, foreign ambassadors accredited to the Porte (the Ottoman administration), very few of whom were fluent in Turkish, had become accustomed to communicating with the sultan and his bureacracy through a class of interpreters, the *truchemen* (Turkish), anglicized to *dragomen*.[14] Paid relatively well (in modern American terms) according to experience, these bureaucrats had been permitted assistants, apprentices called *giovanni di lingua* — "young linguists" — or student interpreters, as the English would later call them, who earned about a quarter to one-half as much. Turkish protocol required the dragomen to wear a kind of uniform, easily identifiable red-and-blue shoes, the cost of which was charged to the employer.[15]

France had concluded with Turkey, in 1536, the first capitulation treaty, granting to its nationals a long list of privileges within the sultan's domains, which would, ultimately, be extended to the citizens of the other important Western nations. In the negotiation of these treaties, the dragomen had played a leading role.[16] Many of them were non-Turks, primarily of Greek and Italian origin, such as the Pisanis, hereditary dragomen to the British Embassy.[17] The Germans were unique in preferring their own nationals whenever possible, among them Dr. Clemens Busch, to become the first undersecretary of the Foreign Office, and Dr. Wilhelm Solf, the last foreign secretary under the Empire.[18] By the 19th century, the German Embassy's first dragoman had held the rank of minister.[19]

All dragomen were, of course, supposed to enjoy the benefits of the capitulatory arrangement. Yet until the late 17th century, those who were Turkish citizens remained subject to the sultan's law, a state of affairs much resented by foreign diplomats, since the loss of a prized interpreter to jail or to the gallows could be most inconvenient!

Early in the 17th century, a Turkish dragoman had been hanged and when his employers' heated protests achieved nothing, the European community had begun a concerted effort to train their own interpreters. Ten young Frenchmen had been sent to a Capuchin monastery in Smyrna to learn Turkish, Arabic and modern Greek,[20] but the enterprise had failed. Berlitz-style methods being as yet unheard of, elegant Turkish proved too difficult to be mastered in a hurry. While the idiom of the man in the street was not particularly hard to learn, the higher the officialdom the more flowery became the prose, until even the Turks could not comprehend it. In fact, a dragoman of the British Embassy had once been complimented by a Turkish official, who had marvelled that "Even I could understand at least a third of it."[21]

But since the diplomatic legations of Constantinople required a consistently large number of interpreters, in 1673 the French had shrewdly negotiated a new capitulatory treaty, whereby all dragomen, *whether Turkish or not,* were to become the legal subjects of the foreign power employing them, entitled to all its privileges and immunities.[22] Moreover, the dragoman's diplomatic immunity was to extend to all members of his family, and it was to be hereditary. The Turks were far from pleased at these coerced concessions, and in 1680 the vizier, Kara Mustapha, had attempted to minimize their impact by decreeing that no one foreign diplomat might employ more than three dragomen.[23] Despite this limitation, the capitulatory agreements, replete with built-in irritations, had remained the major source of friction between Turkey and the Western Powers as late as World War I. Most of this friction stemmed from the ambiguous position of the dragomen, and by 1914, the abolition of all special privileges for foreigners and their hangers-on had become the primary goal of Turkish foreign policy.

During the mid-19th century, the British had made another vain attempt to replace foreign interpreters with their own, by establishing student interpreterships for Turkey and the Levant similar to those already in force in the Far East. The recipients were to study first in Constantinople, then at Oxford or Cambridge. But Stratford de Redcliffe, the ambassador to the Porte at that time, had used as political attachés the two young men sent to him, and had refused to entrust them with any language work, which continued to be done by the traditional dragomen.

It may seem strange that a humble interpreter should find himself, upon occasion, the focus of an "international incident." How could this happen? Because, for one thing, he was not always that "humble." We have already discussed, in an earlier chapter, the powers that interpreters wield, intentionally or otherwise, over their clients, and the likelihood that the truly superb interpreter is fully aware of his potential. Nowhere in Europe were such powers more evident to all parties concerned than in Ottoman Turkey. Paradoxically, it was the Porte's very awareness of the dragoman's dangerous influence that led to his not infrequent persecution.

Consider Giorgio Draperys, aristocrat of ancient family, who had served six British ambassadors, and who had once exploited his intimacy with the vizier to have a rich Jew ousted from his home in order to provide a residence for the new British envoy, but who, later, had diverted gifts intended for that gentleman to his own use. Or Panayoti Nicusi, one-time Greek dragoman at the German embassy, who had manipulated the Porte in order to keep Latin Christians from divesting the Greeks of their custody of the Holy Sepulchre in Jerusalem.[24]

Not only were the dragomen their employer's mouth, they were usually his eyes and ears as well. Because the diplomats had, perforce, to rely upon them extensively, it would have been surprising if some of them had not occasionally betrayed their trust. Since the profession was often hereditary in certain families, two or more close relatives might well be serving different nations that hated each other, and not always were the interpreters discreet in guarding "their" nation's secrets. Some of them, to bolster their reputation for omniscience, would carry fabricated stories to their employers, and some had even been known, while interpreting, to substitute entire speeches of their own.

It is true that inaccuracy often resulted only from the dragoman's fear of saying something which might offend the terrible-tempered Turk. For the dragomen were victims as often as they were victimizers, a fact that may partially excuse their behavior. Not only in the years before they had been granted diplomatic immunity, but oftentimes, even after they had supposedly been placed under the protection of the capitulations, were the interpreters cruelly used. Until rather late in history, the Turks did not subscribe to the generally accepted principle of Western diplomacy that the bearer of bad news is not to be held responsible for his message. Consequently, it had not been uncommon for interpreters to be abused verbally or physically, jailed, even hanged or impaled — only for doing their assigned duty. All of the embassies in Constantinople were faced with the never-ending problem of finding interpreters "at once competent, trustworthy, and brave enough to risk the consequences of transmitting unpalatable messages to the Sultan."[25] A Levantine serving as a first dragoman had once been asked whether he had accurately transmitted a certain distasteful message. He had, said he, but "I rounded off the edges."[26]

One poor dragoman had found himself squarely "in the middle," a victim of incredible pettiness. The new French ambassador to the Porte, the Marquis de Nointel, upon being received by the vizier, had objected that his seat had been placed too low, and had ordered the dragoman, one Mavrocordato, to raise it. But Nointel's order had been promptly countermanded by the rank-conscious vizier, who did not want anyone sitting on the same level with his own "soffah." This see-sawing of the stool, up and down, had continued for some time, until the vizier had ordered Mavrocordato to present his wishes to Nointel in the form of an ultimatum. "The Grand Vizier commands the chair to be placed below," the dragoman said as directed, to which Nointel had replied, "The Grand Vizier may command his chair; he cannot command me." At this point, a servant had snatched the chair away, and Nointel had strode from the room to the accompaniment of a muttered "Gehennem!" from the vizier ("Let him go to hell"). Later, Mavrocordato had been forced to bear the brunt of the vizier's displeasure. [27]

From the standpoint of the Turks, one of the most objectionable features of the capitulations had been the provision that Western nationals could not be questioned in a court, or by Turkish officials, without the presence of a dragoman. This might appear to have been only simple justice; lacking an intermediary familiar with the Turkish language, law and customs, a foreigner could have found himself in a perilous situation. But, according to the Turkish spokesman at an international conference in 1922,

> Whenever a murderer or the perpetrator of a crime succeeds in reaching the abode of a foreigner, the Turkish police [were prevented] from entering and were obliged to suspend the pursuit until the *dragoman* arrived, and in the meantime [the suspect escaped].

Moreover, in a case involving a foreigner,

> When it was foreseen that the judgment would go against a foreigner, or when a judgment unfavorable to a foreigner had been pronounced, the absence of the foreigner or the unjustified refusal of the *dragoman* to sign the judgment prevented the settlement of the dispute.... Witness and *dragoman*, or the latter alone, were able by answering the summons or by refusing to appear, to exercise an influence on the progress of the prosecution. [28]

After Turkey had entered World War I as an ally of the Central Powers, and Germany and Austria had abrogated their capitulatory agreements with her, she had then begun harassing the dragomen serving the Allied Powers in Ottoman territories. A number of such incidents had taken place during 1915 and 1916. Following the war, all capitulatory agreements had been abolished.

We cannot conclude our discussion of the dragomen and of the language professions in early modern Europe without relating the saga of the Cruttas. [29] Throughout the latter part of the 18th century, this colorful, amazing family of politically-minded dragomen, truly the "first family of interpreting," had dominated the profession.

As important as Ottoman Turkey had been to general European affairs during the 15th to 20th centuries, the nations of Eastern Europe had been even more involved with the Porte than those of the West. A thriving commerce between Turkey and the Slavic lands had created a very considerable demand for persons who could translate Oriental tongues, and nowhere had the market been greater than in Poland. Until Antonio Crutta had arrived on the scene, most of the linguists at the Warsaw Chancellery had been Italian, but, for some reason, the Poles had not been happy with their work.

The Cruttas were of Albanian origin, thus nicely placed between "East" and "West." Of the five brothers, only one (a medical doctor) had not adopted a career as interpreter-diplomat. One brother had served the Russian ambassador at Constantinople, another had worked in the Department of Foreign Languages at St. Petersburg, a third had directed a school of languages in Constantinople and had later become a diplomat, while a fourth had served as chief translator to the Polish king, Stanislas-Auguste Poniatowski. (And some of their children had also followed in their footsteps.) All were strongly liberal politically, with a penchant for democratic causes. Of the five, Antonio and Pierre have been best remembered by history.

When war had broken out between Russia and Turkey (1787–1792), with Poland anxious to remain neutral, Antonio Crutta had been in the employ of King Stanislas-Auguste, his delicate task being to interpret during the negotiations in such a way as to "melt the suspicions of the Turks without arousing the suspicions of the Russians." So brilliantly had he fullfilled his mission that, in 1772, the Polish Diet had conferred upon him a title of nobility. A patriot to his death, Antonio had served on Kosciuszko's National Supreme Revolutionary Council, but had resigned his career following the third partition of his country in 1795. He had interpreted one more time during a visit by a Turkish dignitary in 1807, and had died seven years later. With him expired the last of the truly great dragomen.

Brother Pierre's career had been stormier. The language school he had been directing in Constantinople had proved unprofitable, partly because the Polish ambassador there (a German, in accord with the common practice of the time), disliking Pierre, had subtly undermined his efforts. Forced to abandon his school, Pierre had become a dragoman to the British ambassador, and had soon achieved such a degree of influence over that gentleman that, according to a rumor reported to the tsarina, the ambassador had promised Pierre a "golden bridge" if he succeeded in bringing Russia and Turkey to war.[30] Anyone who doubts the "power potential" of an interpreter should consider this story. Whether or not Crutta actually *did* enjoy that much influence, the important thing is that he was *believed* to do so.

Through the good offices of brother Antonio, Pierre had next been appointed first dragoman to the Polish embassy at Constantinople, replacing an Armenian whose work had been unsatisfactory. Later, upon his return to Poland after the April, 1794, uprising, Kosciuszko had hand picked him for a crucial and perilous mission to Revolutionary France's envoy in Constantinople. Pierre's assignment had been to persuade the French to offer their Polish brothers-in-arms a military alliance. In order to afford Crutta a modicum of protection, the English ambassador in Warsaw had provided him with an English passport, and he had arrived in Constantinople in November, 1794, where he had been cordially received by the Frenchman, Descorches. But Pierre's efforts came to naught, for Kosciuzko's government had been overthrown shortly after his arrival in Constantinople. With his hopes (and Antonio's) now dashed, Pierre, together with his son, Jean, had entered the service of France. Although offered the post of chief of the French Chancellery in Tunis, he preferred to remain in Constantinople, where he died in 1797.

Early in the 19th century, European political translating and interpreting were still being performed in much the same manner as in former centuries—by whatever linguist might be found within a nation's diplomatic corps—or, as frequently happened, could be pirated from some other nation's. At the Congress of Vienna (1815) following Napoleon's downfall, translation had been of far greater importance than interpreting, for the Congress had not, in today's terminology, held "sessions." In fact, it had never even formally convened, but had carried on its work through its eight committees, through meetings at the Austrian Foreign Ministry, and (perhaps most important of all) through private conversations at the many and brilliant social gatherings.[31] What had counted at Vienna had been the inclusion of a nation's views and goals in the final documents of the Congress.

Vienna's most eminent translator had been infinitely more than a gifted linguist. Friedrich von Gentz had been an agent and propagandist for the British government since 1800, serving it so admirably that, when Lord Castlereagh had picked a delegation to accompany him to Vienna, Gentz had been chosen as chief translator. Despite his British ties, this "omniscient Berliner with beautiful eyes, a gentle voice and a passion for sweetmeats and social intercourse"[32] had emerged at Vienna as chief assistant to the Austrian, Metternich, powerful secretary-general of the Congress. The secret of Gentz's influence seems to have been that he was on equally good terms with the British, the French and the Austrians, equally privy to the affairs of all, and fully trusted by none of them. In the words of the Westphalian diplomat, Baron Ompteda, "Gentz is the custodian of all the secrets of Europe, just as in a short time he'll possess all the orders [i.e., decorations] of it.... He has, perhaps, been as formidable an opponent to Napoleon as the snow-bound steppes of Russia."[33] Indeed, even the rather xenophobic Russians had been impressed by him.

Long before the Congress of Vienna — around 1806 — Prince Adam Czartoryski had urged Emperor Alexander I to establish a school of international relations and foreign service (Czartoryski had called it a
"diplomatic nursery") to be directed by Gentz, whom he had believed the
most qualified man in Europe for such a project.[34]

In an entry in his bi- and trilingual diary, dated February, 1801,
while on the English payroll, Gentz had noted: "Lord Carysfoot entrusted me with the translation into French of the publication of the
English note against Prussia on the one hand, and shortly afterwards
Graf Haugwitz with that into German of the Prussian note against
England." Here, indeed, is proof of the translator's power over his client
to which we have alluded, a power of which few were more conscious
than Gentz. In a dairy entry of September, 1814, he laments, "What
difficulties and misunderstandings might not be avoided, and how much
time saved, by leaving matters trustfully in the translator's hands!" It had
been Gentz, in fact, who had written the 110 articles of the Treaty of
Vienna, almost unassisted insofar as content had been concerned,
although 26 secretaries, working from morning until night, had been
required to prepare the necessary copies. [36]

Within fifty or sixty years after the Vienna Congress, national
governments had come to feel that, in the interests of security, it would
be most desirable to employ their own citizens whenever possible, for the
translation of "sensitive" materials — or, at the very least, not to employ
persons who were working simultaneously for another power. This conviction marks the establishment of "modern" style language services
within the foreign offices.

Largely because of the prestige of French culture and the magnifi-
cence of the royal court under Louis XII (1498–1515) and Francis I (1515–
1547), by the 16th century the French language had begun its long climb
to status as the foremost diplomatic idiom of the world. By then, the
French themselves were no longer using Latin in documents of international negotiation, and the diplomatic skills of Louis XIV's Cardinal
Richelieu had assured the hegemony of their tongue in world affairs.
From Richelieu's time on, the French Foreign Office had come to regard
the maintenance of this supremacy as an essential of their foreign policy.
When, for example, at the Congress of Westphalia terminating the Thirty Years' War, one of the delegates had requested the drafting of the
treaty in Latin, the Duc de Longueville had replied to him in French.[37]
(Despite Longueville's protests, however, the treaty had been drawn in
Latin.) But at this point, the Spanish had not yet forgotten the glories of
their once-great empire, and their nationalism was to prove as prickly
as that of the French. At the Congress of Nijmegen (1676–1679), where a
peace treaty between France and Spain was being signed, the only

arrangement satisfactory to both parties had been to have two copies of the treaty prepared, one in each language, and laid on the table at which sat the English mediators. On a given signal, three French diplomats entered through one door and their Spanish counterparts through another. All sat and signed the two versions simultaneously.[38] Likewise in both French and Spanish was the Treaty of Utrecht (1713), terminating the War of the Spanish Succession.

But the very next year, 1714, we note the beginning of a curious diplomatic practice, the "reservation" concerning the language to be used. During negotiations for the Treaty of Rastadt, between France and the Holy Roman Empire, Prince Eugene, representing the Empire, had desired the treaty to be drafted in Latin, but the French delegate had insisted upon *his* tongue. Although the Prince had decided to yield, he did so *only with the reservation that his concession was not to be construed as a precedent.* This, in itself, had set a most important precedent, for it enabled the French to state their own "reservations," in the future, regarding the use of Latin. This they did for the first time when they signed documents formalizing the Quadruple Alliance of August 2, 1718.[39]

The now celebrated rivalry between the French and English languages had begun as early as the 18th century. In 1753, when prize claims among Britain, France and Holland had been under negotiation, the French had complained of having received an English-language memo, to which the English had responded that they had used their own medium simply because, on a previous occasion, the French had complained of the quality of their tongue appearing in an English memorandum! However, added the English, this was quite beside the point, for the French had no right whatsoever to insist upon the use of their own language. To emphasize the new policy, this directive soon went out to all British Foreign Office employees:

> It is the King's express command that you should not for the future accept any paper from the French commissaries in their own language unless they shall engage to receive the answer in English.[40]

After the year 1800, foreign diplomats accredited to the Court of St. James had been received in English rather than in French, and Lord Castlereagh, Britain's post-Napoleonic foreign minister, had inaugurated the custom of corresponding with sovereigns and ministries in English.

Bonaparte's conquests, although spreading the French language far and wide over Europe, had resulted in a temporary revulsion against all things French, and at Vienna, France had been a defeated nation, a suppliant. Since England, Austria and Russia had dominated the Congress, one might have expected one of their tongues to have been declared the official medium of expression there, but for two reasons this did not happen. For one thing, none of them enjoyed, at that time, sufficient international prestige to be acceptable to a majority of the conferees.* Secondly, France had the good fortune to be represented at Vienna by a super diplomat in the person of Count Talleyrand, who, to a considerable degree, succeeded in mitigating the French humiliation. The ready acceptance of the tongue of the vanquished as the official language and sole medium of negotiation at Vienna must be accounted an important symbolic victory for France, even though the usual "reservation" (June 19, 1815) had been incorporated in the treaty:

> The French language having been exclusively employed in all copies of the present Treaty, it is recognized by the Powers which have acceded to this Act, that *the use of that language shall have no consequence for the future* [italics added]; so that each Power reserves for itself to adopt in future negotiations and conventions the language which it has hitherto employed in its diplomatic negotiations, without the present Treaty being cited as an example contrary to established usage.[41]

After 1815, however, Britain had pressed its linguistic claims in Europe with accelerating zeal. Foreign Minister George Canning, in 1823, had ordered a subordinate in Lisbon to communicate with the Portuguese Foreign Ministry in English only, and less than thirty years later, Lord Palmerston had established the principle which has ever since been honored in the diplomatic world—the right of any government to use its own language in foreign relations.

Nevertheless, French continued to be the medium in which nearly every important treaty had been drafted in the 100 years between 1814 and 1914. Among them might be cited the Treaty of Paris (1856), Treaty of Berlin (1878), Hague Conventions (1899, 1907), Treaty of Portsmouth (1905), and the Anglo–Russian Treaty (1907). The question of English vs. French had embarrassingly reappeared at the Hague Convention of 1907, however, because the American secretary of state, Elihu Root, had played a leading role in organizing the meeting.[42] At subsequent conferences, it became common practice for speakers to use their own language with a running translation of the speech (consecutive interpreting) into French.[43] Moreover, Article 52 of the Hague Convention for the Pacific Settlement of Disputes (October 18, 1907) was to stipulate that the parties to an arbitral settlement should specify the language to be used by the tribunal in making the award.[44] Thus, French *and* English

---

Years later, communications from the Russian Foreign Ministry to Bismarck's Chancellery piled up unread for some time, the Germans claiming that they had no employee who could read Russian.

were to emerge as the languages of choice before the courts of arbitration, with French more commonly used in Europe, but with English preferred in the Pacific areas and throughout the British Empire. Thanks largely to the prestige of that Empire, many nations other than the Anglo–Saxon began writing their treaties in English. Occasionally, of course, it would be judged expedient to use languages other than the "Big Two."

We should not overlook the linguistic arrangements in vogue for the reception of diplomats during the 19th and early 20th centuries. Nearly everywhere, French remained the court language. Indeed, educated people—the only type the diplomat was ever likely to encounter in those days—were so proud of their fluency in French that they were often offended if addressed in their own tongue! Particularly sensitive on this point were the nobility of the czar's Imperial Court, since they were well aware that Western Europeans regarded their land as only marginally civilized.[45] (One Western diplomat of the 18th century had referred to the Russians as "baptized bears," and with some justice. When Peter the Great and his entourage had stopped off in London on their European tour of 1697–1698, they had totally "trashed" the house in which they were living, wrecking furniture, ruining carpets and smashing windows.)[45] Thus, it would have been a *faux pas* of the worst kind to have addressed a Russian diplomat in Russian, for this would have implied that he was not expected to know French. Upon one occasion, an Englishman named Whitworth, sent to apologize to the czar for an insult suffered by the Russian ambassador in London, had addressed the czar in English, with an immediate interpretation into *French* and *then* into Russian.[46]

On the eve of World War I, in July, 1914, an incident had taken place which clearly indicated the rise of a dangerous degree of nationalism in Europe. At a conference concerning the status of Spitzbergen, although the language used by everyone up to that point had been French, suddenly, as the European political climate had deteriorated, the German and Russian delegates had begun speaking in their own tongues.[47]

The New World

In the exploration of the Western Hemisphere, remarkable contributions were made by interpreters of many different nationalities. Christopher Columbus had taken with him on his first voyage in 1492 one of those Jewish interpreters who had been so useful in Arabic Spain—Luis de Torres, fluent in Hebrew, Chaldean and Arabic.[48] (Since the great Admiral had expected to find the Orient on the other side of the

Atlantic, he had naturally assumed that those languages would be helpful.) When his supply ships had returned to Europe, Columbus had sent
with them six Indians who were to learn Spanish so that they might interpret for future expeditions.[49] And on his fourth and last voyage in 1502,
the explorer — still hopeful of locating the passage to India — had brought
along two men who spoke Arabic.[50]

Much of the communication between Indians and explorers of the
New World had been conducted in sign language. A Spaniard in Florida,
Cabeza de Vaca, had complained in 1528 of this unfortunate necessity,
"for although we knew six languages, we could not in all parts make use
of them, as we found more than a thousand differences of language."[51]
Francisco Vásquez de Coronado likewise comments that it had often
been possible to converse so easily with the Indians via signs that no interpreters had been required, although occasionally, Coronado refers to
the use of an interpreter without mentioning him by name.[52] Sign language
is assuredly not an ideal method. When the Spaniards had tried this
medium upon one occasion, de Vaca notes, the Indians "so insulted us
with their gestures" that they had been forced to discontinue.[53] He goes
on to say that the Gospel had been preached to the natives entirely
through signs, but "if we had had an interpreter ... we should have left
them all Christians."[54]

Hernando de Soto, explorer of Georgia and Florida, had employed
as his interpreter one Juan Ortíz, a Spaniard who had been the last sur-
vivor of the ill-fated Panfilo de Narváez expedition to Tampa Bay in
1521. Held captive by the Indians for 11 years, Ortíz had become so
familiar with their tongue that, by the time de Soto had rescued him, he
had lost much of his fluency in Spanish. According to one authority,
Ortíz as interpreter had been "worth a hundred men to the expedition,"
on several occasions probably saving the Europeans from annihilation.
Once, when the hot-tempered Spaniards had been about to execute some
remarkably unapologetic Indians who had been caught stealing food,
Ortíz deliberately misinterpreted the culprits' scornful, insulting barbs
at the Spaniards as pleas for mercy, thereby mollifying the latter into
sparing their lives — and, no doubt, thus saving many Spanish lives in the
future. So dependent upon his interpreter had de Sota become that, after
Ortíz had died in what is now Louisiana, the leader had found himself in
a serious predicament. "What Ortíz used to get out of the Indians in a
few minutes took nearly a whole day ... and more often than not the
exact opposite of what was said would be understood."[55] Largely because
of his inability to carry on without a reliable interpreter, de Soto had
been forced to abandon his plans to proceed further West.

As in the Orient, missionary priests proved to be the pioneering
linguists and compilers of the earliest grammars and dictionaries of these

hitherto unknown tongues. The friars commonly learned from two to as many as ten different Indian dialects, with the result that textbooks and dictionaries had been printed in sizeable numbers, and chairs in the native tongues had been established at the Universities of Mexico and Peru as early as the 16th century.[56]

Indeed, probably nowhere in the world is the historical importance of the linguist more evident than in the conquests of Mexico and Peru. Eight years before the arrival of Hernán Cortés at Cozumel, a party of 175 Spaniards had been shipwrecked off the coast and seized by the Indians. One of them, Jerónimo de Aguilar, who had once studied for the priesthood, had escaped and made his way to Cortés, who hired him as his first interpreter.[57] Unfortunately, Aguilar had proven to be conversant only with the Mayan dialect of his captors, which, bearing little resemblance to the Aztec, could be of no help to Cortés in his crucial parleys with the latter. Rather, it was a female slave given Cortés by the chief of Tabasco who had most facilitated the conquest of Mexico. Not only had she spoken Aztec "with great elegance," but she also knew Mayan. Thus, it had been relatively simple for Aguilar to transmit the words of the Spaniards in Mayan to Marina (or "Malinche," from the Aztec "Malintzin"), and for her then to render the Mayan into Aztec. "Relay" interpreting is never the most desirable form, but it is better than nothing.

The young woman's history was even more colorful than Aguilar's.[58] Left the widow of a rich and powerful man, her mother had remarried and borne a son to her second husband. To enable this favored boy to inherit the property left to Marina by her father, the mother had invented a tale that her daughter had died (producing a corpse as evidence!), while surreptitiously selling the girl to the chief of Tabasco.

Marina's relations with Cortés are something of a mystery to historians. She became his mistress and bore him a son, Martín Cortés, whom the explorer acknowledged as his son and legal heir. Yet, upon two distinct occasions, Cortés had "given" her to other men as their mistresses. Salvador de Madariaga, feeling that the Spanish leader "had a high opinion of her ability, but he was by no means smitten with love for her," records that he had approached her sexually only at certain times when he considered her personal devotion to be vital to his interests.[59] It would seem that the girl possessed nobility of character as well as high intelligence, for many years after her mother had sold her into servitude, Cortés had caused the terrified woman and her husband to be brought before him, where Marina had freely forgiven her and even presented her with gifts. To the pious Spaniards, this behavior paralleled that of Joseph and his brothers in Egypt, and Marina's reputation among both Spaniards and Indians rose even higher. The latter began referring to

Cortés himself as the "lord of Malinche," and it was thus that Montezuma had addressed him during the interview between them, for which the young woman had interpreted.[60]

Marina is credited with having saved the Spanish from total disaster. While Cortés and his expedition were visiting Cholula, she had discovered, by making friends with the wife of a prominent citizen, that the Cholulans were plotting the murder of the entire company of Europeans. After she had passed this choice bit of information on to Cortés, he speedily disarmed the chieftains and had them slain.[61]

Francisco Pizarro, conqueror of the Incas, had been somewhat less fortunate than Cortés in the interpreters who had fallen to his lot. On his second voyage to the New World in 1528, he had acquired in Panama two young Indians, Martín and Felipillo, and had sent them to Spain to be taught the language (and, of course, baptized as Christians). Both had been employed in Pizarro's negotiations with Atahualpa, the Inca, but it had been Felipillo who had managed to foul things up—whether intentionally or accidentally is still a matter of debate, although his confession just before his death would seem to indicate that it had been intentional. The other boy, Martín, must have performed well enough, for he had been the only Indian to be given by Pizarro a share of Atahualpa's ransom and an *encomienda* grant near Lima.[62]

The priest who had accompanied Pizarro on his visit to the Inca had been quite as unfortunate a choice as Felipillo. In a bullying, condescending manner, Father Vincente de Valverde had lectured Atahualpa on the Church, on the power and glory of Charles V, and on the Inca's duty to submit himself and his kingdom to the Spaniards, on pain of eternal damnation if he did not. But Atahualpa had inquired, reasonably enough, why the Spanish monarch needed the Pope's help if he were really all that powerful, and had further displayed his contempt by casting to the ground a sacred object which Valverde had thrust at him. This being, no doubt, the very excuse the Spaniards had been hoping for, they had seized Atahualpa and imprisoned him. Hernándo de Soto, the Inca's most influential defender, had been lured away on a fake mission, so that during his absence a formal legal charge might be drawn up against the Inca, using Indian witnesses examined through the interpreter Felipillo.[63]

Arrogant though Valverde had been, it is alleged that the interpreter had made things worse by misinterpreting. For example, while the priest had been attempting to explain the concept of the Holy Trinity, Felipillo had rendered it as Four Persons rather than Three. Some have tried to excuse him on the ground of his inadequate knowledge of both Quechua and Spanish, limited mainly to crude soldiers' argot. Others allege that he had not only misinterpreted Atahualpa's remarks to the Spanish and *vice versa,* but had deliberately set abroad false reports of the Inca's military intentions, leading the Spaniards to fear imminent attack and sealing Atahualpa's doom.

Why would Felipillo have wished to cause such mischief? Some believe it was because he had belonged to one of the subject tribes who hated the Incas, but, more importantly, because he had been in love with one of Atahualpa's concubines, and feared the result if he should be discovered. Later, when Pizarro and one of his associates, Diego de Almagro, had quarrelled, Felipillo had deserted to Almagro, who ultimately had him hanged. [64]

How the Spaniards and the Indians had communicated on a mundane, day-to-day basis is explained by an Inca chieftain: "At first, there was almost no comprehension.... Then, as a new race of half-castes grew up, a mixture of the Quechua and Spanish languages became usual, but was still not fully understood by either race." More to the point, the chieftain reveals how the Spanish, knowing so few words of Quechua, had so easily managed to cheat the Indians out of their property: "A Spanish soldier would call out in a loud voice: 'Don't be afraid. I am the Inca.' As the Indians fled in terror, the Spanish would move in." [65]

In 1571, another Inca, the young Tupac Amaru I, fell victim to one of the half-caste interpreters, a *mestizo* named Gonzalo Jiménez, who had misinterpreted at Tupac's trial. After having been viciously tortured, the Inca was killed. [66] Like Felipillo, Jiménez was destined to meet death at the hands of an outraged master.

Far to the North, interpreters had been among the earliest immigrants to French Canada. One of them, Mathieu da Costa (or d'Acosta), had been "the first Black to have come to New France." Apparently a Christian and a well-educated man, he had been kidnapped and brought to Canada on a Portuguese ship, where he had learned the Micmac language and had entered (or been sold into) the service of the Sieur de Monts. He is known to have died in 1607. [67]

Another student of Micmac, who complained of its difficulty, was the Jesuit, Pierre Biard, professor of theology at Lyons, who had arrived in New France in 1610 with the Baron de Poutrincourt. The Baron's son, attempting to act as his father's interpreter, had found the going too rough whenever religion had entered the conversation, for the Micmac tongue utterly lacked any abstract terminology. Biard lamented that the "savages," as he referred to them, who must have had a ribald sense of humor, had frequently suggested to young Poutrincourt "scurrilous and unseemly" word equivalents, which the unsuspecting Frenchman "studiously incorporated into ... the Indian catechism, [producing in] his pupils an effect the reverse of that intended." [68]

Samuel Champlain, the founder of Quebec, had brought with him as interpreter on his first voyage to Canada in 1608 a Huron named

Savignon, who had rendered invaluable service to the French by stressing to his fellow tribesmen how well he had been treated in France and by commending the French to them as their protectors against hostile tribes.[69] Also with Champlain had been two Frenchmen, Étienne Brûlé and Nicholas Marsolet, who had speedily set about learning the two principal Indian tongues. Marsolet, a Norman from Rouen of rather high birth, and founder of "the oldest name among the Canadian colonists," had specialized in Algonquin, while Brûlé had become a master of Huron and an eventual "adopted" member of the tribe. At one time, the latter had been captured by the Iroquois and bound to a stake for torture. When his forceful threats of the wrath of God had been punctuated by the fortuitous onset of a thunderstorm, the awestricken Indians had released him. Later, both Brûlé and Marsolet were to turn traitor to Champlain (or so he regarded their behavior) by entering the service of the English. Brûlé is said to have come to an appropriately bad end, having been eaten by some Indians around 1634.[70]

Historical records reveal that during the first quarter of the 17th century approximately 12 interpreters were at work in New France, and many of their names have been recorded, among them Jean Manet, Jean Nicolet, Jacques Hertel, Jean Richer, Olivier le Tardif, the brothers Thomas and Jean-Paul Godefroy, plus several more mentioned only by their last names.[71] A majority of these, like most Frenchmen in Canada, had been Normans. In July of 1629, out of a total population of 85, Quebec had boasted 11 interpreters, plus 14 clerks and 10 missionaries,[72] most of whom were also bilingual or multilingual. We must add, however, that this enumeration ignores a vitally important group of men in New France, the ubiquitous and largely illegal "courieurs de bois," or "woods runners," whose uncivilized mode of living and intimate relationships with the Indians placed them just outside the pale of respectability. But few knew the Indian tongues, or the Indians themselves, better than they.

The most interesting thing about these French interpreters, even the "respectable" ones, was that the very nature of their work demanded long-term, continued contact with the Indians. To an even greater degree than in most situations where interpreters function, the success of French trading negotiations with the Indians had been crucially dependent upon an atmosphere of mutual trust. So exacting had the work been that few interpreters did anything else for a living.[73]

Roman Catholic priests appear as prominently in the linguistic history of New France as in that of Latin America, but the earliest of the French priests to reach Canada had faced a dilemma unknown to the Spanish. They had soon discovered that most of the Frenchmen who had been living among the Indian tribes for years and who were sufficiently well-versed in their tongues to be able to instruct others were Protestant Huguenots and thus much averse to assisting in the propagation of Catholicism. Said a Jesuit of one such man, "This interpreter never wanted to communicate his knowledge of languages to anyone...."[74] Had there not been a marked similarity among the various Indian tongues of Eastern Canada,* the priests might have found their task even more difficult than it was.

One of the best-known priest-linguists of North America was Jacques Marquette, a Jesuit who, after having learned several Indian languages, had accompanied Louis Joliet on his voyage down the Mississippi in 1673. But Joliet himself, as Marquette recorded, "knows the language spoken in the country of the Outaoacs, where he has passed several years."[75] And René Robert Cavelier, Sieur de la Salle, sent by Louis XIV to extend French dominion over Louisiana, was also said to have been fluent in several "savage languages."[76]

In general, the French leaders proved much more adept at learning Indian speech than their Spanish or English counterparts, a fact which may go far to explain their considerably better record of success in their relations with the tribes. The French cherished the Indian and made the fierce hunting tribes of New France an instrument in the building up of French power; the English, failing to make an agricultural laborer out of the more pliable New England Indian, treated him with indifference and turned him into a sullen enemy.[77] It has been said that, of the treaties between the English and the Indians, "Most were made by negotiators on each side ignorant of the other's language ... and both parties dependent upon interpreters perhaps incapable, sometimes dishonest, and having strong motives to deceive one or both of the contracting parties."[78]

When the Pilgrims had first arrived at Plymouth in the winter of 1620, for approximately three months the Indians had refused to come anywhere near them and had appeared rather hostile. But one day, on March 16, 1621, as the Pilgrim *Chronicles* recall, "there presented himself a savage, who caused an alarm.... He saluted us in English and bade us 'welcome.' For he had learned some broken English among the Englishmen that came to fish at Monhiggon" (i.e., Monhegan Island off the coast of Maine).[79] Samoset had not been particularly fluent, but on his third visit he had brought with him a more articulate Indian, who had actually

---

*The Rev. John Heckenwelder, an authority on Indian languages, quotes a certain French Baron de la Hontan: "There are but two mother tongues in the whole [of eastern Canada].... They are the Huron and the Algonquin. The first is understood by the Iroquois, for the difference between these two is no greater than that between the Norman and the French. The second, namely, the Algonquin, is as much esteemed among the savages as the Greek and Latin are in Europe." (See Heckewelder's History, Manner and Customs of the Indian Nations [Philadelphia: Historical Society of Pennsylvania, 1876], p. 122.)

lived for a time in England. This was Squanto (or Tisquantum), sole sur-
vivor of the Patuxet tribe which had formerly inhabited the region
around Plymouth.

Squanto's story had been a sad one. He and 19 other Patuxets had
been captured by a villainous Englishman, one Captain Hunt,[80] who had
apparently made a career of carrying off Indians to Spain and selling
them into slavery. But Squanto had escaped in London, had been taken
in by a merchant who had treated him kindly, and had later returned to
Newfoundland on one of the merchant's ships, from which it had not
been too difficult for the Indian to make his way back to New England.[81]
Besides helping the English as interpreter and instructor in the means of
survival, Squanto had introduced them to the chief of the Wampanaugs,
Massasoit, leading to a Treaty of Alliance which would be broken only
54 years later, by Massasoit's son (Metacom, or "King Philip"). Squanto,
of course, had usually been the interpreter on such occasions. But he
could not always be present when an Englishman had been trying to
communicate with an Indian, and in any event, his own English had been
less than perfect. Governor Edward Winslow, writing in his *Good News
from New England* two years after the meeting with Massassoit, had admitted, "As for the [Indian] language, it is very copious, large and
difficult. As yet, we cannot attain to any great measure thereof, but can
understand them, and explain ourselves to their understanding, by the
help of those that daily converse with us."[82]

It would seem that the Indians had much less difficulty with strange
tongues. John Brereton, writing to Sir Walter Ralegh from Cape Cod in
1602, had extolled the remarkable linguistic abilities of the Massachusetts
Indians. Upon catching one of these helping himself to some of
Brereton's tobacco, the latter had inquired of the man, "How now,
sirrah, are you so saucy with my tobacco?" The exact words, with perfect
intonation, had been immediately repeated by the Indian, and Brereton
declares that he had observed a number of similar incidents.[83]

Yet we know that there must have been some Englishmen who served
as interpreters at this time, for early records make occasional, scat-
tered references to them. Myles Standish, for example, had often served
in that capacity.[84] And a Joseph and Thomas Staunton (perhaps
brothers or father and son) are recorded as interpreters, but we know
nothing further of them.[85] In Virginia, a letter from a member of the
Committee for Indian Affairs to Robert Harley, the queen's principal
secretary of state, mentions the use of an English interpreter during a
conference with an Indian "queen." (The latter affair, incidentally,
reveals the English ineptitude in their relations with the Indians. They
had been trying to persuade the "queen" to provide them with guides and
other assistance against hostile Indians, but she had refused, pointing out

that, although her husband had lost his life while helping the English some time previously, she had never received any compensation.)[86] A similar lack of diplomatic sensitivity in New England would lead to the outbreak of hostilities there.

Miantonomah, a Narragansett chieftain suspected of conspiring with the Mohawks, had been summoned by Governor Thomas Dudley in 1640 to attend a hearing in Boston. When Miantonomah had objected to a Pequot serving as interpreter for the occasion, he had been given the "shunning" (ostracism) treatment by the Puritans. Such needless offense offered to a powerful leader had naturally made him resentful, and, sensing possible future trouble from that quarter, Massachusetts had later laid claim to his lands, although Roger Williams had declared that the Colony had no right to them whatsoever. When Miantonomah had begun a war against Uncas, a rival Narragansett chieftain allied with the English, and Uncas had captured his enemy, Miantonomah had been slain with the tacit consent of the English.[87]

The precipitating factor in King Philip's War (1676–1677) had been the murder of Sassamon, a Christian convert, erstwhile Harvard student and secretary-interpreter to King Philip. Sassamon had become alarmed at evidence that Philip was plotting treachery against the English, had reported the matter to Governor Winslow, and had been promptly slain by three of Philip's men under circumstances remarkably reminiscent of Thomas à Becket's death. The English had found the culprits and executed them, but 12 days later a party of warriors had attacked a colonist's home in Swansea and the war was on. Philip himself had been killed in August of 1676.[88]

One of the earliest harbingers of French–English conflict on the North American continent had been the construction, in 1722, of a fortress at Oswego, New York, by Governor William Burnet. Very little noted in history textbooks, this was to prove one of the decisive events in American history, for it diverted the main channel of the fur trade away from the French of the St. Lawrence region to the English of the Mohawk Valley.[89] The result was to be an extension of English influence over the warlike Indians of the Northeastern United States, particularly the Mohawks, who had traditionally been allies of the French.

Sir William Johnson, a wealthy fur trader who was also the English manager of Indian affairs for the Colony of New York, so influential with the Indians that he had been accepted as one of their chieftains, had in 1743 been charged with administering the English trade in furs at Oswego. "When Johnson took over the burden at Oswego, he sent his trusted interpreter, Arent Stevens, there, in order to prevent the Indians from going on to Canada with their furs" and "where others had failed,

Stevens achieved favorable results with gifts and all but neutralized the influence of the French"[90] among the Iroquois—the strongest, most militant and most sophisticated of tribes. Within 20 or 25 years, the English had come to realize—as the French always had—that the outcome of the struggle for control of the continent might well depend upon the loyalty of their Indian allies, and their ability to win the "neutral" tribes to their cause.

At the time, most of the English settlers outside the New York–New England area were to be found in the Allegheny region of Pennsylvania, Maryland, Virginia and the Carolinas. By 1748, they were rapidly approaching the Appalachian ranges, and the Ohio Company of Virginia, among whose members was a young officer named George Washington, had been organized to develop the lands along the Ohio River. The great trade and military routes of the time had been the one running from Albany, New York, to the Niagara River and thence West to the north and south of Lake Erie, and the one which stretched from Philadelphia or Baltimore to what is now Pittsburgh and down the Ohio River. By seizing and holding the Niagara River and the junction between the Allegheny and the Monongahela (the present site of Pittsburgh), the English would have their rivals at their mercy, a fact of which the French were only too well aware.

But the latter held one distinct advantage: an abundance of good Indian-language interpreters of the old "courieurs de bois" type, thoroughly familiar with Indian cultures. "The Joncaire brothers, Philip Thomas and Daniel, Sieur de Chabert et de la Clausonne, were two of these officer-interpreters who played a vital part in the drama of forest diplomacy and gifts."[91]

Since the two brothers are vaguely referred to in the official records only by their surname, the researcher cannot always determine with certainty which one is being discussed, particularly since 18th-century spelling was capricious. There is little doubt, however, that one of them was the "Jean Ceur" appearing in a letter from Sir William Johnson to New York's Governor De Witt Clinton in 1750: "Jean Ceur, whom I mentioned to your Excellency some time ago, is now gone among the Ohio Indians in order to spirit them up against the English. I wish he may meet with his proper Deserts."[92] The Joncaires' instructions came from the governor–general of New France, to whom they reported. This indicates how centralized was the French policy toward the Indians.

Among the English, good interpreters were fewer and harder to find. Two such were "Conrad Weiser, religious leader, farmer and head of a large family," and "George Croghan, holder of a military commission and an outstanding trader." Weiser recommended that, to overcome the shortage of interpreters, "young men live among the Indians, possibly with the resident blacksmiths, in order to learn the language" — in effect, a "student interpretership." Other interpreters in the service of the English included Jacobus Clement, William Printup and Daniel Claus, all of New York State, the latter of whom wrote the first textbook on the Mohawk language. Some of these men went far beyond the mere call of duty. After General Jeffrey Amherst had decided upon a policy of economy after 1760, which included a reduction in the expenditures for Indian gifts, "George Croghan was handing out goods to the downcast tribesmen who had been refused gifts by the commanding officer at Fort Pitt, [which act] cost Croghan a year's salary."[93]

But the most remarkable — and certainly the most colorful — of the English interpreters had been Andrew Montour ("Eghuisara" to the Indians), who, although Canadian-born and probably half-French-half-Huron, had preferred to serve the English, much to the irritation of the French. Of striking appearance, with European features set in a painted face and wearing heavy brass earrings,[94] Montour had spoken French, English and several Indian tongues. He had been a figure well-known and well-respected by the officials of all the English colonies, and among those eager to employ him had been George Washington.

The young officer and future father of his country had been one of the few English to realize from the start that, if white men wished to remain on cordial terms with the Indians, gifts were all-important. In a letter to a friend in 1754, he had observed: "...Nothing can be done without [gifts]. All the Indians that come expect presents.... They must be bought; their friendship is not so warm as to prompt them to these services gratis; and that, I believe, every person who is acquainted with the nature of Indians, knows."[95] And whenever a gift was to be presented, it had to be done with style, with much oratory, or the recipient would feel insulted. Influential colonists and — above all — skillful interpreters — were always among the presentation party.

On October 10, 1755, Washington wrote Montour a most cordial and flattering letter, inviting him to settle down in Virginia, and simultaneously urging, in a letter to militia guide Captain Christopher Gist, that he persuade Montour to bring some men with him to Virginia. Gist had been authorized to promise that, if at least 60 men accompanied the interpreter, he would be rewarded with the rank of captain in the Virginia Militia, and a salary of ten shillings per day.[96] Obviously, Washington had known with whom he was dealing. In return for his actions at the Lancaster conference, Montour had already asked that the government of Pennsylvania "build him a house and ... furnish his family with necessarys [sic]...,"[97] demands which Conrad Weiser considered excessive.

Another intriguing character figuring in the French–English conflict had been a Seneca chieftain named Tanacharisson, but better known as "Half King," because he had owed his allegiance to the Six Nations.* Dispatched by the Onondaga Council (located where Syracuse, New York, now is) as a kind of emissary-supervisor to keep tabs on members and satellites of the Six Nations living in the upper Ohio region, Half King, unlike most Indian chieftains, had become renowned not for military prowess but for his diplomatic skill. Although he had failed in his personal goal — to prevent either of the European peoples from taking the Ohio Valley away from the Indians — he is remembered with respect for the suppleness and subtlety of his negotiations. Despite Half King's services to the English at many different times and his open defiance of the French on several occasions, Washington had never fully trusted him.[98] It is impossible, at this date, to determine how valid the latter's suspicions may have been. Yet the facts as recorded seem to affirm Half King's loyalty to the English cause, even after 1754, when he had come to believe that Washington had not dealt fairly with him.

Although, as a chieftain, Half King had been required to spend most of his time with his own people, yet he had often been called upon to serve as Washington's Indian guide, interpreter and general liaison with the Indian tribes whom the English had been hoping to win over to their side.

In 1749, the governor of New France had sent a party of 250 men, headed by Céleron de Bienville, to take possession of the land between the Niagara and Ohio Rivers for the French King and to try to establish rapport with the Indians there. Bienville had found the latter "polite but suspicious and unsatisfactory,"[99] and had been forced to conclude that English influence in the Ohio Valley remained strong. Four years later, the new governor of New France, the Marquis Duquesne, had dispatched another party which had crossed Lake Erie and erected a blockhouse named Fort le Boeuf. Beyond this, a member of the group, one of the Joncaires, had been entrusted with the seizure of an English post at Venango, where the French were hoping to construct another fort. But Governor Dinwiddie of Virginia had been watching the Ohio Valley from Williamsburg as Duquesne had been watching it from Montreal, and one evening some English guests had arrived: a trader and guide named Christopher Gist, an Indian interpreter named Davison, a French interpreter of Dutch nationality called Van Braam, and four rangers, headed by Major George Washington.[100] Proceeding to Fort le Boeuf (after having been warned by Half King not to go there without an

---

*The Six Nations were a confederacy of northeastern tribes the French called the "League of the Iroquois," including the Mohawk, Onondaga, Oneida, Cayuga, Seneca and, ultimately, the Tuscarora.

armed escort[101]), Washington had presented Dinwiddie's letter of warning to the French commander, but the latter had refused to budge from the spot until he had received instructions from Montreal.

During the winter of 1754, Half King learned that the French were about to march against Fort Necessity, which had been hastily constructed by Washington. After a conference with the Indian, and upon his recommendation, the Virginians had sought out the French force and defeated it.* During the attack on the fort, a French officer, Coulon de Jumonville, had been killed, and his brother, Coulon de Villiers, had immediately set out with six hundred men to avenge him. Needless to say, French wrath against Half King was at fever pitch, since they correctly held him responsible for their debacle. Governor Duquesne himself had ordered the commander of the fort to find some way of having the chieftain slain without arousing the suspicion of the English that the French had been responsible, but word of this plot had been immediately reported to Half King by his spies within the French stockade![102]

Following an all-day siege by Villiers, the English had been forced to capitulate. The Frenchman had slyly inserted into the document of surrender, which had been written in French, a phrase implying that his brother had been "assassinated" by the English, instead of having simply been killed in battle. As none of the English were able to read French, they had relied upon the interpreter, Van Braam, whom they had later suspected of having misinterpreted.† The French, of course, had been delighted at the "confession," but Washington had insisted that he had been "wilfully or ignorantly deceived by our interpreter in regard to the word 'assassination.'"[103]

This catastrophe had been followed by a council attended by Half King, among others, where Washington had made the serious error of paying more heed to the advice of Shingas, chief of the Delaware, than to that of his longstanding, faithful ally. Shingas was not popular among the leaders of the Six Nations, being under suspicion of pro-French tendencies. Thus, Half King had been so enraged that he had immediately withdrawn from Washington's camp, taking with him his entire retinue.[104] This did not seem to disturb Washington, but did alarm George Croghan.

---

*Since the junction of the Allegheny and the Monongahela had been so vital to English interests, why they had not more speedily constructed a fortress there? The answer is intercolony rivalry. Both Virginia and Pennsylvania claimed the region; neither wanted to spend money building something which might wind up in the hands of the other.

†This despite the fact that Van Braam was a militia officer, previously on good terms with Washington, to whom he had taught the art of fencing.

Later, Half King would complain that Washington had been arrogant toward the Indians, commanding them like slaves, that he had expected them to do most of the fighting, and that "had he taken the Half King's advice and made such fortifications as the Half King advised him to make, he would certainly have beaten the French off." Yet, before his death in October of 1754, he is reported to have declared, in a last message to the Onondaga Council, he "would live and die with the English."[105]

Interpreting services remained vital in the exploration of the West during the years following the establishment of the United States government. On the Lewis and Clark expedition of 1804–1805, the explorers had hired as their first interpreter one René Jessaume, a Frenchman who had lived in the region of the upper Missouri for many years and who knew the Mandan language well.[106] On November 4, 1804, they had been approached by a half-breed, Toussaint Charbonneau, and his Shoshone wife, Sacajawea, who had been living among the Minitari Indians and who desired to be taken on as interpreters. Although the woman has sometimes been credited by historians beyond her due, the husband had been the actual interpreter for most of the journey. Only as the expedition had approached Shoshone territory and the purchase of portage horses from these Indians had become crucial, were Sacajawea's services to prove truly vital. Lewis and Clark are also known to have had, for a time, at least one other interpreter — George Drouillard, a man who later accompanied the New Orleans Spaniard and fur trader, Manuel Lisa, in his explorations of the upper Missouri in 1807.[107]

At approximately the same time that Lewis and Clark had been pursuing their journey, Zebulon Pike had been doing likewise along the Mississippi, from St. Louis to present-day Minnesota, and as far south as the Mexican border. At Prairie du Chien, Wisconsin, he had hired an interpreter named Rousseau, "probably an out-of-work French *voyageur*," who scouted, hunted, guided and negotiated for Pike's party, which until then had "fumbled along with makeshift interpreters using mutilated [Indian tongues]."[108]

The new United States government had found it necessary to employ translators for the French language, and occasionally for certain other European tongues, even before the infant government had settled permanently in Washington. One George Taylor, a M. Pintard, as well as an anonymous Dutchman (possibly Van Braam?) and the notorious Philip Freneau, are said to have been employed in that capacity by the printers who held the contract for the government's work in New York and Philadelphia.[109] The first of them to come to public attention, however, had been a translator of Spanish named Isaac Pinto, hired in 1786, who had loudly complained, three years later, that his salary for the entire period had amounted to little more than £8.[109]

In 1790, out of a total State Department budget of $8,008.50, Congress had allotted $250 as annual salary for a translator of French, with provision for possible services in other tongues as the need might arise. A year later, the then Secretary of State, Thomas Jefferson, had appointed to the post Philip Freneau, "poet of the American Revolution" — and thereby, indeed, hangs a tale.

Freneau was, and remains, a most controversial figure. Descended from a Huguenot family who had come to these shores in 1705 and settled in New Jersey, Philip had graduated from Princeton — then called the College of New Jersey — and had dabbled in various professions, including journalism with the Philadelphia *Freeman's Journal*, while continuously scribbling the poetry that seems to have been a compulsion with him. Although expressing sympathy for the revolutionary cause, he had somewhat strangely exiled himself to Bermuda during the height of the struggle.[110] Upon his return in 1788, however, he had joined the state militia, serving in it for two years. Subsequently, he had edited, or been associated with, a number of newspapers in the New York–New Jersey area — *The Daily Advertiser,* the *National Gazette,* the *Jersey Chronicle, Time Piece,* and *Literary Companion.* In his capacity as a journalist, he had begun translating French books and articles, which had led to his appointment as official government translator.

Jefferson's political enemies, of whom there were many, had purported to detect a partisan attempt to "buy" an influential journalist. They overlooked the plain fact that there was no need to "buy" Freneau, for he already belonged, heart and soul, to the Jeffersonian camp. Although he had been just as devoted to President Washington, dedicating to him a poem ("To His Excellency, General Washington," September, 1781), this had done nothing to mitigate the suspicions of the skeptical, ever-vigilant President, who had called upon Jefferson to explain his questionable choice of a translator. The Secretary had readily volunteered that, when the government had moved from New York City to Philadelphia, Freneau had been selected as the best-qualified person to succeed M. Pintard, a sophisticated Frenchman who had not wished to leave New York. Stoutly defending his appointment, Jefferson had told Washington, "His paper [referring to the *National Gazette*] has saved our Constitution, which was galloping fast into Monarchy."[111] One cannot help wondering how this statement was received by Washington!

All of this had been bad enough, but Freneau had also become involved in the case of "Citizen Genêt," who had been actively trying to promote the French revolutionary cause in this country despite opposition from the United States government — or, at least, the Federalist faction of it. After Freneau had dedicated some laudatory poems to Genêt, Washington had demanded that Jefferson fire him, but the

Secretary had flatly refused.[112] Although his services were subsequently to be sought by presidents Madison and Monroe, by 1812 Freneau had retired to his farm in New Jersey, never to return to Washington. One student of the poet's life views him as a "frail but passionate figure of protest against all forces tyrannical, monarchical and undemocratic. He was a much-needed factor in the early shaping of the American dream."[113]

Let us now take a look at some of the language problems in United States diplomacy up until World War I, while reserving a consideration of the State Department *per se* for our final chapter.

Because so few American diplomats were then fluent in any tongue other than their own, they had almost invariably required interpreters. At the court of the Turkish sultan, our minister, James B. Angell, had recalled reading his speech to the sultan in English, followed by a Turkish interpretation into that tongue, with the sultan replying in Turkish and the interpreter then rendering the sultan's speech into English. Copies of the addresses in both tongues had previously been submitted to the Turkish Foreign Office to facilitate the interpreter's job.[114] This was, and still is, the usual procedure followed whenever a diplomat has been unable to speak the tongue of the country to which he has been accredited.

It may seem strange that the most linguistically bedevilled of our diplomats should have been, probably, the most literate of them all—the poet, James Russell Lowell, American ambassador to Spain from 1877 to 1880. Lowell had learned pure Castilian Spanish at Harvard, but, as all elder citizens of the United States can attest, language teaching in most American schools and colleges in years past had consisted solely of mastering the skills of reading and writing. To learn to *speak* the language had simply not been considered important! (Nowadays, in the opinion of some, pedagogy has swung too far in the opposite direction.) As Lowell revealed in a letter to a friend, "Although knowing more Spanish than most Spaniards [i.e., in written form], I couldn't speak, and my French and that got so jumbled together that I was dumb in the language of diplomacy also."[115] Lowell describes the puzzlement of the young Spanish tutor whom he soon found it expedient to hire, that the Ambassador could not speak more fluently when his grammatical knowledge was so minute. (We might note that the experience of Carlton J. Hayes, named our ambassador to Spain by President Roosevelt in 1942, had been almost identical. Hayes, a Columbia University professor of modern European history, could read Spanish easily, but could not speak it. Warned by Undersecretary of State Sumner Welles that it would be better not to speak the language at all than to speak it badly,* Hayes had addressed General Franco in English, with the latter responding in Spanish. Both had been presented, prior to their meeting, with translations of each other's remarks.)[116]

A few of our ambassador-linguists have contributed notably to effective foreign relations. Joel Barlow, for instance, emerged as the hero of our war with the Barbary pirates. Barlow, who had been sent to North Africa to negotiate the release of American prisoners, had been chosen for his fluency in French and Italian, the European tongues most familiar to North Africans. The American succeeded in ransoming all captives and in concluding peace treaties with the local rulers, albeit at a cost of $800,000 — somewhat more than the $50,000 Congress had appropriated for that purpose.[117]

Bayard Taylor, dispatched to Russia by President Lincoln in 1862 to try to influence the czar in favor of the Union cause, has depicted the amazement of the Russians that an American could speak French as well as he did. "The fact that I, an American, could speak French, astonishes the Russian Court; the like never before occurred in the memory of the Imperial Family."[118]

And General Horace Porter, our ambassador to France (1897–1905), maintained an exceptionally warm relationship with French officials, largely because of his expertise in the use of their language.[119]

Regrettably, not all of our envoys were so well prepared for their duties. Henry Lane Wilson has left us a graphic demonstration of the possible consequences of a diplomat's not knowing the language of the country to which he has been assigned. The United States had just

---

An excellent piece of advice which ought to be taken more seriously, both in government circles and by tourists. It is not true that awkward floundering in a foreign tongue will be appreciated by the natives on the theory that "it proves you mean well." Sir Vincent Corbett, longtime British diplomat, warned particularly against ambassadors attempting an Oriental tongue: "They [Oriental languages] are full of traps for the unwary, and an Ambassador cannot afford to make himself appear ridiculous" (Corbett, Reminiscences, p. 196). Joseph C. Grew, American ambassador to Japan 1932–1941, felt the same way. He once told a young colleague that he had intentionally never learned Japanese, out of fear that incorrect usage might make him appear foolish (Emmerson, The Japanese Thread, p. 28). Both were wiser than the English notable who had insisted upon trying out his Arabic at a gathering in Zanzibar. After his speech, he had asked the interpreter who had been present but not permitted to function how he had liked the speech. "Very well, Bwana," was the reply. "They asked me what it was about after you left and I read to them from my copy" (Ingram, Arabia and the Isles, p. 13). It is even possible for a foreigner to turn his lack of fluency to advantage, as did Winston Churchill on a visit to Paris in 1944. Refusing an interpreter, he stepped onto the balcony of his hotel and bellowed, "Prenez garde!" ("Watch out!") Having thus won everybody's attention, he continued, "Je vais parler français" ("I'm going to speak French"). From this point, of course, he had his public firmly by the ear (Roetter, Diplomatic Art, pp. 211–212, n.50).

appointed new ambassadors to both Chile and Peru, which, at the time, were on anything but friendly terms with each other. Wilson, who had been named envoy to Chile, had journeyed there on a boat which had made a stop at Callao, Peru. Because the Peruvian officials were expecting *their* new U.S. ambassador to be on that boat, they had assumed that Wilson was he, and had received him, in the absence of any interpreter to clarify the situation, with all the pizzazz of which Latins are capable. When Wilson had finally managed to apprise them of their error, the result had been, so he records, "a considerable cooling of official courtesy." Wilson was the same diplomat who, even after he had "learned" Spanish, had once told the shocked gathering at a formal dinner party that his wife would speak better Spanish "if she wore no stockings," rather than "if she had not been timid."[120] (He had, of course, confused *medias,* "stockings," with *miedos,* "fear.")

The United States stumbled and bumbled along in this fashion, taking potluck as far as language skills were concerned, long after 1881, when John A. Kasson, our minister to the Austro–Hungarian Empire, had sternly warned Congress that, because of our lack of native American linguists and the necessity of relying upon European interpreters abroad, "the real interpreter of our national interests becomes at last an irresponsible and partially educated foreigner."[121] The sad truth is that, until long after World War I, our diplomats in Europe continued to bemoan the scarcity of skilled linguists available to them. (Posts in the Orient, through sheer necessity, fared somewhat better.)

Joseph C. Grew, best known as our envoy to Japan during the difficult pre-World War II period (1932–1941), has left a fascinating account of the language difficulties at the United States embassy in Vienna in 1911. Finding himself working long hours overtime to complete the translations assigned to him, young Grew had begun to wonder why other members of the embassy staff with the same duties always seemed able to leave early. Upon checking up, he learned that the others had been paying an Austrian girl out of their own pockets to do their translating for them! Comments Grew, "The Ambassador [Richard C. Kerens, who himself spoke neither German nor French] was quite unaware of this arrangement, but had wondered why they never translated a note the same day he gave it to them."[122] Bearing in mind that World War I was to burst upon the world within a few short years, one must shudder at the security implications of such an ill-conceived attempt to avoid work. It is quite possible that the young Austrian woman reported to her own government everything she had learned at the American embassy.

CHAPTER IV

East–West Confrontation:
Three Cases

Case One: China

Among China's first civil service appointees, following the introduction of Confucian-type examinations in 165 B.C., were translators
and interpreters.[1] As supervised by the Board of Rites through the
Residence for Envoys,[2] most of the work involved only the ten tongues
spoken in China's tributary states, since "foreign relations," to the
Chinese of that period, signified the empire's relationship with its
satellites in Asia and little more. The *ssui kuan*, one of two separate institutions constituting the Residence, bore responsibility for the translation of foreign messages, while the *hui t'ung* did the interpreting.
Translator-interpreters were known as *i, hsiang chi* or *ti t'i*, according to
whether they dealt with the various peoples of the North, South, East
or West.[3] Once foreign messages had been translated, the product could
legally be transmitted to the emperor only through officials of the Board
of Rites.

By 1579, positions in the *ssui kuan* had begun to be viewed as
hereditary, despite training at an official school, followed by civil service
examinations. If a man died, his son, who had been trained to follow in
his footsteps, took over. However, language posts were of low
prestige—not because of the intrinsic nature of the work, but because
they involved contact with despised "barbarians"—and everyone put forth
a valiant effort to be promoted out of them to something better.[4]
Although the school graduated approximately 100 students per year,
these were not always as knowledgeable as they might have been. When
the king of Siam once responded to a Chinese mission to his court by
dispatching a delegation to Peking bearing a memorandum on gold leaf
which no one could read, the humiliated government pressed into service
as an instructor in Siamese the very man who had led the original
delegation to Siam.[5] After 1748, the two bureaus for translating and

79

interpreting were combined into a single agency bearing total responsibility for the nation's foreign affairs — the *hu t'ung ssui kuan*.[6]

Of particular interest are China's earliest contacts with nonsatellite
foreigners. Her first real awareness (it would be too much to call it
"knowledge") of other lands stems from the Han Dynasty (202
B.C.-A.D. 220), when one Chang Ch'ien arrived in Bactria (northeastern Afghanistan) as envoy from Emperor Wu, who had been seeking
allies against his enemies.[7] The Romans paid their first visit to China to
the court of Emperor Huang-ti of the Han Dynasty in A.D. 166. As the
Han Annals record the event, "The Ta-tsin [Roman] King always desired
to open up relations with the Han, but An-sih [Parthia, i.e., Syria]
wished to trade with Rome in Han silk goods, so that he was obstructed
and could not reach us until [A.D. 166], when Antun [Marcus Aurelius
Antoninus] sent an envoy ... with offerings of ivory, rhinoceros horn and
tortoise shell."[8] We do not know how the Romans and the Chinese communicated.

The Venetians, Marco Polo and his two brothers, who were warmly
received at the court of Kublai Khan in 1275, remaining for 17 years,
knew "enough Persian and Mongol to get along in official circles. It is not
known precisely how much [they] understood of other languages, but
possibly ... knew enough about spoken and written Chinese to conduct
daily affairs in Chinese."[9] Expressing an interest in the Christian religion,
the Khan asked the Polos to request that missionaries be sent to China.
Accordingly, the Franciscan, John de Montecorvino, probably the first
priest ever to set foot in China,[10] came to labor in the country for 11 years
and to baptize several thousand Chinese, although the Khan himself
decided that he preferred Islam. Direct and permanent commercial
relations with the West began about A.D. 1300 and sporadic diplomatic
missions, about 1500.

In the meantime, under Admiral Yung Lo of the Ming Dynasty
(1368–1644), Chinese fleets were "showing the flag" all over Southeast
Asia and as far away as Africa. Between 1405 and 1432, seven such ar-
madas set forth, accompanied by Muslim interpreters of Arabic, perhaps
graduates of a school for "languages of the barbarians" which had been
established following the first such expedition.[11]

Next to Marco Polo, the best known foreigner to have visited China
in premodern times was undoubtedly the Jesuit priest, Matteo Ricci. (As
noted in Chapter III, Roman Catholic missionaries, and particularly the
Jesuits, pioneered in linguistic work on all continents.) After tediously
studying the Chinese language in Europe, Ricci lived in China, as a
protégé of the emperor, from 1538 to 1610. In the journals which he so
carefully compiled is revealed the full extent of Chinese ethnocentrism
and terror of the outside world. For, despite the hospitality granted a few

favored foreigners such as Ricci, even Orientals like the Koreans were hated, feared and made to feel most unwelcome.

Ricci had been permitted to live at court, it seems, for a rather amusing reason. He had presented the emperor with the first striking clocks ever seen in China, and since the nobles of the court feared that, should these ever fail to work properly, the emperor would expect *them* to do the repair work, with dire consequences if they failed, they urged that Father Ricci be allowed to remain at court.[12] (Could this possibility have influenced Ricci in his choice of gifts?)

Language played a most important role in Chinese xenophobia. The authorities resented not only the teaching of their tongue to foreigners, but the teaching of foreign languages (except in the authorized government schools) to Chinese citizens. One Feng Kuei-fen summed up the general Chinese opinion of their countrymen who served as interpreters: "These men are generally frivolous rascals and loafers ... despised in their villages and communities. They serve as interpreters only because they have no other means of making a livelihood."[13]

Father Ricci tells us that the viceroy of Macao decreed the death penalty for any Chinese caught teaching his mother tongue to the foreign priests.[14] In fact, as late as the 19th century, native Chinese interpreters sometimes carried poisons with which they could speedily kill themselves if apprehended, and sundry stratagems were devised for fooling the authorities. Dr. S. Wells Williams, an early American missionary and later Commodore Perry's interpreter in Japan, had a language teacher who always carried an old shoe while coming and going, so that he might pass himself off as a cobbler.[15]

Upon occasion, a Chinese interpreter would rescue his Western employers from harassment or worse, even at great risk to himself. When a foreign-hating mob gullibly accepted the wild story that a Chinese boy had been kidnapped by some Jesuits, it was the interpreter who convinced the governor that the tale was false, and persuaded him to empower the interpreter to make a "citizen's arrest" of anyone who molested the priests in the future.[16]

Upon Ricci's death, a priest named Longobardi had been formally designated as his successor, but the person who actually replaced him as interpreter for Western diplomatic missions during the reigns of the first two Manchu emperors (Sun Ch'ih, 1644–1661, and K'ang Hsi, 1661–1722) was a German Jesuit, Adam Schall von Bell (1591–1666), usually referred to simply as "Father Schall," who arrived at the Peking court in 1623. "At a time when no mandarin in the Court spoke any foreign language and no foreign diplomat spoke Chinese or Manchu, this was a task of peculiar importance and both the Court and the foreign envoys were entirely dependent on the Court interpreters."[17]

That being the case, it was particularly regrettable that Schall's chief ambition seems to have been to frustrate the purposes of the Dutch in China. In 1655, the Netherlands East India Company had sent a mission from Batavia (Java) headed by Fierre de Goyer and Jacques de Keyzer, to obtain the emperor's permission for four Dutch trading vessels to visit Canton each year. Serving as the only interpreter available to them, Father Schall cleverly sabotaged their efforts by informing the emperor, after the Dutch had presented their gifts, that most of them were "not genuine products of Holland."[18] He is also alleged to have told the Chinese, according to one John Nieuhof who was a member of the European party, that the Dutch were not a truly independent people, but belonged by right to Spain, under whose rule they had formerly been.[19] So seriously did the emperor view these aspersions against the integrity of the Dutch that he gave them permission to enter China only *every eight years,* and then *only for the purpose of paying tribute* — [20] not precisely what they had hoped for!

In fact, the Dutch company experienced general ill luck in its relations with the Chinese, and for this the priest was not solely responsible. Back in Batavia, the Dutch were dependent upon Chinese interpreters who possessed an adequate command neither of Dutch nor of standard Chinese, and who were not above lining their pockets through deliberate misrepresentation.[21]

Although the French had sent a diplomatic mission to China as early as 1506, the first Western power to open serious, ongoing relations with that land had been Portugal, and Tomé Pires had been courteously received by the emperor in 1517. But his brother, Simão de Andrade, who arrived later, had behaved in such an execrable fashion* that both brothers had been ousted from the country, a letter from the king of Portugal had been torn up, and Simão's Chinese interpreter had been put to death.[22] It must be said that, in general, the Portuguese did not give a good account of themselves in the Far East. It was unfortunate that the first Europeans to enter the Chinese sphere of influence in force should have so conducted themselves as to appear to justify the innate Chinese suspicions of foreigners. The story of Macao (if we may credit it) is instructive.

In 1557, the Chinese government had granted the Portuguese permission to trade in Macao. According to the respected American diplomat, Chester Holcombe, after repeated racial conflicts in that city a

---

*What Simão de Andrade did was to capture Chinese and carry them off to Africa to be sold into slavery. The Chinese, however, put an even worse interpretation on the body-snatching. They believed that the unfortunates were eaten, and stories were circulated, full of rich detail as to just how the bodies were prepared for the table.

treaty had been drafted in French, Portuguese and Chinese by a Roman Catholic missionary. As was customary at the time, the French version was to be the authoritative one. Holcombe accepts the accusation, first voiced by the Swede, Sir Andrew Ljungstedt, that in the *Chinese* version of the treaty, China's sovereignty over Macao had been recognized, with Portugal to pay an annual rental, but that in the European texts, China had been made to relinquish all sovereignty over the territory.[23] Ljungstedt had quoted a former bishop of Macao to the effect that "by paying ground rent, the Portuguese acquired the *temporary* use and profit of Macao *at the pleasure of the Emperor.*"[24] When the Portuguese later tried to assert their sovereignty over Macao on the basis of an alleged imperial grand chop (which they had unfortunately lost!), the Chinese government denied that any such document had ever existed.

At this late date, we may never know the truth, but we can and should bear in mind the only known fact, that the Portuguese *did* pay rental on the territory up to 1849,[25] and it is surely not customary to pay rental on something one owns. The British Foreign Office says flatly that "the Chinese did not recognize Portuguese sovereignty,"[26] and, in fact, the only non-Portuguese source which does not roundly condemn Portugal waffles in this manner: "The rights of property were not subjected to such scrupulous criticism in the 16th century as Ljungstedt subjected them to in the 19th."[27] This, of course, is tantamount to an admission that Ljungstedt spoke the truth.

Subsequent *ad hoc* diplomatic missions to China included those of the Spanish (1575), the Dutch (1624), the Russians (1689), the British (1793) and two papal legations (1705 and 1720). From the beginning, European diplomats, by contrast with the missionaries, reported insulting treatment at the hands of the Chinese. Until the late 19th century, all foreign envoys, including Britain's Lord Macartney, were classed as *tribute-bearers*, and all their carts, luggage, etc., were required to bear this appellation. Once arrived, the Europeans were virtually prisoners, secluded and kept waiting at the pleasure of the authorities. If permitted into the presence of the Emperor, they were forced to *kowtow* (the literal meaning of which is "head-knocking") to prostrate themselves before him with head touching the floor—although, if they had lacked the foresight to bring gifts, they never did get to see him. (This happened to some stingy Russians twice, in 1567 and 1619.)* One "old China hand" describes his legation's 18th century experience this way:

> They were brought to the capital like malefactors, treated when there like beggars, and then sent back to Canton like mountebanks to

The first time European diplomatic representatives were received without the kowtow was in 1873.

perform the three-times-three [the kowtow] at all times and before anything their conductors saw fit.[28]

Because of geographic proximity and trade potential Russia had
always been keenly interested in China, a sentiment not exactly
reciprocated by the Chinese. The earliest emissaries of the czar, Petrov
and Yallishev, reached Peking as early as 1567, but were rebuffed, as
noted above, because they had come without gifts, and in 1619 Pettlin
and Mundov met with an identical reception for the same reason.[29] In
the meantime, the Russians had built a fort on the Amur (Yalu) River
which the Chinese promptly destroyed, although they did agree to receive
envoys from the czar to discuss the matter.

Linguistic barriers between China and the West came close to being
insurmountable. Nicholas Gavrillovitch Spathary, a Greek czarist envoy
who spoke Russian, Turkish, Arabic, Italian and Latin, and who enjoyed four audiences with the Chinese emperor up to 1676, complained
frequently, when back in his own country, of letters received from China
which he could not read.[30] One reason for the problem in communication was the determination of the Jesuits at the court to
monopolize all diplomatic correspondence, thereby making themselves
indispensable. To this end they insisted upon the use of Latin, a language
as unfamiliar to the czar's courtiers as Chinese itself. (Although Spathary
was one of the few Russians who could *speak* Latin, it is questionable
how well he could *read* it.) By the time the Russian arrived in China,
Father Schall had been succeeded by Father Ferdinand Verbiest, a
Belgian Jesuit who became Spathary's (and every other European's)
Chinese interpreter. Conversing easily in Latin, Spathary and Verbiest
astounded Emperor K'ang Hsi, who had held the inaccurate opinion that
no Europeans from different lands could understand each other.[31] (This
was one reason why the Chinese despised them.)

At Verbiest's request, six additional Jesuits were assigned to China
in 1685. Two of these, Gerbillion and Pereyra, accompanied the Chinese
minister, Prince Su ko-ti, to Nertchinsk in 1689 to negotiate with the
Russian envoy, Prince Golovin.[32] The meeting began not too
auspiciously, with a dispute over which language to use for the conference, the Russians preferring Mongolian and the Chinese insisting upon
Latin, which only the priests knew. But the happy outcome was the first
treaty in which China ever permitted a foreign power to negotiate with
her on an equal basis,[33] delineating the boundary between the two em-
pires and permitting trade across the border. The texts were in Russian,
Chinese and Latin, but with this slight variation—that while the Russian
and Latin versions listed all titles and honors (the so-called "honorifics"),
the Chinese text mentioned nary a one belonging to the Russians.

Language problems attendant upon the 400-man caravan mission led from Russia to China in 1695 by Ibrant Ides (a Russian of Danish origin) led to a decision to make Latin the official language of intercourse between China and the West, thus confirming and perpetuating Jesuit influence at the Court of China.[34] Another result of the Ides mission was to make Europeans, through translations of the leader's account of his journey, much more "China-conscious."

Sava Lukitch Vladislavitch, named by Peter the Great as "ambassador extraordinary and minister plenipotentiary" to China, took with him some language students from a church school in Irkutsk along with a few Latin translators and interpreters of Mongolian, who would, in time, constitute an Orthodox mission in Peking. As formalized by the 1729 Treaty of Kiakhta, the arrangement permitted a permanent Russian delegation of ten, including four priests of the Orthodox Church, to reside in Peking "to study the languages of the land." In all probability, the emperor granted such a concession in order to assure himself of a convenient source of Russian-language interpreters. But the school proved to be something less than a showpiece, for most of the priestly instructors turned out to be disorderly alcoholics, encouraging their charges to fritter away their time with wine, women and song. Nevertheless, at least one student, Hilary Rossokhin, upon his return to St. Petersburg in 1741, was deemed worthy of appointment to a post as professor of Oriental languages.[35]

Nineteenth century Chinese diplomacy is comprehensible only in terms of the Middle Kingdom's abysmal ignorance concerning the world beyond its sphere of influence. And it was wilful ignorance! The Chinese had refused to credit a map of the world shown them by Matteo Ricci, on the ground that "whatever they didn't know wasn't knowledge." Their foggy notions about geography—that the United States was a small island off the coast of England and that Prussia did not exist because they had never heard of it (and therefore they refused to consider treating with it)—greatly handicapped them in their contacts with the West just at a time when the West, whether China liked it or not, was beginning to make a tremendous impact upon the East.[36] At first the Chinese did not even attempt to distinguish one Westerner from another. All were "Franks" *(fo-lang-chi)*, whether Portuguese (to whom the term had first been applied), Spaniards, French or Italians,[37] and all were held in equal contempt.

The underlying problem was that the Chinese simply could not envision the conduct of foreign relations as a tit-for-tat affair between sovereign equals. To them, it had traditionally meant merely a series of ritualized gestures of subservience directed at the Great Central Power (the "Middle Kingdom") by its satellite states. Thus, the Chinese saw no necessity to maintain permanent embassies abroad. What was the need for that, when temporary visiting delegations would serve as well, and would forestall the long-term residence in China of those repulsive barbarians?* Lord Macartney's request, in 1793, for a permanent British mission to China, met with flat rejection, couched in the most arrogant and insulting terms. The ethnocentrism of these people is revealed in all its glory in a diary kept by Kuo Sung T'ao, who headed China's first delegation to Britain, in 1876. Observing the ladies' fashions at a diplomatic reception, he wrote, "That night there were women dressed in the Greek national costumes, in long tunic-like robes with big outer garments, rather like the Chinese robe. That is because *Greece was the first country to be sinicized"*[38] — a statement which must have astounded any Greeks who read it.

As has been said, during the Chou Dynasty relations with foreign states had been placed under the Board of Rites because "diplomacy" consisted almost entirely of presentation ceremonies. During all subsequent dynasties — of which the Ch'in, Han, T'ang, Sung, Yuan and Ming were the most important — foreign political affairs remained affiliated with the Board, a policy continued by the Manchu (Ch'ing) Dynasty until 1861. Commercial relations, however, were left in the hands of local mandarins† or trade associations. By the 1830's, the Co-hong, or guild made up of certain government-approved merchants, had become the liaison between foreign traders and the Chinese government. No one might trade except through the Co-hong, supervised, at the emperor's command, by the imperial high commissioners, Lin Tse-su, Hsu Kwang-tsin and Yeh Meng-chin. These three men, by 1840, had become the sole arbiters of China's foreign affairs.[39] As far as language is concerned, some of the difficulties may be gauged from the story of a British businessman who, seeking an interpreter in 1844, could only rely upon a Chinese from Singapore, who repeated his words in the Fukienese dialect to a Chinese of that locality, to be converted by *him* into Mandarin for the Chinese official![40]

It had been the good fortune of the British East India Company to have acquired the services of some remarkable interpreters of the Chinese language. The first, George Leonard Staunton, had been knighted by George III for service with the Company in India, and later, after studying Chinese at Matteo Ripa's Chinese College in Naples, he and a

*Much of this was pure racial prejudice of a type familiar to Americans. The Chinese regarded blue or grey eyes, for instance, as "cat's eyes."

†A mandarin was a civil service bureaucrat, whose rank was denoted by a button worn in his cap. The word probably comes from the Portuguese mandar ("to command") or, as some think, perhaps from a Malay word (see Cameron, Barbarians and Mandarins, p. 135).

native of China from the College named Dominus Nean had accompanied Lord Macartney to Peking in 1793 as interpreters.[41] Staunton's 12-year-old son, George Thomas, who went along as Macartney's page, proved to be even more gifted than his father. Picking up Chinese at virtuoso speed, he returned to China some eight years later as the Company's Chinese interpreter in Canton. Until the advent of Staunton and his successor, Robert Morrison, the English traders at Canton had been at the mercy of interpreters who were either Macao Chinese or Eurasians. Such men knew little but pidgin English, and, because their own safety was at stake, they had a tendency to alter the Englishman's words in order to make them appear more humble. But with the coming of Staunton, Morrison and their successors, circumlocution disappeared and it seemed to the dismayed mandarins that they were now confronted with an entirely different breed of Englishman.[42]

Upon the expiration of the Company's charter in 1834, the British government had assumed control of its affairs, including supervision of the China trade, in which opium figured largely. When William John Lord Napier, newly appointed chief superintendent of the British China trade, arrived in Canton on July 15, 1834, requesting an audience with the Chinese viceroy, his mission from its inception had been plagued by semantic misunderstandings. The Chinese draw a distinction between a *letter* (which is a communication between equals and for which there are various words, depending upon the type of letter) and a *petition* ("pin" or "ping"), implying subservience. Thus, they took immediate offense that the Englishman's message had been styled a "letter" rather than a "petition" (that he might be received in audience). Napier's secretary, who had been sent to the city gate to deliver the missive, had been kept waiting for hours, while one official after another had appeared but insultingly refused to receive the note. Told that the stalemate would end if he redrafted the "letter" in the form of a "petition," Napier flatly refused to do so. The Chinese viceroy, by implication, then threatened the Co-hong's interpreters with death unless they made Napier understand, and conform to, Chinese law.[43] At this crucial point, Napier's fluent missionary-interpreter, Dr. Morrison, died, leaving his inexperienced son to carry on, and the impasse was broken only by an order from the viceroy cutting off *all* trade with England. But within a very few years, the British were to be avenged with interest, when they won the so-called Opium War (1839) and coerced China, through the Treaty of Nanking (1842), into accepting a humiliating set of conditions. Following this, the chief Chinese negotiator for the Treaty, Ch'i-ying (often anglicized to Kying) had been named governor-general of Canton and authorized to conduct relations with foreigners in all treaty ports, thus uniting responsibility for political and trade relations in one office.[44]

As we have seen, the Chinese had been formally training language students under the supervision of the Board of Rites since at least the 16th century. However, the languages taught were only those of the tributary states. Then, in the early 18th century, the Russians had founded their language school-*cum*-mission in Peking, primarily to train their own nationals in oriental languages. But they had also accepted 24 young men chosen from the "Eight Banners," the ruling Manchu class. This old school had lingered on—in relict form—until the 1860's, by which time it consisted of one decrepit Chinese professor who knew no Russian whatsoever.[45]

Europe had been of little consequence to the Chinese as late as the 18th century, but within another hundred years it had become the gravest of concerns. For one thing, the British were pressing China to establish a regular, systematic exchange of ambassadors, to which the Chinese pleaded every excuse they could dream up—insufficient qualified men, fear of corruption of their citizens abroad, the impossibility of mastering European tongues, etc., etc.[46] In fact, any Chinese so unfortunate as to be required to deal with foreigners was known, for obvious reasons, as "the devils' slave." After 1860, when the evil day could be postponed no longer, the Chinese government found it nearly impossible to recruit qualified citizens for the necessary diplomatic posts. Far from looking upon ambassadorships as the high honor which Westerners hold them to be, the Chinese regarded them as a fate worse than death. Many wept bitter tears, even, on occasion, deliberately mutilating themselves in the hope that they might then be ruled ineligible.[47]

The Treaty of Tientsin (1858) compelled the Chinese government to improve its foreign language instruction, by stipulating that English dispatches would be accompanied by Chinese translations for three more years only, after which the Chinese would be expected to do their own translating. Many of the more sophisticated Chinese now began to grasp the necessity for a thorough overhauling of China's "Foreign Office," and for the promotion of foreign language study, particularly of the Western tongues. The most influential such person was Prince Kung, the emperor's brother, whose involvement in the Napier affair had won him the title of "Devil Number Six" (a devil through "guilt by association" with the foreign devils, and Number Six because he was his father's sixth son). In an official communication to the emperor, the Prince warned, "To know the state of the several nations it is necessary first to understand their language and letters. This is the sole means to protect ourselves from becoming the victims of crafty imposition."[48]

Crafty imposition, indeed! For in the drafting of the Sino–French Treaty of 1860, another priestly linguist pulled a "Macao," concocting discrepant treaties, of which the *Chinese* version permitted French missionaries to enter the interior and to own land there, in contravention of the law of China. This clause was omitted from the French version, evidently out of fear of that government's reaction to such unscrupulousness. (The French government did later repudiate the controversial clause.) For purposes of comparison, the two versions follow:

> *French:* Conformémant a l'édit imperial rendu le 20 Mars, 1846, par l'auguste Empereur Tao-Kouong, les éstablissements religieux et de bienfaisance qui ont été confisqués aux Chrétiens pendant les persecutions dont ils ont été les victimes, seront rendus a leurs propriétaires, par l'entremise de son Excellence le Ministre de France en Chine auquel le Gouvernement Impérial les fera delivrer avec les cimetières et les autres edifices qui en dépendaient.

> *English translation of the French:* In conformity with the Imperial edict of March 20, 1846, by the august Emperor Tao-Kouong, religious and charitable foundations which were confiscated from the Christians during the persecutions of which they were the victims will be returned to their owners, through the good offices of His Excellency the French Minister to China, to whom the Imperial Government will deliver them, together with the cemeteries and other structures appertaining thereto.

> *But in Chinese:* It shall be promulgated throughout the length and breadth of the land in terms of the Imperial Edict of the 20th February, 1846, that it is permitted to all peoples in all parts of China to propagate and practice the "teachings of the Lord of Heaven," to meet together for the preaching of the doctrine, to build churches and to worship; further, all such as indiscriminately arrest (Christians) shall be duly punished; and such churches, schools, cemeteries, lands and buildings as were owned on former occasions by persecuted Christians, shall be paid for, and the money handed to the French Representative at Peking, for transmission to the Christians in the localities concerned. *It is, in addition, permitted to French missionaries to rent and purchase land in all the Provinces and to erect buildings thereon at pleasure* [italics added].[49]

So it came to pass that, in 1860, the Chinese government established the delightfully-named "Soothing Office" *(fu-chu)*, whose main objective was, of course, the appeasement of France and England. A year later, the *fu-chu* became the *Tsungli Yamen* (Office of Foreign Affairs),[50] mandated to execute China's obligations under the various treaties which had been forced upon her. Intimately related to the emperor's Grand Council, the *Tsungli Yamen* included most of the five to seven members of the Council.

Originally, the Office of Foreign Affairs had been organized into eight functional bureaus, four of which corresponded to the major

Western nations with which China dealt, but *based upon the language spoken there*. As late as 1860, with the Russian and French bureaus were included an American and a British bureau, the Chinese being under the impression that the two latter peoples spoke different tongues.[51] After being informed of their error, they replaced the "American" bureau with one for the German language. Throughout the 1880's, eight translators-interpreters *(fan-i-kuan)* were employed, two for each language. These persons were the first true professional linguists to serve the Chinese government, and they were classified as such, rather than as secretaries, but not until 1898 was an official government Office of Translation set up, under the direction of Liang Ch'i-chao.[52]

Supervised by the *Tsungli Yamen,* and primarily to satisfy treaty obligations, a school for Chinese interpreters of foreign languages, known as the "School for Combined Learning" *(Tungwen Kuan)* had been established in 1869. Prince Kung had suggested to the emperor that some Chinese who knew Western languages be recruited in Shanghai and Canton to come to Peking as instructors. When a search turned up only one such person, later found to be poorly qualified, the government, reconciling itself to the unavoidable, hired a number of Europeans to teach the languages representing the four bureaus of the Tsungli Yamen.[53] They were directly accountable to the Office of Foreign Affairs, which relied heavily upon the school's graduates for its language needs. By 1866, similar schools had also been established in Shanghai, in Canton, and at the Foochow Shipyard.[54] Graduates who did well on the horrendous civil service examination, the *takao,* attained that most coveted of all stations in imperial China, the mandarinate, and frequently rose very high in China's diplomatic service.

Following the Boxer Rebellion (1900), the European powers that had mounted an international expeditionary force to rescue the foreign legations in Peking required China to reform the ineffective "Dead Letter Office," as they had contemptuously labelled the *Tsungli Yamen.* Thus, through an Imperial Edict of July 24, 1901,[55] the *Tsungli Yamen* became, first, the *Waiwu Pu,* and, ten years later, the *Wai Chiao Pu* (Ministry of Foreign Affairs), with the understanding that this ministry was to take precedence over the other six. As in the earlier ministries, interpreters and translators of the Department of Intercourse were classified according to their language of expertise — Russian, French, English, German or Japanese.[56]

A frequent subject of comment among the foreign instructors of the *Tungwen Kuan* was the glaring ineptitude of the Chinese for languages, in such contrast to their abilities in science and mathematics. (Fortunately, no student was required to master more than one language, nor was an interpreter or translator expected to offer more.) In view of modern China's abundance of superb linguists, the explanation is obvious. Because the Chinese of that era never really *liked* to speak any language other than their own, even if they had volunteered for a career which demanded that they do so, a kind of psychological inhibition kept them from reaching a peak of true excellence. In their relations with Europeans, their highest regard continued to be reserved for the rare Westerner who was fluent in Chinese—such as the American career diplomat, Nelson Trusler Johnson (1887–1954). A recipient of the State Department interpreter's fellowship to China in 1907, Johnson ultimately mastered the language so well that, at a formal banquet in Peking celebrating his appointment as United States minister to China, his toast in Chinese produced "an electric tension ... followed by ... a low murmur of appreciation."[57]

The work of Chinese–European linguists can be best appreciated if we briefly examine some of the difficulties involved. To the missionaries of yesteryear, Chinese was a language "invented by the devil to prevent the spread of the Gospel in the Middle Kingdom." (Strange how both parties associated the Lord of Darkness with the other!) What has always compounded the Westerner's frustration in dealing with Chinese is the fact that the perplexities present themselves on *two* levels—the mechanical and the philosophical—and today, a third level as well, the ideological.

Philosophical stumbling-blocks are most often encountered in the written word, but are by no means absent from oral communication. Traditional Chinese philosophy is schizoid, embracing two mutually incompatible ways of looking at the universe, the Taoist and the Confucianist. To the former, "things are not what they seem, and thus we should seek reality apart from actuality," but to the latter "things are as they seem but should be better, and literature is the means whereby they may be made better."[58] This being so, should the writer (or speaker) be interpreted through Taoist or Confucianist lenses, or (today) through Marxist or Maoist lenses, or through some odd combination thereof? The following critique of Chinese literature says it all:

> The finest flower of Chinese education is that which, steeped in the Chinese classics, can convey in three pages of allusive writing, to the right readers, what would otherwise take thirty.[59]

Few things have made life more difficult for Western linguists in government service since World War II than the necessity of recognizing communist ideological semantics and of dealing with it in the most effective manner. The attempt to communicate with a communist nation, says Sir William Hayter, may be likened to a purchase from a vending machine: "You put in a penny—your question—and in the end, probably, you will get something out (perhaps a sour ball) when what you wanted was a chocolate. You can sometimes expedite the progress by shaking the machine. It is, however, useless to talk to it."[60]

Robert T. Oliver, pointing out that, to the communists, "words ceased to be symbols for reality and became symbols of intent," enumerates some new meanings for everyday words that have actually appeared in such sources as the *Dictionary of the Russian Language* and the *Soviet Encyclopedia.* The reader may wish to compare them with Webster's version.

> *Cosmopolitanism*—"a reactionary, anti-patriotic, bourgeois outlook on things, hypocritically regarding the whole world as one's fatherland" (how ironic that this was the *ideal* of the original Marxists: "The workers of the world have no fatherland," i.e., they are all of *one*).

> *Morality*—"that which facilitates the destruction of the old world and strengthens the new Communist regime" (i.e., "the end justifies the means").

> *Patriot*—"anyone who believes that the interests of his own country necessarily and always coincide with those of the USSR."

> *Revolutionary*—"he who without argument, unconditionally, openly and honestly, without secret military consultations, is ready to protect and defend the USSR."[61]

As an example of this type of usage, *Izvestia,* on August 27, 1968, gave a new meaning to the word "freedom" when it greeted the entry of foreign tanks into a free city as a "spontaneous, ardently welcomed defense of popular freedom."[62] Faced with this sort of thing, the language professional is in exactly the same dilemma as the citizens of George Orwell's *1984,* in which everyone babbles in Newspeak, whose most salient characteristic is that it means the exact opposite of what it appears to mean.

The United States has had a number of semantic disagreements with the Soviet Union. One such incident occurred when Russia was dickering with the Western powers for removal of troops from Germany. In the proposed agreement, both East and West reserved the right to send reinforcements into Germany if she were attacked. The Russian version, however, reflecting their picture of Germany as *two* nations, specified the right to bring in troops "in case the security of either part *of* Germany is threatened," while the English version, premised on the assumption that Germany is *one* nation, stated, "in case the security of either part *in* Germany is threatened"[63] (italics added).

Whenever communist ideological terminology must be expressed in an Oriental language, such as Chinese or Vietnamese, the potential for trouble is only compounded. One remarkable account of semantic confrontation on the eastern front is that of Colonel Robert B. Ekvall, an American born and raised in China, whose earliest experience as an interpreter had been acquired by explaining *Robinson Crusoe* to his Chinese playmates. In later life, Ekvall served with General Stilwell in Burma and with the OSS (forerunner of the CIA) in Washington, and was then chosen to interpret at the negotiations at Panmunjom for the release of American prisoners after the Korean settlement.[64]

One semantic hassle between the Chinese and the Americans involved the date for the release of 41 Americans being held in Chinese prisons. At the conference between Alexis Johnson and Wang Ping-nan in August of 1955, the United States wished to use the phrase "promptly to exercise their right to return," but the Chinese objected to this as implying a command, since their word for "promptly" is the same as the one for "immediately." But, as the Americans did not like the preferred Chinese phrase "as soon as possible," a compromise was reached with mutual agreement upon the word "expeditiously."[65]

Disagreement also ensued when the matter of withdrawal of all "foreign" troops from Korea was under discussion. North Korean General Nam II defined as "foreign" all troops brought into Korea by their governments. By this definition, the United Nations troops, being "foreign," should withdraw, but since the communists insisted that the Chinese were all there as "volunteers," they were not "foreign."[66]

Perhaps the most amazing feature of the language professions in communist China, unknown in the Soviet Union, has been an attempt to apply the principle of collectivity even in translating, on the theory that "two heads are better than one." Harking back to ancient days, when the translation of Sanscrit Buddhist literature into Chinese had been a collective enterprise, Lu Tien-yang says, "Translation hardly can be done successfully in individual work. Personal response to a stimulus ... and personal linguistic ability may be limited."[67] Thus, the individual variations in a translation which, to a Westerner, seem inevitable or even desirable, from Lu's point of view are indicative of faulty technique. To him and to those like him, proper technique consists in the pursuit of THE ONE elusive, flawless, irreproachable translation.

Mechanically, the Westerner has few problems with Chinese grammar, there being no moods, tenses, personal genders or numbers, conjugations or declensions. Moreover, the same word may serve as noun, verb, adjective or adverb. (But this very simplicity is what makes it excruciatingly hard for a Chinese to learn the more complex Western tongues.) And to Europeans and Americans, spoken Chinese is a

minefield studded with booby traps known as "tones" and "inflections."
"In Chinese, a man ceases to be a man the instant you change your tone
of voice in uttering a word. He may, in fact, become a disease, a night-
ingale, or a carrot."[68]

Aspirated letters present so many pitfalls that "boner" stories
abound, often to the embarrassment of the missionary gentry. Anyone
who has ever tried to learn an Oriental language must feel pity in his
heart for the clergyman who told his flock that the Savior, while on earth,
went about "eating cake," his intended phrase having been, "healing
the sick." No less dismayed was the missionary who saw his congregation
rise and leave the chapel after he had asked them to be seated. Both men
had fallen victim to misplaced aspirates.

Another headache is transliteration—the rendering of a *sound* into
its closest written equivalent in the alphabet of another language. Today,
the transliteration of Chinese is governed by systematic rules, but in centuries past there were no rules, and it was a case of "every man for himself." For fun, an American interpreter once asked a number of
European and American scholars of Chinese how the word "porridge"
should be written in Roman letters. This was the result: *chou, chow,
chew, chau, tcheau, djou,* and *tseau* (this word is the origin of our slang
word "chow" meaning food).[69]

Derk Bodde has pointed out that, when a foreign term or name must
be transliterated by a compound of many characters (such as "Prince of
Wales," *wei-erh-shih*), the Chinese prefer to be as laconic as possible,
using only a few characters, and *with regard for the literal meanings of
the syllables.* Such economy can lead to confusion, as was the case with
the Chinese lady who, in 1949, thought the United States was ruled by an
emperor, because (communist) Chinese newspapers habitually shortened
one of their pet expressions, *mei-kuo ti-kuo chu-yi* ("American im-
perialism") to *mei ti* ("American emperor").[70] Most Americans would
probably regard as the extreme of silliness this attempt on the part of
Chiang Kai-shek to analyze world affairs through linguistic hocus-pocus:

> The Japanese call China "Chihna," [meaning] "half dead man." What
> do they call Russia? They call it "Lusiya," [meaning] "dew." ... The
> Japanese compare Japan to the sun and Russia to the dew. Once the
> sun shines, the dew dries instantly. From this, it is obvious that long
> ago Japan had decided upon her national policy. She is determined to
> destroy Russia.... What do the Japanese call the United States of
> America? We Chinese call her "Meilichien," or "Beauty Sharp
> Strong." But the Japanese call her "Milichi," or "Mikuo." The word
> "mi" means "rice." ... The Japanese reveal that they have long in-
> tended to eat [the United States] up. From this we can understand how
> painstakingly the enemy has been making preparations to acquire
> supremacy.[71]

It doesn't matter whether Chiang really believed this nonsense. Clearly, he thought it would influence his audience, and his information service judged it worth translating and distributing in English. But that sort of thing had unpleasant consequences in earlier centuries because of the Chinese fondness for placing the *least* pleasant interpretation on any foreigner's name. When the head Hong man sent his calling-card to Lord Napier, he refused to use the characters which had been suggested by Napier's interpreter as representing the Englishman's name, picking others—Lao Pi—which meant, literally, "laboriously vile." (If an Englishman were to do this to a Chinese name, he might, for example, transliterate Mr. Li Hung-chang (meaning "Mr. Great Elegance Plum") as "Lie Hung in Chains."[72]

Case Two: Japan

Western communication with Japan is an equally fascinating story, although it does not go back quite so far in time. The earliest recorded contact with the West dates from 1543, when three Portuguese seamen had been shipwrecked off the coast.[73] Within six years, St. Francis Xavier had arrived and initiated a process that was to have the direst consequences, both for Japan and for the entire future history of the Far East—the attempted conversion of the Japanese to Christianity. This strange land having been recognized as a fertile mission field, European Catholics, particularly the Jesuits, went all-out in their efforts to convert the population. In the beginning, the Portuguese were in the majority, augmented from time to time by Spaniards from the Philippines and by a few Italians. Since the priests soon realized that the Japanese wanted to hear religious services in their own tongue rather than in Latin, Balthasar Gago, a Portuguese Jesuit, was sent to Japan in 1553 with instructions to learn the language, which he proceeded to do, with the aid of another Jesuit and a Japanese convert. Two years later, in a letter to Europe, he included six characters in Chinese and Japanese, which are supposed to have been the first examples of those two tongues ever published in Europe, although St. Francis Xavier had also sent back some samples.[74]

It became the practice, in 16th century Portugal, for boys who displayed intelligence to be plucked from the Lisbon orphanage and sent to the Far East as assistants to the priests, and with the particular injunction that they learn the native tongue so that they might, in time, serve as interpreters.[75] These were, in fact, history's earliest "student interpreters," as such young men came to be designated in the 19th century. A number of them earned reputations as outstanding linguists, laying the foundations for Western scholarship in the Japanese language. Of them all, none more deserves a place in history than João Rodrigues, who arrived in Japan at 16, remained there for more than 30 years, and became known to the Japanese as "Rodrigues *tsuji*" ("Rodrigues the Interpreter").

Between 1192 and 1868, the effective rulers of Japan, governing in the name of the emperor, were the *shoguns* (military dictators). Much like the emperors of ancient Rome, many of the shoguns feared above all else the "subversive" influence of Christianity, not least because a number of their own vassals had undergone conversion. But, exactly as had been the case in Rome, persecution of the Christians was a sometime thing. Much depended upon the temper of the particular shogun, the advice given him by his leading vassals, and, above all, the political and economic conditions of the land at any given moment. Undoubtedly, the Japanese government would have ousted the priests long before it did had it not been for a greedy desire for trade with the Portuguese. Nowhere is this vacillation more apparent than in the behavior of the great Toyotomi Hideyoshi (1536–1598).

In 1579, when Alexandro Valignano arrived in Japan as visitor general (inspector) of the Jesuit mission there, he picked as his personal interpreter João Rodrigues, who had learned the Japanese language by travelling widely with another priest. Although Hideyoshi had previously ordered the missionaries expelled from Japan, he took a fancy to young Rodrigues at first sight, and on many occasions received him graciously when he would see no other Europeans. In the years to come, Rodrigues several times rescued his fellow priests from expulsion or worse, purely through Hideyoshi's regard for him. In fact, from 1592 until the dictator's death in 1598, Rodrigues was the only Jesuit whose presence in Japan was legal,[76] although a few always remained there in hiding.

Tokugawa Ieyasu (1542–1616; the "Toranaga" of James Clavell's novel *Shogun*), behaved as capriciously as had his predecessor. Although much was made of the fact that Ieyasu received Rodrigues in person and named him to be his commercial agent in Nagasaki (i.e., interpreter and mediator between the Portuguese and the Japanese merchants),[77] in 1609 the interpreter fell from grace for business reasons and was ordered into exile. The last years of Rodrigues were spent in China where, in middle age, he set about learning the Chinese language.

To eradicate what he had come to regard as an un-Japanese ideology, Ieyasu expelled all priests in 1614,[78] and 22 years later an earlier kind of "iron curtain" was slammed down on the land, with the death penalty decreed for any missionaries or for any Japanese converting to Christianity.[79] No person could legally leave the country, and the only Europeans permitted entrance were the Dutch. These, being totally devoid of any missionary impulses, were allowed a limited trade at one port,

Nagasaki. Since the Japanese despised these "favored" Hollanders and treated them virtually as prisoners, it is remarkable how attractive, to young Japanese men, the so-called "Dutch studies" (*rangaku*—i.e., Western scientific education) proved to be. Through the Dutch, Western books continued to circulate in Japan, provided only that they did not propagate Christianity.[80] In 1803, in fact, the shogunate established an office at the Edo observatory for the translation of Dutch scientific materials, followed eight years later by a similar office for more general translation. It is also known that, by the end of the 18th century and the early years of the 19th, a few Japanese were actually studying other languages besides Dutch—Russian, French and English.[81]

One of the most gifted students of Dutch was the interpreter Nishi Zenzaburo, who in 1767 began compiling a Dutch–English dictionary, but who died before he had gone beyond the letter "B." Some of the Japanese interpreters, including Nishi, tried to guard Dutch lore as their private preserve, and when two Japanese doctors applied to learn the language in order to be able to read European medical texts, Nishi discouraged them by telling them it would be too difficult.[82]

The Japanese managed to keep themselves fairly well-informed on the Western world (much better informed than did the Chinese) through this one, narrow channel. When the American Commodore Perry arrived in 1853 to force the door wide open—primarily to assure the protection of United States seamen shipwrecked off the coast of Japan—the Japanese were by no means as ignorant of the West as historians have sometimes implied. But there was definitely a serious problem in communication!

Perry had brought with him two interpreters, Dr. S. Wells Williams (1812–1884), a Protestant missionary and an authority on the Chinese language, and one Portman, who spoke only Dutch. On the Great Lew Chew (Ryuku) Islands, Perry's first port-of-call, he also found as local interpreter a Dr. Bettelheim, a Christian missionary who had converted from Judaism. Williams, the chief interpreter, had learned Japanese from some shipwrecked sailors of that nation who had been picked up, as an act of mercy, by American naval vessels. Perhaps it should be explained that one of the headaches for the Western powers during Japan's period of isolation had been the refusal of the Japanese manning shore batteries to permit a foreign ship to approach close enough to the coast to return one of their own nationals. Any Good Samaritan vessel therefore found itself stuck with the Japanese sailor. However, the little which Westerners knew of Japan at that time came either from such rescued persons or from the Dutch.[83]

The Japanese also found one of their former involuntary expatriates to be of service during the negotiations with Perry. Makahama Manjiro had been rescued by an American vessel, spending several years in the United States before returning home. While the Treaty of Kanagawa was being negotiated, the Japanese had secreted Manjiro in an inner room accessible only to themselves, where, quite unknown to the Americans, he could pick up off-the-cuff remarks and rapidly translate any materials written in English.[84]

Upon the conclusion of the first conference in 1853, it is reported, the two Dutch-speaking Japanese interpreters, Hori Tatsunosuke and Hatshisuko Tokushumo, lingered as long as possible on the American ship and were very loth to say goodbye. Tatsunosuke confided, *sotto voce,* that President Fillmore's demands stood a very good chance of being accepted.[85] This man, who apparently soaked up new languages like a sponge, was distinctly heard to say, upon leaving Perry's flagship, "Want to go home."[86]

When Perry returned a year later to receive the Japanese government's reply, he found a new man added to the roster of Japanese interpreters. This was Moriyama Einosuke, who could actually speak some English, having learned it from a captive American sailor. On March 31, 1854, a treaty granting practically everything the Americans had asked for was signed in English and translated into Dutch, Chinese and Japanese. (Some minor semantic problems arose over its exact wording. The Japanese found that their copy called for ratification *after* 18 months, while the European and Chinese versions said *within* 18 months. The Japanese text being the only discrepant one, they agreed to alteration.)[87]

Before departing for home, Perry had decided that he would "show the flag" by entering Edo Bay with two of his ships and making a slow turn around the Bay. The Japanese authorities had forbidden him to enter the city himself, which irritated Perry because his crew had been looking forward to doing exactly that. After some argument, the authorities consented to a turn about the Bay, provided a few Japanese were allowed to remain on board the flagship. One of these, the interpreter Einosuke, had heard of the Western custom of firing gun salutes and was terrified lest Perry fire such a salvo, thereby causing the people of Edo to think they were being attacked. Einosuke had decided, privately, that if Perry made ready to fire his cannon, he would position himself in front of the gun's mouth and offer himself as a sacrifice to the cause of peace.[88] Happily, Perry had the good sense not to fire the gun.

Throughout the Americans' sojourn, no one treated them with greater cordiality than did the Japanese interpreters. Until the day Perry sailed for home, they continued coming on board nearly every day, bringing small gifts for the crew. Perhaps they felt that the Americans treated them with more consideration than did their own superiors, for, according to the official United States government record of the expedition, the Japanese interpreters had been required, during both the 1853 and 1854 parleys, to perform their duties *on their knees*.[89]

Since there was only one Dr. Williams, the first Westerners to enter Japan after 1854 had little choice but to rely upon a group of interpreters attached to the Dutch settlement at Nagasaki, not all of whom were either Dutch or reliable, although they were very well paid. (Some Englishmen, a Swiss and a South African Boer were numbered among them.) As for the Japanese interpreters, *their* status was hereditary, being handed down from father to son. All of them had descended from interpreting families at Hirado where the Dutch and Portuguese had established their first "factories" some 300 years before.[90]

Westerners who went to Japan in those days were prone to two serious errors regarding language. First, some of them actually believed that Dutch was the official language of the Japanese court, simply because it was the only European tongue which the Japanese seemed to know. Secondly, *most* foreigners at the time—including Foreign Office officials—held the misconception that a knowledge of Chinese was a prerequisite to learning Japanese, and that anyone who knew the former could rather easily learn the latter. They were to discover that this was not exactly true.

In 1856, President Franklin Pierce, on the joint recommendation of Commodore Perry and William H. Seward,[91] appointed a well-to-do merchant in the Asian trade, Townsend Harris, as his special emissary to Japan. Harris was to conclude a commercial treaty with the Japanese and also one with the Siamese. As his interpreter, he took with him a Dutch-born American, Henry Heusken. This gentleman merits some attention.

Born in Amsterdam in 1832, Heusken had emigrated to the United States at the age of 21. Shortly after his arrival, he had learned from the Reverend Thomas de Witt of the Collegiate Reformed Church of New York[92] that Mr. Harris was seeking a secretary who spoke Dutch. Applying for the post, he had immediately been hired, and he remained in Japan until murdered in 1861 by some ultra-nationalistic fanatics.

Townsend Harris is given well-deserved credit for his accomplishments in six short years, within a still largely hostile land, of whose tongue he spoke not a word. But few are aware of Henry Heusken, to whom Harris's achievements are so largely owing. And Heusken's difficulties were many. He found that the Japanese authorities were inclined to blame their own interpreters (since there was nothing they could do about those of the other party) whenever any difficulty arose in the negotiations. When Moriyama Einosuke, serving the Harris mission as he had Perry's expedition, displeased them, they replaced him with two new men who knew less Dutch than Einosuke. Aside from this, the

Dutch they used was archaic, with a vocabulary limited to words spoken by sailors and traders of 300 years before, and the Japanese insisted upon forcing this quaint Dutch into their own grammatical structure, word for word. Harris himself complained of having to struggle for hours in an attempt to convey even the simplest idea.[93]

It is clear that Heusken's special talents were widely appreciated, for Harris was asked to lend him, at various times, to other Western diplomats—the British and the Prussian, for example. Yet he was being paid only $1,500 a year, which was less than what other Western interpreters were making. Apparently, Heusken decided on a polite form of blackmail. He went AWOL, a fact duly reported by Harris to the State Department. Yet, when Heusken later voluntarily returned, not only was he welcomed back, but his superior concocted a coverup story for State Department consumption, and succeeded in obtaining for him the salary of $2,500 which he had been demanding, as well as an advancement in rank to First Secretary of the Legation. The ultimate accolade was his funeral in 1861, at which five national flags flew at half-mast.

Shortly after the opening of Japan, the British government had begun offering scholarships (student interpreterships) for language study in that country, as well as in China. Later, these scholarships were to be extended to other lands. As of 1903, the examination was a (possibly) five-day ordeal encompassing mandatory tests in handwriting and spelling, arithmetic and English composition, while optional papers might be offered in précis-writing, geography, geometry, the elements of law and contracts, and Latin, French or German.[94] A major purpose of the tests was to evaluate the candidate's aptitude for learning languages, rather than his present knowledge.

In such a manner began the colorful eight-year career of Sir Ernest Satow, whose good fortune it was not only to serve in Japan during some of the most breathtaking years of its history, but to be right in the middle of most of the history-making events. Yet the task with which he found himself faced, upon his arrival in 1861, had been truly formidable. When Satow first set foot in Japan, in the company of another young Englishman (Russell Brooke Robinson), he discovered that the second-ranking officer of the British Legation, charged with handling all correspondence with the Japanese government, knew *not one word* of the language. Even worse was the lack of instructional material. Arriving in Japan without any textbook or dictionary, Satow had been able to beg the sheets of a new Japanese–English dictionary, written by a missionary, Dr. S.R. Brown, "virtually as they came off the press."*[95] This material, together with remarkably haphazard instruction from the said

*The first European–Japanese dictionary was a Dutch–Japanese one in 1796.

missionary and a couple of Japanese—punctuated by the crack of balls rolling down the bowling alley next door—enabled Satow to make considerable progress. Unfortunately, as he records, he never learned to write as well as he could speak, because each of his three mentors tried to teach him a different style of Japanese writing!

Some of the more intriguing assignments that fell to Satow's lot during these years included interpreting for negotiations with the antiforeign Choshu clan, for the reception marking the retirement of Japan's last shogun, and for the presentation of the English ambassador's credentials to the new Meiji emperor. Upon one occasion, Sir Ernest was put to the ultimate test: he was required to interpret from English to Japanese *and vice versa* for eight hours.

Satow provides us with a first-hand description of the negotiations which took place between 12 Englishmen and three Japanese, the shogun's Council. The matter at issue, not successfully resolved by the conference, had been reparations for the murder of two English nationals.[96] Two interpreters were present, one speaking Dutch and English, the other Japanese and English. Recalls Satow,

> The conversation proceeded at a very slow pace.... This gave rise to misunderstandings and the Japanese Ministers seemed every now and then to profit by the double instruction [i.e., two separate interpreters] to answer very much from the purpose, so that Col. Neale's observations had to be repeated all over again, and interpreted and reinterpreted.[97]

During the years following the reopening of their country, the Japanese set about modernizing themselves as if there were to be no tomorrow. Inviting Western experts to come and show them how to do it, they shrewdly picked their advisors from those nations whose expertise in certain areas was, at that time, internationally renowned. The Western language which a Japanese would choose to learn would depend, therefore, pretty much upon his field of interest. As a 19th century student of Japanese culture explains,

> When you visit one of the purely political offices, say the Foreign Office, you find yourself in an English atmosphere and you speak English. When you visit the University, on the other hand, you find all the bottles of the Medical School labelled in German, the inscriptions over the patients' heads in Latin and German, and unless you know Japanese you must speak German to be understood. The Department of Police is modelled entirely upon the French system, and you must speak French there if you are a visitor, and be tried in the French style if you are a prisoner.[98]

There was a time when the American public school system was the envy of the world, and for this reason the Japanese government in the 1860s turned to the United States for help in modernizing their own. Marion K. Scott, an educator from Hawaii, arrived in 1872 as special advisor to the Minister of Education. Since he chose to use only American books and materials, and to conduct the teachers' training classes in English with the use of interpreters, it is not strange that the English language acquired, just as it had in China, a foothold in the country which it would never quite lose. Mr. Scott was soon joined by Dr. David Murray from Rutgers University, during whose six-year tenure English became the required secondary language in all high schools, universities and colleges, and in the 1880s was even introduced on the elementary level.[99] From that time onward, however, in keeping with the growing trend toward militaristic nationalism and the indoctrination of school children in such values, the Ministry of Education turned somewhat away from the United States and became more receptive to German influence. But by 1891, a government-sponsored Foreign Language School had been established in Tokyo.[100]

Case Three: India

Britain's language problems in the strikingly multilingual land of India must have been particularly challenging. To this day, the government of India acknowledges in its Constitution 14 tongues, in addition to which English is commonly spoken by the educated.

The earliest record of a Western interpreter at work in India comes from the time of Vasco da Gama, the Portuguese who had been the first European to reach that land in 1498. A countryman of his, Pedro Alvares Cabral, had picked up one Guaspare, a Jew from Posen who had been working his way around the Red Sea and Persian Gulf on Arab ships, eventually winding up in Goa, on the coast of India. The Goan ruler sent him to da Gama, who compelled him to undergo conversion to Christianity and to change his name to "Guaspare da Gama." Knowing many languages, from this time on Guaspare sailed with the Admiral as his interpreter and confidant, and also made a second voyage to India with Cabral, in 1500.[101]

As elsewhere in Asia, the Jesuits were the pioneers in language study. By 1548, the superior of southern coastal India, Antonio Criminale, had learned Tamil, and his successor, Henrique Henriques, continued his efforts. Between the two of them, a Tamil grammar was prepared and sent to Europe in the hope that the Jesuits would make a rule requiring all missionaries in India to write *only* in a native tongue.

Akbar, the great Moghul Emperor, received a group of Jesuits in 1595, and, while speaking a few words to them in Portuguese, suggested that they learn Persian (the language of his court), in order that he might converse with them without an interpreter. They took his advice to heart and, by the end of the century, were translating Christian literature into Persian.[102]

But *secular* translating and interpreting were the province of the British East India Company. Chartered in 1600, the Company had at first been greatly handicapped by an inadequate number of employees who knew any Indian tongues. In 1634, an officer complained that they had only one clerk who could speak any language except English, and some 40 years later, the Company began a policy of hiring tutors for its employees.[103] Between 1714 and 1806, personnel were chosen strictly by the patronage system, but in 1800, Fort William College had been founded at Calcutta to train employees of the Bengal Civil Service in Indian languages, and similar arrangements were made for the presidencies of Madras and Bombay. (Calcutta, Madras and Bombay, were the "three legs of the stool" on which imperial power rested.) Fort William came to boast some distinguished Orientalists as teachers of Sanscrit, Persian, Arabic and Bengali, but after 1860, Hailybury College in England somewhat reduced the importance of Fort William. Students (male only, of course) were admitted at 15 for a three year course, which included both Oriental languages, especially Arabic and Persian, and "general" college-type work.[104] A limited degree of patronage prevailed between 1833 and 1837 (meaning that those who would even be allowed to take the civil service examination were screened, in order to keep out "the wrong sort"). But by Charter Act of 1853, the competitions were thrown open to all male British subjects.

The lowest rank in the Indian Civil Service was that of "writer." In the beginning, before the establishment of the training schools, writers had been required to know only bookkeeping. But after arrival in India, they had been expected to learn the vernacular of whichever part of the country they were stationed in, tutors were hired for them, and they received a salary supplement as soon as they had proven their mastery of a tongue by passing an examination in it. Sometimes these exams must have been curious affairs indeed. One veteran of the I.C.S. recalls that it used to be customary to prepare to examine a student both by hiring an "educated" Indian gentleman and also waylaying some "ignorant" passerby who would both converse with the applicant, thus testing the latter's ability to carry on a conversation in the refined and the not-so-refined idiom. Once, while this was going on, everyone present had been startled by a loud shriek of dismay, as a villager who had been pressed into service was seen on his knees before the examinee, vehemently protesting his innocence. The applicant, simply to make conversation, had exercised his creative imagination and had asked the Indian why he had come to Lucknow, and being told that the villager had a court suit pending, had then demanded to know if he had bribed the judge![105]

After 1842, writers were not eligible to permanent appointments until they had attained competence in Persian and Hindi (if they were to be stationed in the Northwest) or Bengali and either Persian or Urdu (if they were going to Bengal). Although supposedly required to qualify within a year, they might be permitted another three months if they failed. But a third failure sent them home to England. From the 1850's, new arrivals were detained in Calcutta or Bombay until they had perfected the language of the province to which they had been appointed, which might take as long as a year-and-a-half. There were three periodic examinations at half-yearly intervals and a final test at the end of two years.[106]

In 1858, the Civil Service Commission, which had been established for recruitment to the Home Civil Service, was given jurisdiction over the I.C.S. also. From then on, recruitment was by written examination, stressing both European languages (any of Greek, Latin, French, German or Italian) and Oriental languages, law and culture.[107]

As an illustration of the level of language competence expected of the candidate for an I.C.S. appointment, for the French exam of 1903,[108] the candidate had been required to write a short essay in French on one of four specified topics, presented to him in French, two of them being "la simplicité est la plus belle parure d'une pièce de Shakespeare," and "Le duel est contraire aux principes de la civilisation moderne." He had also to answer eight general questions on French grammar — for example, "Quels sont les verbes correspondant à *bride, ordre, élan, veut, main, visage, grand, profond, mou, ridicule, gris, fort*?" Finally, there were 12 questions on French literature and passages to translate both ways. A unique feature of civil service examinations before the advent of the typewriter had been the stress placed on handwriting. Candidates for language posts would commonly be given a page of script in a foreign language and asked to copy it precisely.

It should not be forgotten that, while the I.C.S. was recruiting men with language potential, so was the Army. In the same year (1903), candidates for posts as language officers in the Indian Army might conceivably have been subjected to three days of examinations, depending upon the number of languages in which they chose to be examined.[109] On the first day, there was translation from and into the language, an essay, copying of French manuscript, translation into Spanish or Arabic and dictation in and translation into Portuguese or Turkish. The second and third days followed the same pattern, except that other languages — German, Japanese, Russian, Italian or modern Greek — were substituted.

An English poet of considerable experience in India once satirically compared what a writer for the East India Company was required to undergo, only to wind up as a "seventh sub-assistant," while some young district officer, an army man, was assumed to possess an "intuitive" knowledge of languages:

> All you've to learn are some few dialects, (you'll do it if
> You don't, why you're *deported* in about a year;)
> That's for you Writers, but such knowledge is intuitive
> In soldiers old or young — at least, that's what we hear;
> Ensigns, day by day, poor boys, dragged roaring from their mess away;
> Forced to rule whole districts, hit or miss, surmise or guess away;
> Meanwhile you, lucky dog, in happy ease, your bile expectorate
> As seventh sub-assistant in some excellent collectorate.[110]

District and subdivisional officers had to deal with two forms of petition, which required either a knowledge of the vernacular on their part or expert service from an interpreter-translator. The "peshi" was the "placing before," or submission of documents requiring the officer's attention. Those in a vernacular he did not know would be read to him by his *peshkar,* or clerk, who obviously had to be bilingual. A good peshkar would have studied the document in advance and summarized it for his superior.

The "sawalkhama" was the oral hearing of complaints (or "cases"), with double records kept by the peshkar in English and in the vernacular. It was not uncommon for the peshkar to be an old man on the verge of retirement, who would insist upon reading every paper from page one to page zillion, "intoning its elaborate phrases in a maddening singsong and swaying his body back and forwards in time to his own music." Although the Englishman would usually know what was coming next, he had to sit through it to the bitter end.[111]

The art of translating had been of special importance in British India because, according to Sir George Campbell, "all business is conducted in writing to an extent quite beyond anything known [in Britain], even in our most important courts of record. All petitions, statements, applications of every description, are filed in writing; all evidence is recorded in writing, and all orders and instructions of every kind are formally written and signed."[112] Because of this, during the early part of the 19th century the East India Company found it expedient to hire a kind of super-linguist or "grand translator," who would be versed in a number of tongues, such as Hindustani, Gujarati, Marathi, Persian, Urdu, etc. He came to be officially known as the "Oriental Translator to Government," but was more commonly referred to simply as the "O.T."[113]

The Political Department (of which the O.T. was a functionary) had been the diplomatic arm of the British Indian Government. Some of its work related to foreign countries on or near the frontier—Afghanistan, Persia, Tibet, Nepal—but most of it concerned the so-called "princely states," Indian states still under native rulers.[114] Of these there were some 562, covering 60,000 square miles, and their relations with the British government were defined by treaty.

Persian being the court language of the decaying Moghul Empire, a Persian Department had first been established, separate from, but loosely affiliated with, the Political Department. In charge of it was the "deputy secretary and translator," later rechristened the O.T. Until 1854, the post had always been filled by an Englishman, appointed by the governor. So multifarious were his duties that they must have been far from boring. He (and his underlings) were responsible for the translation of all central and provincial bills, acts, rules and miscellaneous papers. He interpreted for the governor, supplied to the district officers any required materials in a vernacular tongue, served as secretary of the language examinations for the recruitment of linguists, reported on the native press and made summaries of it for the government, conducted the correspondence with the "princely states," looked after the comfort of the princes on their official visits to Bombay, and did such odd-job work as the compilation of glossaries of useful terms in the native tongues. One of the strangest of his duties had been to pass judgment on the acceptability of any Indian who desired entrée to a government social event.[115]

In 1862, the O.T. had been given an assistant, a Marathi and a Gujarati expert, a writer, and six menial helpers. But because the staff was still so small for such an immense volume of work, much translating continued to be done by other agencies, such as the military or the High Court.

Some of the O.T.s made a better showing than others, and a number of them were outstandingly brilliant, despite Lord Elphinstone's patronizing words of caution when he appointed Vinayak Wasoodev (1854–1879) to be the first Indian O.T. Wasoodev, warned the Governor, "should constantly remember how much the Government may be influenced by his conduct in the future selection of his countrymen for places of trust and responsibility."[116]

Wasoodev did well enough, but his immediate successor, Shankar Pandarang Pandit, who served from 1879 to 1894, had been nothing short of a prodigy. At the age of 18, Shankar had been earning all of two rupees per month as a village bookkeeper. Only ten years later, he had received an M.A. degree at Bombay University and was a brilliant scholar of English, Sanscrit and Latin. All of this came about simply because some clerks from the Political Agent's Office who had one day visited his village had so impressed Shankar with their lifestyle that he had determined, then and there, to acquire a similar status. Having no money to pay for schooling, he eavesdropped near outdoor classes until a wealthy man, noticing him, offered to finance his education. By the time Shankar was appointed O.T., he had become proficient in *ten* Indian and European languages, an unparalleled record.[117]

Much later, it was the fate of one of the few Muslim O.T.s, Syed Shamsuddin Kadri (1906–1938), to become involved, in his official capacity, in the 1908 sedition trial of Bal Tilak,* that notorious nationalist firebrand. Tilak had been publishing a newspaper, *Kesari,* in the Marathi language, and it fell to Kadri's office to translate the allegedly seditious articles and to explain the various nuances of meaning in open court. The trial's outcome, in fact, hinged entirely upon semantics. *Were* Tilak's words indeed as disloyal as the government claimed they were? Apparently so, for the jury, refusing to accept Tilak's version of his intentions, sentenced him to six years in prison.[118]

All Oriental languages present many difficulties to the Westerner that he does not encounter even in those European tongues most unlike his own. It is much easier for an American to learn a Slavic tongue than to learn Japanese or Arabic, because grammatical differences are perhaps the least of the problem.

Infinitely harder to surmount are the psychological and cultural differences, of which language is a mere reflection. Since it takes many years of exposure to an Oriental tongue and its background culture before one feels truly secure in it, the best time to start learning is clearly in childhood. But it is rare enough for American youngsters to be introduced even to such a popular language as French at that early age, much less Chinese. The result, as should become evident in our final chapter, has been a heavy burden placed upon the conduct of our foreign policy, and the commission of errors ranging from the trivial to the most grave, in our negotiation with foreign states. In an age when the world is rapidly shrinking, the United States can ill afford an educational system which de-emphasizes foreign languages and cultures, or which, at best, stresses only those most like English.

It was Tilak, not Gandhi, who coined the word swaraj *meaning self-government (Speer, India, p. 319).*

CHAPTER V

The Language
Professionals of Today

International Organizations and Conferences

At Versailles in 1919, the "Big Four" met either at the private apartment of President Wilson or in the French War Office. At these parleys among Wilson, Lloyd George, Georges Clemenceau and Vittorio Orlando (occasionally with the Japanese delegate), only one "outsider" had been present for the first three weeks. He was the interpreter, Paul Joseph Mantoux, a towering figure of all time in his exacting profession.* The Supreme War Council of the Inter-Allied War Organization had, in November of 1918, appointed 12 interpreters, of whom M. Mantoux and M. Camerlynck were to become particularly notable.† Four bilingual secretaries had soon been added, one for each delegate, thus affording the professional interpreters some relief. In an amusing coincidence, the British secretary's title and last name had been Major Caccia and the Italian secretary's, Maggiore Jones!

During the course of some three hundred meetings over a period of a hundred days, including several Sundays, the "Big Four" had produced nearly seven hundred decisions, filling ten large volumes of typed material.[1] Whereas at the Congress of Vienna (in 1815) only eight com-

---

*An historian, Mantoux, at the end of the Peace Conference, became head of the Political Section of the League of Nations. In 1927, with William Rappard, he founded the Graduate Institute of International Studies in Geneva. Mantoux was the interpreter referred to in Chapter I who rendered ex tempore a poem by Shelley into French at a League session. He was, in fact, such a public attraction that people attended the sessions just to watch him in action.

†In 1929, in a speech before the League Assembly announcing Camerlynck's retirement, Britain's Ramsay MacDonald said he was "one of the most distinguished servants of this League and this Assembly" (see Shenton, Cosmopolitan Conversation, p.385).

mittees had functioned, the Versailles Conference had 58, which were to hold 1,646 meetings.[2]

It had been necessary to devote two preliminary Council sessions to the question of the language medium to be used at the conferences. As might have been predicted, both the French foreign minister, Stephen Pichon, and the official French delegate, Clemenceau, had argued at length for their own tongue as the *sole* working language. But Wilson and Lloyd George had reminded the Frenchmen that the English-speaking world at (then) 170 million people now outnumbered the French-speaking. Neither Wilson nor George spoke any language except English, while Clemenceau had not only lived and taught in the United States, but had an American wife.[3] Nevertheless, he was far from being an unreserved admirer of American culture.

What concerned the French was the *political advantage* accruing to the use of English. But since it had soon become clear that French as the sole language would not be tolerated by the English-speaking delegates, Clemenceau, to minimize the English advantage as much as possible, had suggested that *all three* languages of the "Big Four" (French, English *and* Italian) be recognized as official tongues of the Conference, *with the French version to be authoritative.* Much to the displeasure of Clemenceau and his colleagues,* both French and English (but not Italian) were finally chosen as official languages of the Conference and for the Treaty of Versailles (Articles 1–26 constituting the Covenant of the League of Nations), *both texts to be equally authoritative.*[4] Thus ended more than two hundred years of French language dominance on the international scene.

Within the League, the Rules of Procedure for the Assembly decreed official equality of the two languages at meetings and in the drafting of documents. Rule 16 stated the following: that speeches in French were to be summarized in English and *vice versa* by an interpreter of the League, that a delegate might speak in any other language but would then be required to furnish his own translation into one of the official tongues, that all official documents would be rendered in both French and English, but that any delegate might circulate documents in another language at his own expense, and that any Member(s) of the League might request the regular translation of League documents and publications into a nonofficial tongue, subject to their paying the cost.[5]

The French sentiment about the use of their tongue as a diplomatic medium is revealed in a statement by former Minister of Culture Maurice Druon, in a 1973 speech before the Alliance Française, as reported in Le Monde: *"If it is well used, French does not allow men to lie."*

In practice seldom had a nonofficial tongue been spoken by the delegates, both because of the requirement that they bear the expense of an interpreter, and because each interpretation slowed down the work appreciably. "The states ... therefore renounce what is always a question of prestige and not of necessity, and send delegates who understand and speak French and English."[6] Of course, there had been exceptions. Although the German representatives had spoken the official languages at committee meetings, on the Council itself they had generally used their own tongue, purely out of national pride. Haile Selassie, emperor of Ethiopia, even though he had been fluent in French, had spoken Amharic when he had addressed the League Assembly in 1936 to request help for his nation against Italian aggression.

On the administrative side of the League, the Secretariat had been organized into three divisions, according to the type of duty performed by the employee. Ranked within the First Division had been all staff whose work "directly gives effect to the Resolutions of the Assembly, the Council and the organization of the League and carries out the preparatory work on which their decisions may be based." But the League's linguists had not been classified within the First Division until 1930, following a recommendation that "officials of this category might, having regard to the class of candidates recruited, their high qualifications, and the importance of their duties, be assimilated to Members of the Section." This meant that interpreters, translators, revisors and précis-writers, further subdivided into A or B categories according to their Junior or Senior status, had then become official members of the First Division. Henceforth they would be equal in status, salary and conditions of employment to the other members, would enjoy the same diplomatic privileges and immunities, and would be placed directly under the authority of the League Assembly and Council, rather than the Secretariat. The Staff List of 1921 bears the names of 31 persons in that category; by 1930 they had grown to 51.[7]

The *League Year-Book* of 1934 reveals an organizational breakdown comprising a "French [and an English] Interpreting, Translating and Précis-writing Service," which included a head, four interpreters, ten translators and précis-writers, three revisors and two stenographers.[8] In addition to the two main Services, there had also been French and English Verbatim Reporting Services, each consisting of a head reporter and two verbatim reporters. Until 1921, the English-language Service, rather remarkably for those days, had been directed by a woman, a Lady Blennerhassett.

But one should not conclude that the two official languages were the only tongues with which the language services had to deal. As early as 1920, the director of the Translating Service had boasted that his underlings were capable of working in 12 others as well,* and this was to be only a beginning. As the years passed, many more languages were added to the repertoire.

Within the League itself, as we have said, nearly everyone used the official tongues. Most governments, too, out of longstanding tradition, couched their messages to the League in either French or English. Nevertheless, a vast amount of textual material sent in support of the official communications would be in the language of the country of origin, and it was this circumstance that necessitated the broad array of language skills. Actually, mother-tongue material probably gave the League fewer headaches than those communications helpfully rendered into French or English by Foreign Office personnel. Coming from a government, such missives had to be treated with due respect, but what if the text were ambiguous, misleading or downright wrong? The League's translators were probably the best in the world; Foreign Office employees were not. The linguists of the League would, therefore, administer whatever doctoring seemed called for — but very carefully, to avoid giving offense.

Two organs associated with the League of Nations are of particular interest for their language practices — the International Labor Organization (ILO) and the Permanent Court of International Justice. The ILO's Standing Orders, Article 13, had been almost identical with those of the League Assembly with respect to language rules,[9] except that, after World War II, Spanish had been introduced as a third official language. Simultaneous interpretation had been used at plenary sessions, but within committees the consecutive technique had continued. (See Chapter I.) Approximately 16 translators and interpreters had worked for the ILO.[10]

Between 40 and 50 states were represented in this organization from time to time, speaking nearly every world tongue. Although most of the work had been done in French or English, German had been more widely spoken by the worker delegates than any other language, simply because Germany had been the pioneer in workingmen's movements. In 1929, therefore, the prickly question had arisen as to whether a man might be an officer of the ILO Conference if he could speak neither French nor English. Dr. Brauns, former German minister of labor, had been elected president of the Conference, and although he had understood some French, he had been permitted to make long speeches in German.[11]

The "Statute for the Permanent Court of International Justice," Article 39, had provided that French and English would be the official

---

They were: German, Arabic, Czech, Danish, Spanish, Dutch, Italian, Norwegian, Portuguese, Russian, Serbo-Croatian and Swedish (see Ranshofen-Wertheimer, International Secretariat, *p. 138).*

tongues of the Court, even though not all of the judges thereof could understand or speak either.[12] However, the parties involved in a dispute might specify which of the two would be used, but if no such decision had been made, each party might use whichever one it chose. In that case, the judgment of the Court would be rendered in *both* languages and the Court would determine which should be considered authoritative. At the request of the interested parties, the Court might also permit the use of a language other than English or French.

One of the most difficult aspects of the post–World War II period, so far as international relations are concerned, has been the proliferation of tongues which their nationalistic speakers insist upon using for the purpose of international negotiation. Thus, language considerations occupied an inordinate amount of time at the San Francisco Conference (April to June 1945), convened to complete work on the Charter of the United Nations.

The preliminary arrangements for language services at San Francisco, on the part of the hosting United States, had been negligent, to say the least. Secretary of State Edward Stettinius, evidently having expected English to be the *only* medium of expression, had been astonished to find that French Foreign Minister Georges Bidault's interpreters, whom he had observed at work, were, in fact, linguists rather than delegates![13]

Thus the first question that had arisen at San Francisco concerned the official languages in which the conferences would be conducted. The French delegate, Bidault, reconciling himself to the inevitable, had acquiesced in the equality of French and English. But some of the South American delegates, notably those of Chile, Venezuela and Peru, had insisted upon French as the *only* official tongue, which led the delegates of Honduras and Brazil to condition their support of French upon the inclusion of Spanish and Portuguese as official languages.[14] The Chinese delegate, on the other hand, had demanded that English be the sole "working" language of the Conference, simply because it was the only European tongue which any of the Chinese purported to know.

The Russian delegate, V.M. Molotov, had pressed for a clarification, for the first time in the history of international conferences, of the distinction between "working" and official" languages. Since the difference is important, a word of explanation is in order. According to pre–World War II understanding of the terms, "official" languages are those in which delegates are ordinarily expected to make their speeches, or, if they cannot, their speeches will always be interpreted into those languages. All documents (such as any treaties which may be signed) and official records will be printed in the "official" tongues. "Working" languages will be *additional* tongues (besides the "official" ones) whose use is sanctioned in the particular organization or conference, and the rules adopted will determine precisely to what extent these languages may be used. Nationalistic fervor had been responsible for the use of such auxiliary tongues. Most nations seek prestige through the use of their language on the international level, but if it is not acknowledged by all to be a worldwide medium of expression, there is no chance of it being adopted as an "official" tongue. The "working" language compromise very expensively salvages national pride.

The most interesting thing about San Francisco, however, was a virtual reversal of the definition. English, French, Russian, Chinese and Spanish had all been designated as "official" tongues, thus permitting delegates to use any of them, provided they then accepted responsibility for the translation of their remarks into a "working" language upon request, with English and French to be the sole "working" languages. This meant that, at plenary sessions, addresses in French or English would not be interpreted into any other language unless the speaker so requested, but a subsequent translation would appear in the Minutes. All documents had been produced at once in both English and French and as soon as possible in the other "official" languages.[15] San Francisco had been the greatest "word factory" of modern times, generating *78 tons* of paper, or an average daily output of half a million sheets.[16] The same arrangement prevailed at meetings of special commissions, committees and subcommittees of the Conference.

Another interesting thing about San Francisco was that it afforded a preview of what happens when Chinese is made an official language in an international organization consisting primarily of peoples using Roman characters. Brand-new Chinese words had to be invented for the expression of concepts presented at the Conference, as well as new type with which to print them. Moreover, the "English-speaking" Chinese at San Francisco had proven so incomprehensible that their speeches had first to be interpreted *into English,* and from this into French and the other official tongues![17] The (Nationalist) Chinese mounted in the U.N. a futile campaign to have their language adopted as one of the "working" tongues, a proposal which was voted down by the Fifth Committee in 1958 with 27 opposing votes, 12 abstentions and 6 in favor. Purely as an "official" language (a status it retains at the U.N.), Chinese has caused enough problems. Eleanor Roosevelt has recalled that a Chinese calligrapher had to sit in on all meetings and make a "longhand"—if Chinese calligraphy may be called such—transcript of the proceedings, which had then been photographed in the print shop and reproduced.[18]

At the first meeting of the U.N. General Assembly in London in 1946, the language question had once more been subjected to a thorough consideration, resulting in the Language Rules within the Rules of Procedure of the General Assembly. As at San Francisco, the "working" languages in all U.N. organs except the International Court of Justice would be English and French, but the "official" tongues would be French, English, Russian, Spanish and Chinese. However, egged on by the Philippine representative, the Spanish-speaking delegates of Latin American were to continue pressing for the adoption of their tongue as a "working" language. Although, at the time, the Spanish-speaking countries in the U.N. amounted to a third of the total membership, there had been many objections to the adoption of that tongue for "working" purposes. Spanish was not a true medium of international communication except in the Western hemisphere, there were four times as many speakers of Russian and Chinese as of Spanish, which might have justified those persons in making similar demands, and, finally, the Spanish-speaking lands contributed less than 5 per cent of the total U.N. budget. To add Spanish to the repertoire, had warned the Secretary-General, would cost the U.N. an additional $1,236,031 per year.[19]

There is no doubt that within any international organization, multiplicity of languages multiplies costs. It has been estimated that the average production of a translator is five pages per day, although, if the revisor's work is calculated in, the average output of the entire translation unit would fall to around three pages per day.[20] To translate a 40-page document into five languages (assuming an absolutely equal output from all translators, which is never the case) would, therefore, require a total of 63.5 "person days," as follows. A French, a Spanish, an Arabic, a Russian and a Chinese translator at five pages a day each is eight "person days" each or 40 person days overall; the work of revisors for each language at 15 pages a day (2.7 person days each) is 13.5 person days overall; and four typists and a Chinese calligrapher-and-typist working a total of 10 person days, yields 63.5 person days total.[21]

Nevertheless, the Latin Americans were to have their way. In December, 1948, Rules 44–48 of the Rules of Procedure were amended by Resolution to adopt Spanish as the United Nations' third "working language. Five years later, it had also been so adopted for the work of the Economic and Social Council (ECOSOC) and it is, of course, one of the two "working" tongues of the Organization of American States (the other being English), while the "official" languages of that body remain English, Spanish, French and Portuguese.[22]

All interpreters and translators at the United Nations are appointed by the Secretary-General and are subject to the rules of the International Civil Service. They retain their national citizenship, but owe their allegiance to the United Nations, and they are the only employees of that organization who, for obvious reasons, are exempt from the usual U.N. requirement of broad geographic distribution.[23] Within the organizational structure of the U.N., linguists belong to the Office of

Conference Services, headed by an under-secretary directly responsible to the secretary-general. This Office encompasses the Language and Meetings Services, Publishing Service, and Library and Stenographic Service, with English, Russian, French, Spanish and Chinese units.[24]

Linguists of the United Nations provide interpretation services for conferences and meetings, translate documents and edit and publish the U.N.'s journals and official records. In 1980 there were approximately 110 interpreters at the U.N., who are required to be fluent in two languages besides their own, to possess a good voice and good diction, to have perfect hearing, and to undergo special training, after which they will be called upon to service between seven and ten meetings per week. At no time in a two-year probation period, may they be over 50 years of age. As late as 1965, there had been only one native-born American among them, a Californian specializing in Spanish who had frequently visited Mexico and who had enjoyed close friendships with Mexicans.[25]

Translators are in greater demand than interpreters at the U.N., with about three hundred employed there, turning out some 7,000 pages of material per day.[26] Here, also, the age limit for beginners is 50. All applicants, selected on the basis of a written examination, must possess a university degree or equivalent education with special language training and several years of experience as translators. Of particular advantage is a knowledge of law, economics or technical subjects. If an applicant's native tongue is English, he or she must be able to translate from French into English, possess a knowledge of French culture and institutions, and be able also to translate either Russian or Spanish. Those whose mother tongue is Spanish, Russian, French or Chinese must offer English as one of their two foreign tongues.

Beyond the actual interpreters and translators, the United Nations hires about 100 young women from 20 to 31 years of age, who conduct visitors on tours around the premises (about 1¼ miles) four times daily. These women are required to speak one language besides English, which will most commonly be French, Spanish or German. Bilingual secretaries are also in demand, most of them offering English, French or Spanish.

The auxiliary agencies of the United Nations afford many opportunities for translators and interpreters, but generally prefer to hire nationals of the country in which the particular agency is located. Although many people think the headquarters of all the agencies of the U.N. are in New York, this is not the case. The Food and Agricultural Organization, for instance, is domiciled in Rome, UNESCO is in Paris, the World Health Organization is in Geneva, and the International Civil Aviation Organization is in Montreal.

Unlike other organs associated with the U.N., the International Court of Justice (successor to the old Permanent Court of Justice under the League of Nations) does not mandate the use of English and French as "working" languages. Following the practice of its predecessor, the Court is required, by Article 39, Paragraph 3 of its Statutes,[27] to use *any* language at the request of a party to a case. However, the "official" languages remain French and English and most judgments are rendered in both tongues, with English nowadays more popular than French. Article 58 of the Rule requires interpretation from one "official" language to the other, and translations of pleadings are usually made in this manner, but the Court is permitted to make exceptions. Until 1965, speeches were interrupted for interpretation at 10 to 15 minute intervals, but since that time, simultaneous interpretation has been used at all public hearings.[28]

The European Economic Community also has its own Court of Justice, founded in 1959. Articles 39–41 of the Court's Rules of Procedure specify the languages to be used: French, German, Italian and Dutch, all of which are on an equal footing. Under the Rules of this Court, it is the plaintiff *(requérant)* who determines which tongue shall be used, and be it noted that, prudence sometimes rising superior to chauvinism, he frequently picks his attorney's tongue rather than his own![29] Exceptions are provided for, however.

No interpreters are permanently attached to the EEC Court, but are lent to it from the European Economic Commission in Luxembourg. There is, however, a full complement of translators and revisors, divided into four sections corresponding to the four official languages. This Court is unusual in having the rule that only licensed attorneys (under the laws of their own country) are eligible to apply for positions as linguists, and each applicant must know two of the "official" tongues in addition to his own.[30]

The European Parliament (Council of Europe), with headquarters in Strasbourg, France, produces about six times more paper than any other parliamentary body in the world, for its members speak nine different tongues — French, German, Italian, Danish, Swedish, Norwegian, English, Dutch and Irish. Consequently, an average of at least 120 interpreters, both staff and freelance, work there every week of the year,[31] plus some 1,200 free-lancers from time to time. Translating for this organization presents peculiar hazards. Although linguists need offer only two languages plus their own, circumstances are such that often they find themselves forced to work in others, and no one can possibly know intimately the cultures of so many different nations. For instance, one translator at Strasbourg, aware that cheese is a major product of the Netherlands and that the Dutch word for it is "kaas," had once rendered "pinda kaas" as "pinda cheese," when in fact it is "peanut butter."[32]

The "official" languages at Strasbourg are English and French, with speeches normally given in one of those tongues, and with simultaneous interpretation supplied for the other.[33] (Members may speak in any of the other tongues but in that case must supply their own interpreter.) Since 1954, simultaneous interpretation has also been provided for German and Italian, since it had long been suspected that the non-English or French speaking delegates had been playing a more passive role in the proceedings than had the British, French and Belgians.[34]

Between the two world wars, there occurred a striking proliferation in the number of conferences sponsored by international organizations, ranging from the scientific to the literary, some affiliated with national governments and some not. In the ten years between 1840 and 1850, there had been, on the average, only one such conference per year, but by 1910 the annual number had jumped to nearly 120, and by the early 1930's, to around 250. Today, approximately 2000 such conferences are held each year. Throughout the 1930's, for 67 per cent of the meetings French had been chosen as the official tongue, English for 49 per cent and German for 40 per cent, followed at some distance by Italian, Spanish and Dutch.[35]

At most such conferences, the old method of interpreting had long continued in use. Delegates would be seated in sections corresponding to their language group, and at the end of each speech a partition would be drawn while an interpreter rendered the speech for his particular clients. Since some organizations did not bother with the partition, and even had the interpreters working during pauses in a speech, the assembly hall might well be so noisy that most of the delegates could hear little. Today, these problems have been largely eliminated through the use of simultaneous interpretation.

The Foreign Offices

France

Replacing four previous state secretaries, Louis de Révol had been appointed, in 1589, the first real French secretary of state for foreign affairs, to be responsible for all correspondence with other lands. From that time on, but particularly under Cardinal Richelieu, a modern-style bureaucracy had gradually developed. The most important innovations had been the organization of a corps of student interpreters for the Levant from 1662 to 1683,[36] the separation of the work of the Foreign Office under Louis XIV into two geographic divisions, and a total reorganization in 1825. This latter event had resulted in three specialized divisions: political, commercial, and chancelleries and archives.

Translation, along with secretarial, accounting and cyphering functions, had been placed under the Cabinet du Ministre, the foreign minister's own office,[37] and remained that way unaltered throughout the 1800's.

As early as 1712, the then foreign secretary, Torcy, had persuaded Louis XIV to establish an Académie Politique for the training of diplomats, but it had failed because of inadequate funding.[38] Under Napoleon, however, a School of Oriental Languages had been set up within the Foreign Ministry. In general, the lower the bureaucrat in the Ministry, the better his language expertise, although, on a number of occasions, Napoleon had selected ambassadors at least partially on the basis of their fluency in foreign tongues.[39]

After 1875, university students desirous of entering the Foreign Service had been required to prepare for either of two types of examination, the Grand Concours (much the more difficult) or the Petit Concours. Under the former, the first examination, in English and German, counting for *one-quarter* of the total grade, would be administered by a committee of university professors chaired by a Foreign Office official. The few hopeful survivors then appeared before a committee of five members of the Foreign Service for futher examinations of increasing difficulty. Those who passed the Petit Concours had been required to go through an intermediate stage known as a Vice Consulate, whereas graduates of the Grand Concours had immediately become Consuls of the Third Class.[40] In 1945, the École Nationale d'Administration had been empowered to recruit Foreign Office personnel, and today, virtually all entrants to the French diplomatic corps come from one of two schools — that mentioned above, or the École Nationale des Langues Orientales.[41]

The difficulties of these examinations reflect the French belief, often incomprehensible to antiintellectual Americans, that a diplomat ought to be representative of the *best* that his country has to offer, able to hold his own in give-and-take with the finest brains from any other land. It is not accidental that a number of eminent French literary figures, such as the poets Paul Claudel and St. Jean-Perse (Alexis Saint Léger-Léger) had served their nation in the diplomatic corps. Contrast this with American diplomat Bayard Taylor's comments to a friend, regarding Cassius Clay, President Lincoln's (and then Johnson's) minister to Russia from 1861 to 1869: "Ignorance of any European language, I knew, was a necessary qualification, with our Government, for a diplomatic post. I have now learned that ignorance of English is still more necessary."[42]

The French Foreign Service remains very small in proportion to the British. Between the two World Wars, it maintained a Section de Traducteurs, consisting of only three persons who did no other work.[43] Early in the post–World War II years, out of 1,033 Foreign Service officers, only seven were classed as translators.[44]

Germany

The Foreign Office of Germany had its origins in the state of Brandenburg where, in the 17th century, the Privy Council was broken into two sections, with one part of it, the Geheimer Etatssekretarius, responsible for foreign relations. This office was still further developed under Frederick William I (1713–1740), who had authorized one of the Privy Councillors to countersign all of his decisions in foreign affairs, and in 1733 an official Department of Foreign Affairs, the Cabinets-Ministerium, was established, ranking above the other two departments of government. Language and secretarial work for the Ministry were the responsibility of the Privy State Chancellery (Geheime Staatskanzlei).[45]

Always, under the Empire, the German Foreign Office was monopolized by sons of the nobility or near-nobility. (In 1914, of 122 employees, only 11 were "common.")[46] It is true that candidates were subjected to examinations, which were not particularly easy, stressing expertise in law and in languages. But the determination to exclude anyone who did not move in the proper circles sometimes resulted in the selection of men less qualified than others. The kaiser himself appointed the diplomats purely on his own initiative, and all officers of the Consular Service in consultation with the Bundesrat.[47] Just before World War II, the Diplomatic and Consular services were combined, with recruits spending part of their careers in each.

Count Otto von Bismarck, appointed foreign minister in 1862, was himself a superb linguist, speaking English, French, Italian, Russian and Latin.[48] Yet he was sometimes known to relax the language requirements for a candidate whom he especially favored. Once, addressing an ambitious mother trying to secure a post for her multilingual son, Bismarck commented that, while a gift for languages might be essential to a restaurant headwaiter, he would prefer to see as a diplomat "a man with an open mind who spoke Plattdeutsch to an ass who could prattle in seven tongues."[49]

In 1908, a Translation Service (Sprachendienst) was established within the Foreign Office. Applicants for such posts were required to be university graduates, to speak at least French and English, with a knowledge of a third language "very desirable," to know law, and to have typing skill and some business experience.[50] After undergoing two-hour written examinations and 20-minute oral tests in the foreign tongues, they were admitted to the Foreign Office as *Anwärter* (probationers) for one year. At the end of this period, they were subjected to another examination, and, if successful, entered upon a second probationary year on a mission abroad.[51] Following this, approximately 30 to 40 surviving candidates[52] had eventually been recalled to Germany, where, after three months of intensive study, they had endured the *Abschlußprüfung,* a gruelling final examination in economics, history and international law, plus three hours of testing in French and English. Only after all this did they receive the coveted title of *attaché.* No other European nation has subjected its diplomatic candidates to such lengthy periods of probation.

Hitler's government had maintained a special staff of three interpreters and seven translators, in addition to "a large number" of unofficial assistants, and bonuses had been awarded to those familiar with the more obscure tongues.[53]

Russia

It is often asserted that Western scholarship and scientific knowledge had been almost unknown in Russia before the rule of Peter the Great (1682–1725). However, in the early 17th century, prior to Peter's accession to the throne, a Greco–Latin college, the "School for the Teaching of Letters," was founded in Moscow by one Arsenius, a Greek, and in 1665, three secretaries of the "Office of Secret Affairs" (probably the forerunner of the secret police) and of the "Office of the Courts" (the diplomatic service) were commanded by the government to go there to receive instruction in Latin and Greek.[54] It was to become customary for upperclass Russians to have their children tutored in the tongues of Western Europe, and many of the czar's diplomats, particularly A.L. Ordin-Nastchokin and Prince V.V. Golitzin, were gifted linguists who were most cosmopolitan in their outlook. The practice of studying Western tongues only intensified after Peter came to the throne. Because, in the effecting of his policy of rapid westernization, a quite impossible number of books would have required translation, the Russian aristocrats and upper middle classes solved the problem by learning the languages *themselves,* thus minimizing the number of translations that would be necessary.[55] Prior to the 18th century, the most popular tongue had been German, but the Age of the Enlightenment elevated French to first preference (Catherine the Great had corresponded warmly with Voltaire), and Italian became the usual third choice.

It is amusing to note that, even at this early date, Western diplomats found the Russian government devious and hard to deal with. In 1710, the Russians demanded that the Danish envoy give them his credentials in cypher with a translation on the back—which would, of course, have revealed the Danish cypher. When the Danes protested, the Russians blandly said, "there should be no secrets between the Tsar and the Danish."[56]

Moscow was the site of two rather interesting language schools during Peter's reign. In 1701, a gentleman named Schwimmer first

organized such a school in the German enclave of Moscow and then trans-
ferred, as a translator, to the Posolski Prikaz, the old Foreign Office,
where he taught German, French and Latin to a few sons of civil servants, the intention being that they would ultimately become government
translators. At about this same time, a well-educated German missionary
named Gluck had been captured by the Russian Army when they seized
the Livonian town of Marienburg in 1702. Sent to Moscow, Gluck had
been encouraged to start a school for the sons of noble and mercantile
families, which Peter had subsidized with 3,000 rubles annually. Latin,
German, French, Swedish and Italian were taught, as well as other
Western academic subjects. The school survived until 1715, with approximately 40 students, and Foreign Office employees were actually
coerced by Peter into sending their sons to it.[57]

By *ukase* (imperial decree) of 1718, Peter established eight
"colleges," of which one, the Collegium Chuzhestrannich Diel (College
of Foreign Affairs), was intended to supersede the earlier Posolski
Prikaz, and to both of which the government's interpreters and translators were attached.[58]

Because of the intensive training of the aristocracy in foreign
tongues from childhood, and because the members of this class were the
only men who would ever become diplomats, very few translators were
needed by the Russian Foreign Office until after World War I, by which
time the communist government was in power. Moreover, even in the
early days of that regime, Lenin felt constrained to appoint to Foreign
Office and diplomatic posts persons of aristocratic or upper-bourgeois
origin, who were acquainted with foreign languages and with the cultures
of Western Europe. Neither Georgy Chicherin, the Soviet commissar for
foreign affairs during the 1920's, who spoke four languages[59], nor
Alexandra Kollontai, the world's first woman ambassador (to Finland
and Mexico), who spoke 11[60], was of proletarian origin.

But Lenin had been pragmatic and possessed of sound common
sense. Under Stalin, party status, ideological purity, and unswerving
devotion to the dictator himself became the first requirements for any
government position. The civil service was to be purged, not only of most
people whose parents did not meet the test of proletariansim, but also of
nearly all "old Bolsheviks," those who had served under Lenin. Like all
the other government agencies, the Foreign Service came to be filled with
narrow, provincial party hacks who usually knew no language except
Russian. One such person was V.M. Molotov, Soviet foreign minister
from 1939 to 1949, of whom the British ambassador, Sir William Seeds,
complained, "he knows ... no foreign language; has, so far as I am aware,
never been outside Russia and has no practical experience in the conduct
of foreign affairs or knowledge of the psychology of foreign countries."[61]

After Stalin's death, steps were taken to make the Soviet Union's administrative practices more commensurate with the nation's status in the world. Henceforth, greater emphasis would be placed upon both the supply and the quality of government linguists. Since the Russians are secretive about the details of their administrative bureaus, it is difficult to obtain substantial information on them. We do know, however, that all students from secondary school level onward are required to learn a foreign language.[62] Those who aspire to a diplomatic career will then attend the International Relations Institute, operated jointly by the Foreign Ministry, the KGB (secret police), the Party Central Committee and the Ministry of Higher Education, at which 40 per cent of the student's time during the six-year program will be devoted to language(s).[63] An intimate knowledge of at least two foreign tongues is required for graduation, under a rather curious arrangement. A student must learn the language of the country in which he is specializing, and, for the second tongue, the foreign language which is most frequently spoken in that country! Moreover, not the student, but the admission committee, decides which country and which languages an applicant is to specialize in.[64]

Approximately 2,000 students are enrolled at any given time, and admission is only by recommendation of a Party district committee, which will take into account the applicant's record in the Komsomol (communist youth organization). Beyond this, there is a Higher Diplomatic School where those who are already in the Foreign Service may attend a kind of postgraduate course, lasting two years.

Most of those who wish simply to become translators or interpreters receive their training at the Moscow Pedagogical Institute for Foreign Languages, unless they do so through one of the Army's training programs. Once in government service, they will probably be under the authority of the Diplomatic Corps Servicing Board within the Ministry of Foreign Affairs. Under the jurisdiction of this Board fall the Press Department, Higher Diplomatic School, Department of International Organizations, Department of International Economic Organizations, and Department of Cultural Relations with Foreign Countries, in addition to various geographic units.[65] It is not uncommon for a government linguist to step up into a diplomatic career, as did Oleg Troyanovsky, Soviet permanent representative to the United Nations.

The Institute's program has been subsidized by the United Nations, which in 1976-1977 appropriated $275,000 for the training of 40 to 50 Soviet linguists. The Russians had agreed to accept this arrangement only in condition that, in the future, Russian-language interpreters and translators at the U.N. would be recruited solely from the U.S.S.R.[66] Ever since the birth of the U.N., the Soviet government had objected to the employment of non-Soviet Russian linguists—many of them expatriate "white" or anticommunist Russians—on the ground that the language in the homeland had undergone great changes since the Revolution, and that the oldtimers would not be up to date on the variations—which, in itself, was probably true enough.

Britain

Before 1872, the British Foreign Office had been divided into two departments under two secretaries of state, each directing 10 or 12 clerks who were supervised by a couple of under-secretaries. Usually, one of the latter did the translating, limited primarily to French and German. Not until 1821 had a functionary been specifically designated as a "translator," to be paid about £300 per year.[67] Because of Britain's concern with Turkey at the time, an interpreter of Turkish had also been on the payroll.

After 1842, when the first "treaty ports" were opened in China, the government established a special Consular Service for that nation, which from its inception included "student interpreters," and a few years later this scholarship system had been extended to Japan, Siam, and the Levant.[68] By the early 20th century, England enjoyed the largest and most efficient Oriental consular representation in the world, maintaining 33 consuls and consuls-general in the Orient, with 75 lesser officers and many student interpreters. Only the Austrian consular service, which also stressed knowledge of languages, came near to rivalling it in size and efficiency.[69]

The first examinations for administrative-level Foreign Office personnel were introduced in 1856, designed to test the candidate's aptitude for learning languages, rather than his current proficiency.[70] From the beginning, French was regarded as the most important tongue but the rule soon came to be that if two candidates showed equal ability on other parts of the test (handwriting, spelling, précis-writing and French translation), preference would be given to the one who demonstrated a knowledge of German also. In 1871, when the examinations were totally revised, Latin and German had been made compulsory, with Greek, Spanish or Italian optional.[71] The applicant's knowledge of French was tested in every possible manner—in conversation, translation both ways, and writing from dictation.[72] With some further reforms in 1882 and 1891, the system as outlined above remained virtually unaltered until World War I.

On missions abroad, it remained customary to engage local residents as translators or interpreters. But within the Foreign Office in London, the task of translating European languages other than French (the latter having been required of *all* Foreign Office personnel) had come to be assigned to three junior clerks classified as part of the diplomatic staff, one of whom worked in Russian, one in Spanish, one in Italian, and three in German. These had been chosen through competitive examinations and, as an inducement to all clerks to learn a foreign tongue beyond French, they were to be paid a stipend if selected for language duties.[73] The expectation was that the chosen three would not then rest on their laurels but would go on to proficiency in additional languages. Special "cram" schools of the type so popular with American students, aimed at preparing people to pass difficult examinations, had also been known to young 19th and early 20th century Englishmen hoping to pass the Foreign Office tests. Most candidates seemed to feel the need for special tutoring of this type, and upon return from a year or two abroad where they had worked on a foreign tongue or two, they would enter such a class, perhaps the well-known Scoones on Garrick Street.[74]

If these governmental arrangements for linguists seem meager by today's standards, the reader should be reminded that there had been no great need for such services prior to the First World War. During the 1860's, Britain had maintained only four embassies in European capitals, and only one in Asia — the Persian.[75] On the eve of the Great War, the Foreign Office itself had employed a total of 176 people, inclusive of doorkeepers and charwomen.[76] After the war began this small staff underwent considerable expansion through the addition of nondiplomatic personnel, most of whom were favorably received. In 1921, indeed, a committee charged by the Foreign Office with making recommendations for the improvement of language services suggested that the wartime policy of recruiting bilinguals from among the nondiplomatic branches of the civil service be continued. The first examinations for such posts were held the following year, leading to the appointment of three persons, a chief translator and two assistants, which arrangement remained unchanged from 1922 until World War II.[77] The language standards of the Service between the two world wars was very high, with emphasis placed on French, German, Spanish and Italian.

By an order-in-council of May 20, 1943, the British Foreign Service revamped its recruitment and training through the so-called "Eden Reforms."[78] Of the 25 to 30 Foreign Service officers to be recruited annually for the United Kingdom, half would be assigned to study a "hard" (lesser-known) language — usually Oriental or African. The probationer would commence his study at home and might later be one of the lucky few selected to continue it abroad. Those learning Arabic, for instance, would take courses at the Middle East Center in Lebanon, following which the best (only two or three) would be chosen to spend three to six months in intensive study in some other Arab land. Applicants for China would study first for three months at the School of Oriental Studies in London, followed by a year-and-a-half in China, and those destined for Japan, Iran, Turkey, Thailand and Burma were similarly treated, as were candidates in the more common, or "easy," languages. Following the training period, civil service commissioners for the Foreign Service would conduct language examinations.

Britain in the 1980's has the third largest diplomatic service in the world. Between 1970 and 1975, administrative entrants possessed 22 degrees in modern languages, exceeded only by those with degrees in history (35) and economics or law (29). Today's applicants must pass one-and-a-half days of language examinations, which now stress précis-writing — the reduction of a 1,500-page passage to 350 pages. Within the Service, new officers are subjected to training in one of some 25 languages at the Diplomatic Service Language Center, London, whose classes are so arranged that, for the easier tongues, employees can spend an hour or two on them at their convenience. The Center also arranges full-time residential training, lasting about a month, for certain European tongues, during which time the student lives abroad with a foreign family. The British Government invests a considerable amount of money in the training of linguists, especially since it continues its long-standing policy of granting bonuses to those who master a foreign tongue. As of 1975, the Foreign Office claimed 182 fluent Arabists, 159 Russian experts and 35 Chinese specialists.[79]

The United States

The origins of the U.S. State Department's language services, under Philip Freneau, have already been discussed. Louis McLane, Andrew Jackson's secretary of state, reorganized the Department in 1833, establishing a "Translating and Miscellaneous Bureau," the "miscellaneous" referring primarily to librarianship. From time to time over the years, the State Department translator was expected to perform library duties also, as did McLane's translator, Robert Greenhow. The latter was paid a sum so munificent it would have astonished Freneau — $1,000 per year![80]

McLane's successor, John Forsythe, carried out further changes in 1836, setting up five bureaus within the Department: Diplomatic, Consular, Home, Disbursing Agent, and Translator. The latter's duties continued to be nebulous. In addition to his language work, he was charged with "such other duties as may from time to time be assigned to him." Such vagueness is understandable, of course. At that time, there had been hardly enough translating and/or interpreting work to enable the employee to earn his generous salary.

Secretary Hamilton Fish, in 1870, effected an even more sweeping reorganization, setting up 13 departments, of which one was to be Translating — but still with only one translator, now to earn $2,000.[81] Henry L. Thomas held this post for 33 years, from 1869 until his death in 1903. Without any college training, Thomas became renowned as an expert on modern Greek, and he had once ventured to correct the Spanish of a Latin American diplomat. There must have been something in the position which encouraged longevity, for Thomas's successor, Wilfred Stevens, reputed to know some 30 languages, remained on the job for 20 years, and *his* successor, John S. Martin, for 30.[82]

As late as 1909, when the Department once more underwent reorganization, a single translator still remained. But by 1911, references to translators, in the plural, begin to appear in the literature. Many different tongues must have been represented among them, for it is known that communications were by then being received at the Department of State in at least 13 languages. In common with employees of the printing office, stationery room, carpentry workshop, mailroom and livery stable, the translators had been subordinates of the chief clerk, who reported to the secretary of state.[83]

Under the leadership of Secretary Frank B. Kellogg, in 1928 a true Translating Bureau was finally established within the Department, consisting of a translator (the first being Emerson B. Christie) and four assistants.[84] At that time, the duties of these men were specified as the translating of communications received from foreign embassies or legations or any messages received at the White House, the translating of treaties and proceedings of international conferences, and the checking of foreign texts of treaties. By 1936, the Bureau's employees had grown to five translators and two clerks.[85] (Interpreting was not so important at that time, since anyone who moved in diplomatic circles was assumed to know French.)

Largely because of loud complaints from such professionals in the field as John B. Kasson (see Chapter III), the Department of State, in 1895, began its first language training programs. The earliest student interpreters (in emulation of the British system) were assigned to American legations in the lands whose languages were adjudged "difficult," such as Persia, Korea, China and Siam.[86] Under executive orders of 1905 through 1909, admission to the diplomatic and consular services was to be (at least in theory) contingent upon passing a test in a language other than English — ordinarily French, German or Spanish. But this rule was not rigidly enforced until nearly 1913, and in that year, only 27.7 per cent of those who took the test succeeded in passing it.[87] In any event, the requirement did not apply to those of ambassadorial rank, who were political appointees, but only to the lower-level staff serving the embassies and legations. This may, perhaps, have been unfortunate, at least in the opinion of one former American ambassador, who believed that a diplomat's reliance upon an interpreter might mean that "intonations and emphasis are lost; or a touch of humor, so that a delegate may think a thing has been said in ill temper, that was really uttered as a jest."[88] However, as we have tried to make clear, the best interpreters are quite as sensitive to such nuances as the diplomat himself — perhaps more so.

The Rogers Act (1924) establishing a Foreign Service within the Department of State, resulted in a new policy of language training for all Foreign Service officers. Under Title VII of the Act, a Foreign Service Institute was established, to consist of a School of Foreign Affairs and a School of Languages.[89] Moreover, a set of "Regulations Governing Foreign Service Officers Assigned to Language Study in China and Japan" had been promulgated. Between 1902 and 1926, 53 student interpreters, later dubbed "language attachés," studied and worked in China, 27 in Japan and a few in Turkey,[90] with subsequent extension of such training to Russian and Arabic. As an example of the procedure followed, in 1936 the United States had eight Foreign Service officers in Japan assigned to the study of Japanese, the largest number ever until after World War II. It had then been the custom to hire private native tutors who gave lessons at their students' homes, the supervisor of the tutors being an eminent Japanese professor who had written a number of books on his native tongue.[91]

One distinguished American State Department careerist who began as a language student was George F. Kennan, destined to become (briefly) United States ambassador to the Soviet Union in 1952. Kennan, a Princeton graduate who had applied in 1928 as a trainee in the Russian language, received the usual treatment of the time — 12 to 18 months of work in the field in the regular Foreign Service, followed by three years of study at a foreign university. Since the United States then had no diplomatic relations with the U.S.S.R., language trainees could not go to that country, but had studied Russian either in Estonia (as Kennan did, followed by work in Berlin) or in Latvia or Lithuania. Kennan recalls complaining that he had believed he was receiving inadequate instruction in "hard core sovietology" — politics, economics, etc. — but that his State Department superior had admonished him that cultural subjects, such as languages, would do him more good in the long run, and Kennan declares that he never subsequently had any cause to regret that advice.[92]

Under Chapter I, Sec. 13, of the Foreign Service Regulations of 1941, the secretary of state had been authorized to designate particular Foreign

Service officers as language officers for any area of the world, or as language secretaries to supervise the studies of the language officers. In the order of precedence within Foreign Service protocol, language officers follow counselors and first and second secretaries.[93]

At the end of World War II, training at the Foreign Service Institute had consisted of three months of intensive language instruction on the premises (given today in more than 50 languages) combined with a semester of courses in public opinion and international political communication at a university.[94] After 1946, Foreign Service officers assigned abroad (including chiefs of mission) were required to possess "to the maximum practicable extent a useful knowledge" of the principal language or dialect of the country in which they served, wording which, obviously, leaves a king-sized loophole for the unqualified to slip through. At the same time, a spokesman for the State Department had declared that, while inability to speak a foreign language would not necessarily bar one from entering the Foreign Service, such an officer would not receive more than one promotion until he had reached a level of "useful competence" in a foreign tongue.[95] Those who spoke no language other than English upon entrance to the Service would receive intensive instruction prior to their departure from the United States, and higher salaries (bonuses) would be paid to junior officers who entered with competence in certain "hard" languages, all recently appointed officers to be tested soon after entering upon their posts.

Since 1975, written language examinations have no longer been required of Foreign Service officer candidates, but everyone accepted into the Service is still expected to master at least one language during his tenure. In fulfillment of these demands, language proficiency of State Department employees is rated on the following scale:

S/1 (Speaking)–R/1 (Reading) — elementary knowledge
S/2–R/2 — limited knowledge
S/3–R/3 — minimum professional proficiency
S/4–R/4 — full proficiency
S/5–R/5 — native-level proficiency.[6]

It is the Department's objective that before reaching senior level, all officers should attain an S/3–R/3 rating in two foreign languages, as well as job-level proficiency in the language required wherever they may be stationed. At present, every officer on home leave must report to the Foreign Service Institute for language tests. Retesting is not required after the maximum (S/5–R/5) rating is attained, nor after S/4–R/4 has been acquired on two FSI tests at least two years apart.[7]

Some 10 per cent of the diplomatic corps is undergoing intensive training in a language at any given time, while about 100 are training as language and area specialists.[98] If, by the time of appointment to a post, an officer has acquired a reading and speaking proficiency in one language, he or she is taken off the probation list and two years are given in which to pass the language exam, making the officer eligible for promotion. In the late 1960's, it had been estimated that about 70 per cent of U.S. Foreign Service personnel had been proficient in one tongue, but only 14 per cent in a "hard" language.[99]

Despite all of the foregoing, in 1979 former Senator William J. Fulbright publicly revealed that, in Teheran (where, only a few months later, the U.S. was to be faced with one of the worst crises in its national history), only nine of 60 Foreign Service officers could speak Farsi (Persian), while in Pakistan, another critical area, a mere five of our 32 diplomats were proficient in the Urdu language.[100] Moreover, as revealed by Charles W. Bray III, deputy director of USICA, the United States has only 12 Foreign Service officers who speak Chinese at a truly useful level.[101] (This should come as no surprise to those who remember the McCarthyite purge of the State Department in the 1950's.)

One circumstance which does nothing to improve matters is the total lack of guarantee that any government employee will be sent to the land whose language he has so carefully acquired. For example, the background of one officer at a U.S. diplomatic post had been entirely Spanish until he had been shifted to the Netherlands, where he could function in neither Dutch, French nor German.[102] This sort of thing, however, is not unique to the United States. It has been a longstanding joke in the Swedish diplomatic service that the one sure way to avoid being sent to the Soviet Union is to learn Russian.

Fundamentally, of course, the problem is insufficient language instruction in American schools and colleges. Only 8 per cent of all American institutions of higher learning now require students to study a foreign language, as compared with 34 per cent in 1966 and 85 per cent in 1915. *There are more teachers of English in the U.S.S.R. than there are students of Russian in the United States.*[103]

The diplomatic fiascos and possible catastrophes to which Americans are almost certainly condemning themselves were dramatically previewed in an incident of September, 1980, in which the United States embassy in Kabul, Afghanistan, could not find a single Russian-speaking American officer to question a Soviet soldier who had requested asylum at the embassy. When this news reached the United States, a group of 21 congressmen fired off a letter to Secretary of State Edmund Muskie, declaring the episode "inexcusable and outrageous."[104] The Russian involved in the incident had later changed his mind about defecting, perhaps—as columnist Richard Reeves had suggested—because he "got tired of using sign language."[105]

The State Department's Division of Language Services engages in
four distinct types of duties, which result in the production of more than
50,000 pages of written material each year, in over 50 languages:

(a) translations for the Department itself, for the White House, or (by
special arrangement) for other agencies of the government;
(b) interpretation, translation and bilingual secretarial services for international conferences in which the United States participates;
(c) review of draft treaties before they are signed, to assure conformity
of texts;
(d) interpretation and escort services for distinguished foreign visitors
and others in this country under a variety of exchange programs.[106]

Besides the Department of State, many other agencies of the
American government require translators and interpreters, either permanently or on an *ad hoc* basis. Some of them include the Agency for International Development (AID); the United States Information Agency,
which operates the Voice of America broadcasts in 35 languages and
provides materials about the United States in print and in film; the Central Intelligence Agency; the Peace Corps; the departments of Agriculture, Commerce, Justice, Labor, Treasury and Defense; and the
bureaus of Standards and the Census. The Foreign Service Institute also
employs approximately 100 language instructors in Washington and
several hundred more overseas, who are almost always "native" speakers.
However, it is worth noting that fewer than 150 full-time interpreters are
required by *all* U.S. government agencies, although many more are hired
on a part-time basis.[107]

The Free-lance Trade

A very large number of professional linguists do not work permanently for any government or organization, preferring to pursue their
careers as free-lancers. Most of them avoid starvation by servicing international conferences, of which there are now more than 2000 per year,
convening on all continents. How do these people get their assignments?

Almost the first thing the sponsors of a conference will do is to hire a
linguist of acknowledged reputation as chief interpreter. He or she will
then recruit at least two people per language as required, or possibly a
larger number if more than three languages, or little-known tongues, are
to be used. Frequently, concurrent meetings are planned for a conference,
in which case several teams of interpreters may be required. It is not
unusual for a conference to hire 15 or even 25 interpreters, a number

seldom to be found in any one locality. Thus, interpreters of all nationalities commute constantly among the "conference capitals" of North America—Washington, New York, Montreal and Mexico City.[108]

As an example of conference language requirements, an "International Symposium on Industrial Development," held in Athens in 1967, utilized 93 interpreters, translators, revisors and précis-writers, while the conference rooms were equipped for simultaneous interpretation into four tongues, and 75 trilingual typewriters were supplied.[109]

Once hired, the interpreters will receive briefing sessions of one or two days on full pay, during which time they will study relevant documentation and inform themselves of any special terminology which is to be used. (The vocabulary for an airline pilots' conference will obviously be quite different from that for a conference of surgeons! And what about the June, 1975, Inuit, the world's first All-Eskimo Peoples' Circumpolar Conference, at Point Barrow, Alaska, where four different Eskimo dialects from both sides of the Bering Strait were spoken?[110]) At a well-planned conference, interpreters will be informed in advance of the program's subject, its speakers and participants, the constitution and by-laws of the organization, and will be provided with any essential financial or statistical reports, or other background material.

Surveys have found the average translator or interpreter of today to be about age 40 and free-lance, possessed of three working languages (one "active" and two "passive"), and employed about 160 days per year.[111] In fact, however, these people come in all ages from 25 to 80 and two-thirds of them are women; 45 per cent have a university degree, 25 per cent have attended a special school for translators/interpreters, but a surprising 30 per cent are "self-taught," although only 5 per cent of the latter work for international organizations.[112]

At the present time, these are some of the colleges and universities which, as members of the Standing Conference of University Translator and Interpreter Institutes, feature programs specifically designed to produce linguists of internationally recognized excellence: Bath, Paris, Geneva, Heidelburg (the oldest, dating from 1930), Mainz, Saarbrucken, Munich, Trieste, Vienna, Antwerp, Mons, Copenhagen and Montreal.[113] The major criticism of such schools, as far as interpreters are concerned, is that they tend to stress conversion *from* one's mother tongue, despite the fact that, as explained in Chapter I, the opposite is most commonly demanded of the interpreter. Such a policy is, no doubt, based upon the assumption that the more difficult task should be the one emphasized, but the actual result has been to place the graduates of such schools at a loss when faced with the concrete demands of the job. Often, the very people who did the best in school make the worst showing on the employment examinations.[114]

The most prestigious of the professional associations for interpreters, the Association des Interprètes de Conférence, acknowledges some 16 fields of specialization within the general category of language specialist. They include general translator, conference interpreter, conference translator, interpreter/translator, terminology specialist, multilingual secretary; translator for press, publicity and information services; language teacher, revisor, document specialist, *procès verbalist**, movie-TV translator, editor, literary translator, and court interpreter or translator.[115] In a formal course of study, the student will usually choose to concentrate in some such specialized field as simultaneous or consecutive conference interpreting, or financial-commercial translating.

Some Career Interpreters

It might be enlightening to take a peek at the careers of a few of the more outstanding interpreters of the 20th century. As should have become apparent by now, the best linguists are bonafide intellectuals, as the career of Jean Herbert[116] amply testifies.

A specialist in Oriental philosophy and a professor of French in Scotland before World War I, Herbert served as an officer with the British, French and American armies during the war, writing a bilingual glossary of artillery and ballistics terminology that was published in 1919. During the 1917 Anglo–French financial negotiations in London, he began his career as a conference interpreter. Throughout the 1920's and 1930's, he worked at most of the great international conferences sponsored by the League of Nations and for over a hundred different international organizations. The list of world leaders for whom he had interpreted includes nearly all the notables of that period. Upon the establishment of the United Nations in 1945, Herbert was invited to organize the corps of interpreters, which he then directed for three years.

An even more colorful life was that of A.H. Birse.[117] Born in St. Petersburg, Russia, in 1891, Birse may have had his future career predetermined for him simply because his parents, unlike most overseas Britons, did not return him to England for his schooling, thus enabling him to acquire native fluency in Russian. In 1917, at the age of 28, he joined the British Military Commission as one of their interpreters, and soon became an officer. After the Bolshevik accession to power, he returned to England to work for a bank, which sent him first to Poland, where he acquired a knowledge of Polish, and later to Italy, where he

A language expert specializing in the preparation of legal documents or of certified résumés, or accounts, of whatever has been said, decided upon, etc.

learned Italian. By the outbreak of World War II, Birse had been enjoying a high position as a banker. Then, in 1939, he found himself a second lieutenant in the Intelligence Department of the British Army, assigned to the daily reading of a half-dozen foreign newspapers. Upon Hitler's invasion of Russia in June, 1941, Birse was dispatched to Moscow to interpret for the chief of the British Military Mission, which duty included a number of high-level conferences between Stalin and Churchill and a stint in Teheran. Following the war, believing that his international career had come to an end, he returned to banking while teaching some interpreting courses at Cambridge. But in 1953, Australia caught a network of Russian spies, planned to put them on trial, and needed a person of indubitable loyalty but expert knowledge of Russian to examine both the relevant documents and the more than 200 witnesses. Birse worked at this task for ten months, although subjected, like everyone else connected with the trial to constant harassment by communist sympathizers. The trial ended with the conviction of the spies.

On the Russian side, Alexander Barmine,[118] son of a school master, finished high school in 1918 and worked for a time as a tutor. After he had joined the Communist Party and given a good account of himself during the civil war that followed World War I, he received permission to attend the School of Officer Learners of the Red Army, later attaining the status of political commissar and regimental commander. Sent to War College for advanced training, Barmine enrolled in its Department of Oriental Languages, and studied *five languages simultaneously*—French, English, Persian, Hindustani, and Arabic. The war minister, Leon Trotsky, next sent Barmine to Bokhara as a language officer for the Russian ambassador, and later he became an assistant to Georgy Chicherin, the foreign minister. Having concentrated primarily in Persian (Farsi), Barmine eventually became a Soviet consul to Iran. By 1935 he had reached the rank of first secretary of the Soviet embassy in Athens, but resigned two years later because of his dislike of Stalin.

Alexander Kaznacheev,[119] whose father had been a Party member and head of a research laboratory in the Academy of Science, was accepted in 1951 by the Moscow Oriental Institute, which had been founded by V.M. Molotov several years before. Enrolling in its five-year program, he specialized in China and the Chinese language, but during his third year decided to learn Burmese as well, primarily because knowledge of that language in Russia had been nil. (He had to learn it entirely on his own, being unable to find anyone who could teach him.) It was this that had determined his career. When, three years later, the Oriental Institute dissolved, Kaznacheev was one of the lucky quarter of its students who were permitted to transfer to the International Relations Institute, training school for the Soviet Diplomatic Service. Since, in 1955, there was not one Burmese specialist to be found in all of the huge Soviet Union, Kaznacheev had no trouble obtaining permission to specialize in the language, graduating in 1957. Since then, he has remained the dean of Soviet "Burmologists."

Hans Jacob,[120] born in Berlin in 1896, was educated there at the Collège Royal Français (founded by Huguenot refugees), where he discovered within himself an extraordinary affinity for the French language. Later studying at the universities of Berlin and Munich, he began in 1919 to write under a French *nom-de-plume,* translating many of the great classics into German. After Germany joined the League of Nations in 1926, Jacob was appointed Foreign Office interpreter at the request of the minister, Gustav Stresemann, for whom he had interpreted at all of the latter's conferences with Aristide Briand. In fact, between 1926 and 1933, Jacob was present at all of the major international conferences in which the Weimar Republic had participated. On assignment in Geneva at the time Hitler came to power, he sagely decided not to return to Germany but to exile himself to Paris, where he helped to edit the anti-Nazi daily German-language newspaper, *Pariser Tageblatt.* Later he became the chief of a team producing anti-Nazi broadcasts for Radio Strasbourg.

After France's surrender in 1940, Jacob escaped to the United States, where, in New York, he resumed his anti-Nazi broadcasts to the German resistance movement. (Among his more noteworthy comments was a prediction of Hitler's defeat at Stalingrad.) Following World War II, Jacob returned to his linguistic career, becoming senior interpreter with UNESCO in Paris and, in 1960, a recipient of the French Legion of Honor. He was also the first president of the Association des Interprètes de Conférence, which he helped to found.

In striking contrast to Jacob's story is that of the Austrian, Eugen Dollmann.[121] Born in 1914 to an upperclass family, he studied art history in Munich, then in 1927 accepted a grant for research in Rome, where he seemed to have enjoyed association with most of the intellectual coterie of that period, remaining in Italy for 16 years. In 1934, he joined the Nazi Party (as Member No. 3,402,541, he assures us) and soon thereafter began his linguistic career by translating Marshal Pietro Badoglio's *The Abyssinian War* into German. That project, plus his high-level social connections, led to opportunities to translate a number of other books. But Dollmann had not been destined to remain a translator, for when the Nazi youth leader, Baldur von Schirach, visited Italy, he was recruited as interpreter, and later performed similar services during a visit by the S.S. chief, Heinrich Himmler, to the police chief of Rome.

As Dollmann delicately puts it, "On November 9, 1937, I woke up one morning in a hotel in Germany to find myself in the S.S."[122] Ac-

cording to him, he had not been eaten up by any great desire to join the
S.S., and would probably never have done so had he been called upon to
interpret for "some educators or agriculturalists" rather than the head of
the S.S. From this point on, he became a kind of Axis interpreter-
resident-in-Italy. (One of the more interesting highlights of Dollmann's
career was his embroilment in the internecine S.S. feud between Himmler
and his most dangerous rival, Reinhard Heydrich—the only man, says
Dollmann, who ever frightened him.) In September, 1938, Dollmann interpreted at the Munich conference between Hitler and Mussolini, and
again when they met in the Ukraine August 20–30, 1941. Throughout
1939, he served as interpreter and travelling companion for Italian
Foreign Minister Galeazzo Ciano, Mussolini's son-in-law. At the conclusion of the war, Dollmann was captured and interrogated by the
Allies. In an ironic vein, the Austrian declares that a British officer had
demanded to know why he had not prevented Italy from entering the
war.

This might be an appropriate point at which to raise the question of
ethical standards for language professionals. Do interpreters (or translators) bear any responsibility for the use which may ultimately be made
of their labors? Do they have a moral obligation to reject assignments
proffered by those to whose cause they cannot conscientiously subscribe?
There are some who would answer "yes" to both questions—some, indeed, who argue that all linguists should remain free-lancers, in a
position to accept or reject assignments at will, thus retaining their in-
dependence and moral integrity.[123] Others disagree: for example, "I ...
refuse to take the blame for environmental pollution just because I
sometimes translate Operating Instructions for heavy machinery....
Hitler would have been just as bad without an interpreter."[124]

Together with the examples cited in Chapter IV, of the ignoble role
played by two missionary-interpreters in the drafting of the treaties of
Macao and Tientsin, another comparatively recent example of an interpreter who ignored the whispers of conscience to serve an evil cause was
Sir John Bowring, author of two of Protestantism's most popular hymns,
"In the Crown of Christ I Glory," and "Watchman, Tell Us of the
Night." Bowring had been both an apologist for the British opium
traffic in the Far East during the 1830's, in contravention of Chinese law,
and the interpreter servicing the negotiations that followed Chinese
capture of the opium cargo ship, the *Arrow*.[125] Then, there was a
Prussian missionary and interpreter for the East India Company, Karl A.
Gutzlaff, who likewise had seen nothing wrong with the opium trade.
Perhaps significantly, it had been from Gutzlaff's translation of the *Bible*
that the leader of the Taiping Rebellion (1851–1864) had acquired his very
weird notions of Christianity. As Nigel Cameron succinctly puts it,

"When Gutzlaff died, all that remained of Christian endeavor [in China] was a very putrescent smell in the West's Christian nose."[126]

Not until after World War II was much attention paid to the question of ethical conduct for linguists, a development owing chiefly to the activities of some of the Axis interpreters during the war.

Dr. Paul Schmidt, often styled "Hitler's interpreter," is undoubtedly the best-known of these—though by no means the most heinous. However, Schmidt had been interpreting for some ten years, for six different chancellors, before Hitler arrived on the scene. His first opportunity for high-level work had come about in 1924, because the man who had been performing for Germany at the London Conference on Reparations had committed the interpreter's unpardonable sin—allowing himself to be carried away by patriotic passion, he had ruined the negotiations. Schmidt had replaced him, and from this point his star had steadily risen. The first time he interpreted for Hitler was on March 25, 1935, during the Chancellor's conversations with Sir John Simon and Anthony Eden over German rearmament.[127]

Nominally, Schmidt remained attached to the Language Services of the German Foreign Office (which he directed during World War II), with Joachim von Ribbentrop, therefore, his immediate superior. In that capacity, Schmidt interpreted for many other high-ranking Nazis besides Hitler, such as Göring. Among his more important assignments were Neville Chamberlain's meeting with Hitler, the French capitulation in June, 1940, the ultimatum to the Russians in 1941 and the deportation of Hungarian Jews in 1943.

To one reading Schmidt's book with a critical eye, it is clear that, for him, the villain of the opus is not Hitler, but Ribbentrop. Despite his protestations during a BBC interview on March 31, 1971, that he had disliked Hitler from the beginning and had agreed to work for him because the job would afford "an unparalleled involvement in high-level diplomacy,"[128] his autobiography does not quite bear this out. Although the book was written long after it had become safe to criticize Hitler, his general tone in writing of the Chancellor could best be described as one of admiration. He is at great pains, for example, to discredit the many legends about Hitler's temper tantrums, his lack of mental balance, even the bad quality of his grammar. "He expressed himself clearly and adroitly," says Schmidt, "was clearly very sure of his arguments, was easily understood, and not difficult to translate into English.... The only unusual thing about him was the length at which he spoke."[129] Schmidt may have asserted on the radio that he disliked Hitler, but no such statement appears in his book.

In April of 1945, Schmidt was arrested in Salzburg by the United States Army Counter-Intelligence Corps and for the next three years lived, alternately, in prison and under house arrest. At no time was he charged with having personally participated in any atrocities or with having encouraged anyone else to commit such deeds, but his intimate contacts with the leading Nazis and his valuable services on their behalf made him suspect to the Allied Powers—if only by contrast with other figures, such as Hans Jacob. On the other hand, the provable fact that, until 1943, he had resisted strong pressure to join the Nazi Party,[130] might bespeak something less than overwhelming enthusiasm for the cause, if not for Hitler himself. This, apparently, was the conclusion reached by those who held his fate in their hands at Nuremburg, where he testified as a witness both for the defense and for the prosecution. The U.S. Army, in fact, put his skills to use in the interrogation of the major war criminals. He himself was absolved of any wrongdoing.

Dr. Schmidt's moral responsibility is perhaps best left to the philosophers. Quite another case, however, is that of the Dutch millionaire, Pieter Menten,[131] who served the Nazis as a translator during the war, and who, in December, 1977, was found guilty of having assisted in a mass execution of Polish Jews and sentenced to 15 years in prison. The noted art collector, whose wealth was estimated at $100 million, was convicted of having participated in the massacre of 20 to 30 persons at the village of Podhoroce on July 7, 1941. (For want of sufficient evidence, Menten had been acquitted of a similar role in the slaying of more than 175 other persons at a different town.)

On the other side of the world, a number of Japanese interpreters were found guilty of appalling crimes during the war. One, a civilian, had been sentenced to hang for having actively taken part in the rape, torture and murder of unarmed civilians in the Philippines in 1945.[132] Another had abused the Dutch inmates of a prisoner-of-war camp on Java. And there were at least two "hell ship" incidents involving interpreters. In the curious case of the *Oryoku Maru,* en route from the Philippines to Japan in 1944, the interpreter, Shusuke Wada, received the death sentence for mistreatment of prisoners on board, although the captain of the ship was acquitted on the ground that he had been unable to prevent the atrocities.[133]

The worst story of all is undoubtedly that of Nimori,[134] sadistic master of a Japanese ship carrying British prisoners-of-war. Nimori was chief interpreter at the Japanese prison camp in Hong Kong. On September 25, 1945, the *Lisbon Maru* set out from that port bound for Japan, with 1,816 English and Scottish prisoners packed into three holds, plus 2,000 Japanese soldiers returning home. Nimori was assigned to sail with them as executive in charge. Apparently, he had not treated them with undue brutality until after a torpedo struck their ship. No prisoners were injured in that attack but, perhaps out of rage at the torpedoing,

Nimori set out to make their lives intolerable from then on. The first thing he did was to confine all 1,816 men to the holds with no water and no sanitary facilities, despite the fact that many were already ill. When they requested water, he sent down buckets of urine.

Out of desperation, a few men tried to dig their way out of the hold, but the Japanese fired on them, inflicting some casualties. Eventually, when the ship began to sink because of the torpedo damage, many prisoners escaped, to be picked up by Chinese fishermen who treated them kindly but who were then forced to surrender them to the Japanese who had come looking for them. Of the original number, only six men had managed to make good their escape; 846 had died in one way or another, while 970 had been recaptured. Most of the latter, so weak they could hardly stand, had been either personally beaten by Nimori, or ordered by him to be beaten.

In October, 1946, Nimori went on trial in British Military Court in Hong Kong on eight charges of war crimes and had been found guilty of all. Strangely, he did not receive the death sentence, but was remanded to prison for 15 years.

It may be argued that such peoples' language skills have nothing to do with the case—that a sadist is a sadist whatever his occupation. True enough, but the point is precisely that any profession may be misused for vile purposes. A physician may poison a patient, a lawyer may embezzle from a client, a teacher may exploit a child sexually—all of which point to the necessity for universally-accepted codes of ethics in all occupations. As we have seen, it is quite possible for a linguist, particularly in wartime, to grossly abuse his powers, or, at the least, to abet an unworthy cause.

Concern over this matter was what led the Congress of the International Federation of Translators (FIT) to adopt in 1966 a Code of Honor stating, among other things, that a translator/interpreter ought to refuse any task which he or she thinks has illegal or indefensible aims, or which is contrary to the public interest.[135] In other words, the politically responsible linguist will seek out and accept only those assignments whose aims are "socially acceptable." Clearly, this is no panacea. For one thing, it assumes an ability on the part of the linguist to distinguish between good and evil, a sensitivity notoriously lacking among those subjected to totalitarian brainwashing. But it *is* a step in the right direction, because it places solidly on the record as in favor of its members' political and social responsibility, the world's highest-level organization for language professionals.

Professional Associations

There is an international organization for interpreters, the previously mentioned Association des Interprètes de Conférence, based in Paris, which has drafted a Code of Professional Conduct, determines what should be minimum fees and working conditions, and publishes a yearbook listing persons who meet its high standards of proficiency. Its members are rated as A, B or C according to how many "active" and "passive" languages they possess. An "active" language is one *into* which a member can interpret (considered, as we have said, the harder task), while a "passive" language is one *from* which he or she is able to interpret. An "A" is one's principal active language, a "B" is a secondary active language, while a "C" is a passive language.[136] As of 1962, few interpreters possessed more than one "A" rating, while about 20 per cent had two "A's" and only three out of the then total membership of 444 had three "A's." In 1976, total membership in the organization was over 1,300, located in 53 countries.[137]

At the moment, fewer than a thousand men and women, worldwide, are considered the élite, being masters of three languages and having at least 200 days of conference experience. But the high standards of the professional associations should not unduly discourage young aspiring linguists, for a large number of successful practicing interpreters do not belong to any such organization.

For translators, there is the International Federation of Translators, whose members are not individuals, but the national associations throughout the world. This organization will, upon request, furnish to conference organizers lists of qualified personnel. The American Translators Association (ATA), organized in New York City in 1959 with only 30 members, now numbers over 1,200 individuals and 40 institutions or corporations. It maintains a registry of American translators, nonrestrictive and nonselective, of over 2,000 names, as well as a Professional Services Directory, which is limited to members of ATA. The organization also sponsors tests for the accreditation of translators, consisting of five passages of about 200 words each, of which three must be translated "well." Dictionaries are permitted and the pass rate is about 60 per cent.[138]

We can think of nothing more appropriate with which to conclude our account of the ups and downs of a linguist's career than this true story from the old Austro–Hungarian Empire.[139]

The annexation of Bosnia-Herzogovina by Austria-Hungary in 1908 had given rise to political unrest throughout the Balkan region, an insurgence that was to culminate in the assassination of Archduke

Francis Ferdinand at Sarajevo. With armed bands of guerrillas roving the mountains of Bosnia, one Feld-Marschall-Leutnant Ottokar Putz von Eichensieg decided that the first order of business should be to approach and coerce the most powerful of the dissident chieftains, Mehmed Hussein Ali. But when the German–Serbian interpreter who had been hired to service the meeting became ill, a substitute had been hastily rounded up — a Croat named Zdenko Sabotic.

During the conference, the fierce Mehmed Hussein Ali proved amazingly conciliatory, in view of the fact that Field Marshal Eichensieg's first words to him were an ultimatum for the immediate disbanding of his forces. In fact, the conversation had become more amicable by the moment, and was concluded with a signed peace agreement! Word of the Marshal's sensational triumph was wired to Vienna at once.

The next morning, a pale, trembling Zdenko Sabotic came to the Marshal and confessed that what he had interpreted the day before had been "statements by fine Vrsac wine, the very spirit of 'peace to all'." An outraged Marshal ordered Sabotic jailed, to be shot the following day, and then sat down to ponder what his own future might hold. While he was thus engaged, a telegram arrived from his Imperial Majesty, informing the Marshal that he would shortly be the happy recipient of a Decoration. Scarcely had he digested this news than an emissary arrived with gifts from Mehmed Hussein Ali.

A speedily liberated interpreter was commended to Emperor Franz Joseph for receipt of a minor order and a pension.

Chapter Notes

Chapter I

1. Benjamin Lee Whorf, "Language, Thought and Reality," quoted in Theodore Thass-Thienemann, *The Interpretation of Language* (New York: Jason Aronson, 1973), p. 77.

2. Robert B. Ekvall, *Faithful Echo* (New York: Twayne Publishers, 1960), pp. 80–81.

3. Claude Piron and Humphrey Tonkin, *Translation in International Organizations* (Rotterdam: Universal Esperanto Assoc., 1979 [Esperanto Documents, n.s., 20A]), p. 17.

4. Mario Pei, *The Story of Language* (Philadelphia: J.B. Lippincott, 1965), p. 405.

5. Vincent Sheean, "An Error in Translation," *United Nations World,* Sept. 1947, pp. 28–29. However, in a subsequent issue of this magazine, a reader wrote in to take exception to Sheean's understanding of German, saying *Menschlichkeit* may quite appropriately be used to designate "humanity."

6. For the account of this semantic disagreement as related here, see *The Atlanta Constitution,* Jan. 9, 1981.

7. Dexter Perkins, *A History of the Monroe Doctrine* (Boston: Little, Brown, 1963), p. 297.

8. Charles Roetter, *The Diplomatic Art; An Informal History of World Diplomacy* (Philadelphia: Macrae Smith Co., 1963), pp. 216–217.

9. For this exposition, I am indebted to Piron and Tonkin, *op. cit.,* p. 5.

10. Jean Herbert, *The Interpreters Handbook* (Geneva: Université de Genève, École d' Interprètes, 1952), p. 6.

11. An exception: in 1961, the Federal Republic of West Germany introduced identical pay scales for translators and interpreters in the federal service. See *Babel* VIII (Nov. 1, 1962).

12. Quoted from Charles W. Frerk, F.I.L., "The Organization of Translation Services for International Congresses," *Babel* VI, 2 (June 1960), p. 1.

13. Bertrand Russell, "Logical Postivism," *Revue Internationale de Philosophie* IV (1950), p. 18.

14. This story is recounted in A.H. Birse, *Memoirs of an Interpreter* (London: Michael Joseph, 1967), p. 111.

15. *The Diplomat* 17 (July 15, 1951), p. 5.

16. C. Rajagopalachari, in Theodore Savory, *The Art of Translation* (Boston: The Writer, 1968), p. 6.

17. Jacques Barzun, "In Favor of Particular Clichés," *Translation* 73 I, 1 (1973), p. 51.

18. Richard Wolkomir, "A Manic Professor Tries to Close the Language Gap," *Smithsonian,* May 1980.

19. Carl Rowan, "Why U.S. Keeps Falling Behind in World Community," *Atlanta Constitution,* Jan. 14, 1981, citing Paul Simon, *The Tongue-Tied American: Confronting the Foreign Language Crisis.*

20. Sweden: Hakon Auerbach, "Professional Translators in Sweden," *Babel* XI, 4 (1965), pp. 175–176; Finland: *Babel* XV, 2 (1969), pp. 124–125.

21. Barzun, *op. cit.,* p. 49.

22. See, for example, Helen Wolff, "Translator and Publisher," *Translation 73* I, 1 (1973).

23. Alexander Ostrower, *Language, Law and Diplomacy; A Study of Linguistic Diversity in International Relations and International Law,* Vol. I (Philadelphia: University of Pennsylvania Press, 1965), p. 531.

24. It was William Nash Locke and A. Donald Booth, *Machine Translation of Languages* (Cambridge, Mass.: M.I.T. Press, 1955).

25. SERNA: Peter Toma, "An Operational Machine Translation System," in Richard W. Brislin, *Translation: Applications and Research* (New York: Gardner Press, 1976), p. 248; *Pravda*: Ostrower, *op. cit.,* p. 532.

26. Ostrower, *ibid.*

27. For these two examples of successful idiom translation, I thank Nino lo Bello, "Many Languages Spoken Here — at the Same Time," *Parade [Washington Post],* August 21, 1977, p. 14.

28. Alexander Lane, "Quelques Aspects de la terminologie juridique et administrative," *Babel* XV, 1 (1969), pp. 35–36.

29. *Language and Machines: Computers in Translation and Linguistics,* a Report by the Automatic Language Processing Advisory Committee, National Academy of Sciences, Div. of Behavioral Sciences, National Research Council, 1966, p. 78.

30. Victor Yngve, "Implications of Mechanical Translation Research," *Proceedings of the American Philosophical Society* 108 (1964), p. 275.

31. See Patricia E. Longley, *Conference Interpreting* (London: Pitman & Sons, 1968), pp. 57–59.

32. Lord Strang, *The Foreign Office* (London: George Allen & Unwin, 1957 [New Whitehall Series]), p. 193.

33. Robert Confino, Foreword to Longley, *op. cit.* For qualifications see June L. Sherif, *Careers in Foreign Languages: A Handbook* (New York: Regents Pub. Co., 1975), p. 116.

34. Jean Herbert, "How Conference Interpretation Grew," in *Proceedings of the Symposium on Language Interpretation and Communication,* San Giorgio Maggiore, Venice, Sept. 26–Oct. 1, 1977, ed. David Gerver and H. Wallace Sinaiko (New York: Plenum, 1978), p. 7.

35. A.H. Birse, *Memoirs of an Interpreter* (London: Michael Joseph, 1967), p. 104.

36. Longley, *op. cit.,* p. 4.

37. For an excellent treatment of interpreters' notation systems, see John A. Henderson, "Note-taking for Consecutive Interpreting," *Babel* XXII, 2 (1976), *passim.*

38. Francis Graham Wilson, *Labor in the League System; A Study of the International Organization in Relation to International Administration* (Stanford, Calif.: Stanford University Press, 1934), p. 123.

39. All of the rules quoted are taken from the Standing Orders of the International Labor Organization, as found in Vladimir D. Pastuhov, *A Guide to the Practice of International Conferences* (Washington, D.C.: Carnegie Endowment for International Peace, 1945), p. 131, n32.

40. U.S. Government. Department of State. *Agreement for the Establishment of an International Military Tribunal [and] Charter of the International Military Tribunal* (Washington, D.C.: U.S. Gov. Printing Office, 1945 [Department of State Publication 2420]).

41. *Rules of Procedure of the International Military Tribunal,* adopted at Nuremburg, Oct. 29, 1945. See Rules 2 and 9.

42. Whitney R. Harris, *Tyranny on Trial: The Evidence at Nuremberg* (Dallas: Southern Methodist University Press, 1954), Foreword.

43. Solis Horwitz, "The Tokyo Trial," *International Conciliation,* No. 465 (New York: Carnegie Endowment for International Peace, Nov. 1950), p. 538, *n29.*

44. *Charter of the International Military Tribunal for the Far East,* Art. 9 (b), in *Trial of Japanese War Criminals,* Washington, D.C.: U.S. Gov. Printing Office, 1946 [Department of State Publication No. 3613]).

45. Horwitz, *loc. cit.*

46. John Pritchard, "The Nature and Significance of British Post-War Trials of Japanese War Criminals 1945-1948," in *Proceedings of the British Association for Japanese Studies,* Vol. I, Part I: History and International Relations (Sheffield, England: University Centre of Japanese Studies, 1976), pp. 133-134.

47. See Simone Signoret, *Nostalgia Isn't What It Used to Be* (New York: Harper & Row, 1978), p. 81.

48. D. Gerver, "The Effects of Source Language Presentation Rate on the Performance of Simultaneous Conference Reporters," in E. Foulke (ed.), *Proceedings of the 2nd Louisville Conference on Rate And/Or Frequency Controlled Speech* (Louisville, Ky.: University of Louisville Press, 1969), pp. 162-184.

49. Ekvall, *op. cit.,* pp. 64-65.

50. George J. Mathieu, "Words Before Peace," *United Nations World,* January 1949, p. 59. But suppose the principal had never happened to address a question of that nature before?

51. See, for instance, David L. Gold, "On Quality in Interpreting," *Babel* XIX, 3 (1973), pp. 154-155.

52. Eleanor Roosevelt and William De Witt, *The UN: Today and Tomorrow* (New York: Harper & Bros., 1953), pp. 45-46.

53. Leo Rosten, "Diversions," *Saturday Review World,* April 6, 1974, p. 37.

54. Brislin, *op. cit.,* pp. 33-34.

55. Edmund B. D'Auvergne, *Envoys Extraordinary* (London: Geo. B. Harrap & Co., 1937), pp. 238-239.

56. Egon F. Ranshofen-Wertheimer, *The International Secretariat* (Washington, D.C.: Carnegie Endowment for International Peace, 1925), p. 141.

57. Brislin, *op. cit.,* pp. 28-29. He calls them "attraction," "reward," "coercive," and "legitimate" powers.

58. Joseph F. Fletcher, "China and Central Asia, 1368-1884," in John K. Fairbank (ed.), *The Chinese World Order: Traditional China's Foreign Relations* (Cambridge, Mass.: Harvard University Press, 1968), p. 209.

59. Charles Wheeler Thayer, *Diplomat* (New York: Harper & Row, 1959), p. 90ff.

60. Walter Bedell Smith, *My Three Years in Moscow* (Philadelphia: J.B. Lippincott, 1950), p. 73.

61. Ranshofen-Wertheimer, *op. cit.,* p. 140.

62. Humphrey Trevelyan, *Diplomatic Channels* (London: Macmillan, 1973), p. 81.

63. Longley, *op. cit.,* p. 4.

64. Dr. Paul Schmidt, *Hitler's Interpreter,* ed. R.H. Steed (New York: Macmillan, 1951), pp. 103, 110.

65. For this amusing tale, I am most grateful to Dr. Andor C. Klay, "Interpretive Diplomacy," *U.S. Foreign Service Journal* 36, 11 (November 1959). His story reminds me of the one about a British ambassador, Lord Ponsonby, back in the days when few Turks knew English, whose custom it was to count to fifty, gesticulating and varying his tone, thus persuading his Turkish hearers that he was making a speech. See D.C.M. Platt, *The Cinderella Service: British Consuls Since 1825* (London: Longman, 1971), p. 173.

66. Roetter, *op. cit.,* p. 215.

67. Lo Bello, *op. cit.,* p. 14.

68. Matthew Smith Anderson, *Britain's Discovery of Russia* (New York: St. Martin's Press, 1958), p. 15.

69. William Manchester, *American Caesar: Douglas MacArthur 1880-1864* (New York: Dell Pub. Co., 1978), p. 517.

70. Brislin, *op. cit.,* p. 28.

71. John K. Emmerson, *The Japanese Thread: A Life in the U.S. Foreign Service* (New York: Holt, Rinehart & Winston, 1978), p. 32.

72. See, for example, *Atlanta Constitution,* Dec. 31, 1977.
73. Again, see, for example, *Atlanta Constitution,* Jan. 1, and Jan. 10, 1978.

Chapter II

1. Ragnar Numelin, *The Beginnings of Diplomacy: A Sociological Study of Intertribal and International Relations* (New York: Philosophical Library, 1950), pp. 166–167.

2. Rev. James Baikie, F.R.A.S., *The Amarna Age: A Study of the Crisis of the Ancient World* (London, A. & C. Black, 1926), pp. 201–202.

3. Patricia Longley, *Conference Interpreting* (London: Pitman & Son, 1968), p. 2.

4. Henry Snyder Gehman, *The Interpreters of Foreign Languages Among the Ancients,* Ph.D. dissertation (University of Pennsylvania, 1914), p. 17.

5. Strabo, *The Geography of Strabo,* trans. H.C. Hamilton (London: Geo. Bell & Son, 1892), p. 149. One Eudoxes accompanied the Indian, bringing with him on his return to Egypt a number of marvelous items, including "stones which they dig out of the earth, where they have been formed by the moisture, as crystals are with us." Diamonds?

6. A.H.L. Heeren, *Historical Researches into the Politics, Intercourse, and Trade of the Carthaginians, Ethiopians and Egyptians,* Vol. II (Oxford, England: D.A. Talboys, Vol. II, 1832; reprinted by Negro Universities Press, New York, 1959), pp. 121–123, p. 143.

7. Gehman, *op. cit.,* pp. 17–18.

8. *Ibid.*

9. Through his *Constitutio Antoniana de Civitate.* One of the few commentaries on this document is Alvaro D'ors Perez-Peix, "Estudios Sobre la Constitutio Antoniniana," *Emerita* (Madrid) XI (1943), pp. 297–337.

10. Gehman, *op. cit.,* p. 53.

11. Harold Nicolson, *The Evolution of Diplomatic Method* (London: Constable, 1954), p. 4.

12. Coleman Philipson, *The International Law and Customs of Ancient Greece and Rome,* Vol. I (London: Macmillan, 1931), p. 329.

13. Numelin, *op. cit.,* p. 62. It is not unknown for modern linguists to fall afoul of national or world politics. Sydney Rittenberg, of a distinguished South Carolina family, who had learned Chinese as one of the first volunteers in the U.S. Army's World War II language program, volunteered for relief duty in China after the war as a Chinese-language interpreter, remained there and became an enthusiast of the Revolution, for a time helping to run Radio Peking. But he fell from grace when suspected of having participated in a conspiracy against Chou En-lai, and was imprisoned for ten years. Briefly released at one time, he was reincarcerated because Mao's wife, the notorious Jing Quing, took a dislike to him. On November 18, 1977, the Chinese suddenly freed him with profound apologies. See Dusko Doder, "Chinese Jail Term Ends for American," *Washington Post,* Dec. 17, 1977.

14. The Semitic tongue spoken in Mesopotamia from the 3rd to the 1st millennium B.C. Spreading from the Mediterranean to the Persian Gulf during the time of Sargon (c.2,344–2,379 B.C.), it had, by 2,000 B.C., supplanted Sumerian as the spoken language of southern Mesopotamia. Actually, Phoenician and its cousin, Hebrew, were the dominant commercial languages of the Near East, but they never "caught on" as diplomatic idioms, nor did the Egyptian language, even though the papyrus used for the inscription of hieroglyphics was more conveniently inscribed, transported and stored than were the clay tablets on which the Sumerians scratched their cuneiform. See Gerrit P. Judd, *A History of Civilization* (New York: Macmillan, 1966), p. 23. For an intriguing suggestion as to why Egyptian never became an international tongue, see George Steiner, *After Babel: Aspects of Language and Translation* (London: Oxford University Press, 1975), pp. 23–24. It is Steiner's contention that languages which become "universal" are those most susceptible to metaphor, which Egyptian (unlike Greek, for instance) was not. Steiner cites the literary treatment of physical blindness as an example. In many cultures,

this disability represents "a supreme infirmity and abdication from life," but in Greek mythology the poet and the seer are blind in order that they may actually see further.

15. Mesilim, the non-Sumerian: Alexander Ostrower, *Language, Law and Diplomacy: A Study of Linguistic Diversity in Official International Relations and International Law,* Vol. I (Philadelphia: University of Pennsylvania Press, 1965), p. 166; Tell-el-Amarna tablet: A.T. Olmstead, *History of the Persian Empire, Achaeminid Period* (Chicago: University of Chicago Press, 1948), p. 34 — Tell el-Amarna is the name given to the ruins and tombs of the city of Akhetaton in Upper Egypt, built around 1,375 B.C. by Akhenaton (Amenhotep IV); the tablets themselves are 300 cuneiform blocks discovered in 1887; Rameses II temple: Dennis J. McCarthy, S.J., *Treaty and Covenant, Analecta Biblica 21* (Rome: Pontifical Bible Institute, 1963), pp. 23–24; Egyptian–Hittite variances: Baikie, *op. cit.,* p. 188.

16. Derived from Semitic, Aramaic gradually supplanted Akkadian as the *lingua franca* of the Near East and became the official language of the Persian Empire. Replacing Hebrew as the language of the Jews, it was spoken by Christ and his disciples, but was supplanted by Arabic by A.D. 100. As a detail of interest, the language lives on today as the *alphabetical* basis for — of all things! — the Mongol and Manchu tongues. This is the explanation: Manchu is derived from Mongolian, and both peoples got their alphabet from the Uigurs, a Turkic people who arrived on the scene sometime after the 13th century. *They* had obtained their alphabet from the Sogdians, an Iranian tribe, and the Sogdian alphabet is an adaptation of the Aramaic. See *Encyclopaedia Britannica,* Vol. 15 (1973), p. 734.

17. James Breasted, *A History of Egypt* (New York: C. Scribner's Sons, 1954), p. 188.

18. Olmstead, *op cit.,* pp. 354, 177.

19. Nicolson, *op. cit.,* p. 4.

20. D.J. Mosley, *Envoys and Diplomacy in Ancient Greece* (Wiesbaden: Franz Steiner Verlag, 1973), p. 43.

21. Demosthenes, *De Corona and De Falso Legatione,* trans. C.A. Vance (London: William Heinemann, n.d. [Loeb Classical Library]), pp. 363–364. Cicero, the greatest of Roman orators, said virtually the same thing: "I lay it down as a maxim that upon the prudence and abilities of an accomplished orator not only his own dignity, but the welfare of vast numbers of individuals, nay of the whole government, rests." See *Three Dialogues of Marcus Tullius Cicero on the Orator,* trans. W. Guthrie (New York, 1947).

22. Charles Roetter, *The Diplomatic Art: An Informal History of World Diplomacy* (Philadelphia: Macrae Smith, 1963), p. 23; Mosley, *op. cit.,* p. 69.

23. Quintus Curtius Rufus, *The History of the Life and Reign of Alexander the Great,* Vol. I (London: James Moyes, 1809), pp. 328–329. Darius came to a suitably bad end: after fleeing the scene of combat again at the Battle of Gaugamela in 331, he was killed by a Bactrian (Afghan) chieftain.

24. Quintus Curcius (Quintus Curtius Rufus), *The Actes of the Greate Alexander* (London, 1553; reprinted by Da Capo Press, New York, 1971), fol. 105–106.

25. Strabo, *op. cit.,* pp. 113–114. Others of more recent times have held a similar opinion of translators and interpreters, as witness the frequently cited Italian expression, "Tradutore, traditore!" ("Translators, traitors"). In the same vein is Woodrow Wilson's statement that a translation is a "compound fracture of an idea." Actually, the priest was only making a point now universally accepted by professional linguists — that when working with a technical or specialized subject, one must know the subject as well as the languages.

26. Arrian, *The Campaigns of Alexander,* trans. Aubrey D. Selincourt (Harmondsworth, England: Penguin Books, 1971), p. 349.

27. King Tiridates: Gehman, *op. cit.,* p. 48; Sulla–Bocchus: Sallustius Crispus C., *The Conspiracy of Catiline and the War of Jugurtha,* trans. Thomas Heywood, 1608 (New York: AMS Press, 1967), p. 241; Menander: Gehman, *op. cit.,* p. 47.

28. Josephus Flavius, *The Jewish War,* trans. G.A. Williamson (Harmondsworth, England: Penguin Classics, 1959), *passim* but particularly pp. 284–289.

29. Martin P. Nilsson, *Imperial Rome,* trans. Rev. G.C. Richards (New York: Harcourt, Brace, n.d.), pp. 174–175.
30. T. Rice Holmes, *The Roman Republic and the Founder of the Empire,* Vol. I (Oxford, England: Clarendon Press, 1923), p. 83.
31. Slang and Publius Crassus: A.F. Whitley, *The Tremulous Hero: The Age and Life of Cicero* (London: Pallas Pub. Co., 1939), p. 82; Pilate: Ostrower, *op. cit.,* p. 207.
32. Holmes, *The Roman Republic, op. cit.,* p. 84. As Bismarck once commented that no Englishman who was fluent in French could be trusted.
33. See Salvatore Rossi, "Quando Cattone il Censore Apprese la Lingua Greca," *Atti della R. Accademia Peloritana,* Anno XVI (Messina: Tipografia d'Amico, 1902–1903), pp. 1–8, *passim.*
34. Gehman, *op. cit.,* p. 47.
35. C. Suetonius Tranquillus, *The Lives of the Twelve Caesars,* trans. Alexander Thomson (London: Geo. Bell & Sons, 1909), pp. 235–236.
36. Naphtali Lewis and Meyer Reinhold, *Roman Civilization; Selected Readings,* Vol. I, *The Republic* (New York: Columbia University Press, 1951), p. 492.
37. Toynbee, *op. cit.,* p. 554.
38. Gehman, *op. cit.,* pp. 25–26.
39. Will Durant, *The Story of Civilization: Caesar and Christ* (New York: Simon & Schuster, 1944), p. 45. In case one is tempted to feel pity for them, author Durant tells us that they, themselves, had cut off the hands and feet of 700 prisoners, including those of Gesco, and had then thrown all the prisoners into a mass grave.
40. B.H. Warmington, *Carthage* (London: Robert Hale, 1960), p. 98. See also Gehman, *op. cit.,* pp. 30–31.
41. Arnold Toynbee, *Constantine Porphyrogenitus and His World* (London: Oxford University Press, 1973), p. 556. Yet the author tells us that the Byzantine fire brigade was summoned in Latin — *"Omnes collegiati adeste"* — or, "All colleagues hasten hither," which, in the interests of speed, might perhaps be better recorded as "Come!" (*ibid.,* p. 560).
42. Ramsay MacMullen, *Constantine* (New York: Dial Press, 1969), pp. 164, 172.
43. Romilly Jenkins, "Byzantium and Byzantinism," lecture at the University of Cincinnati, 1963, p. 7.
44. See N. Iorga, *The Byzantine Empire,* trans. Allen H. Powles (London: Colston & Co., 1927), p. 33; Toynbee, *op. cit.,* p. 559.
45. Toynbee, *op. cit.,* pp. 559 and 558.
46. Iorga, *loc. cit.,* p. 33.
47. Roman army: Peter Brown, *The World of Late Antiquity: From Marcus Aurelius to Mohammed* (London: Thames & Hudson, 1971), p. 138; Greek commands and legislative purposes: Bertha Diener, *Imperial Byzantium,* trans. Eden & Cedar Paul (Boston: Little, Brown, 1938), p. 109.
48. Pope Gregory: Toynbee, *op. cit.,* p. 560; few Latin words: Iorga, *loc. cit.*
49. Toynbee, *op. cit.,* p. 552.
50. Dimitri Obolenski, *The Byzantine Commonwealth: Eastern Europe 500–1453* (New York: Praeger Publishers, 1971), p. 152.
51. The Pisan: Charles M. Brand, *Byzantium Confronts the West, 1180–1204* (Cambridge, Mass.: Harvard University Press, 1968), pp. 66–67; the Hetairea: Miller, *op. cit.,* p. 149.
52. George Ostrogorsky, *History of the Byzantine State,* trans. Joan Hussey (New Brunswick, N.J.: Rutgers University Press, 1969), pp. 414–415.
53. Brand, *op. cit.,* p. 223.
54. Diener, *op. cit.,* p. 43, 108.
55. Miller, *op. cit.,* p. 91.
56. Brand, *op. cit.,* p. 180.
57. *Ibid.,* p. 235. The Crusaders responded that Alexius had usurped the throne of his nephew, young Alexius, who was among them, and they assaulted the city on July 17, 1203. Alexis fled and his brother Isaac was placed on the throne. See Villehardouin and de

Joinville, *Memoires of the Crusades,* trans. Sir Frank T. Marzials (New York: E.P. Dutton, 1958), pp. 34–35.

48. Obolenski, *op. cit.,* p. 326.

59. Francis Dvornik, *Byzantine Missions among the Slavs: Ss. Constantine-Cyril and Methodius* (New Brunswick, N.J.: Rutgers University Press, 1970), pp. 146–148.

60. Ashit Chakraborty, "Translation in Medieval Bulgaria, Theory and Practice of Translation Throughout the Ages," *Subarnarekha 73* (New Delhi) 2, 4 (1972), p. 76.

61. Obolenski, *op. cit.,* p. 198.

62. *The Russian Primary Chronicle,* Laurentian text, trans. & ed. Samuel Hazzard Cross and Olgerd P. Sherbowitz-Wetzor (Cambridge, Mass.: Crimson Pub. Co., 1953 [Medieval Academy of America, no. 60]), p. 137.

63. Kitab Futûh Al-Buldân, *The Origins of the Islamic State,* Part I, trans. Philip K. Hitti (New York: Columbia University and AMS Press, n.d. [Studies in History, Economics and Public Law, vol. 68, no. 163]), p. 301. The translator, Hitti, ridicules the inkwell story. See his own book, *History of the Arabs from the Earliest Times to the Present* (New York: St. Martin's Press, 1967), p. 217.

64. For information on the Ottoman civil service, see Speros Vryonis, Jr., "The Byzantine Legacy and Ottoman Forms," *Dumbarton Oaks Paper No. 23–24* (Washington, D.C.: Center for Byzantine Studies, 1969–1970), pp. 275–276.

65. Katavolenos: Apostolos E. Vacalopoulos, *The Greek Nation, 1453–1669* (New Brunswick, N.J.: Rutgers University Press, 1976), p. 4; Nicousios: Deno John Geanokoplos, *Interaction of the 'Sibling' Byzantine and Western Cultures in the Middle Ages and Italian Renaissance (300–1600)* (New Haven, Conn.: Yale University Press, 1976), p. 51.

66. Edwin Pears, *The Destruction of the Greek Empire and the Story of the Capture of Constantinople by the Turks* (London: Longmans, Green, 1903), p. 410.

67. *Ibid.,* p. 412.

68. Geanokoplos, *Sibling, op. cit.,* p. 194.

69. Deno John Geanokoplos, *Byzantine East and Latin West: Two Worlds of Christendom in the Middle Ages and Renaissance* (Hamden, Conn.: Archon Books, 1976), p. 123.

70. Geanokoplos, *Sibling, op. cit.,* p. 187.

71. Lord Eversley and Sir Valentine Chirol, *The Turkish Empire from 1288 to 1914* (New York: Howard Fertig, 1969), p. 230.

72. See, for instance, Vacalopoulos, *op. cit.,* p. 213.

73. Pepin delegation: Norman Daniel, *The Arabs and Medieval Europe* (London: Longman, Librairie du Liban, 1975), p. 50; St. Willibald: *ibid.,* p. 49.

74. Bertram Thomas, *The Arabs* (London: Thornton Butterworth, 1966), p. 224.

75. Bernard Lewis, *The Arabs in History* (London: Hutchinson, 1966), p. 89.

76. Philip K. Hitti, *The Arab Heritage,* ed. Nabim Amin Faris (New York: Russell & Russell, 1963), p. 68.

77. Fulcher of Chartres, *A History of the Expedition to Jerusalem, 1095–1127,* trans. Frances Rita Ryan (Knoxville: University of Tennessee Press, 1969), p. 4. Fulcher (c.1059–c.1127), chaplain to Stephen of Blois, accompanied his sovereign on the First Crusade and became its chief chronicler. In 1097, he became chaplain to Baldwin of Flanders and remained with him thereafter. Author of the three-part *Gesta Francorum Jherusalem Peregrinatium,* compiled between 1101 and 1127.

78. Zoë Oldenbourg, *The Crusades,* trans. Anne Carter (New York: Pantheon Books, 1966), p. 503.

79. Thomas, *op. cit.,* p. 225, *n1.*

80. See, for instance, Oldenbourg, *op. cit.,* pp. 484–486, and Daniel, *op. cit.,* p. 199.

81. Villehardouin, *op. cit.,* p. 217.

82. See Hitti, *Heritage, op. cit.,* p. 5.

83. Gustave E. von Grunebaum, *Medieval Islam; A Study in Cultural Orientation* (Chicago: University of Chicago Press, 1954), p. 38.

84. Grunebaum, *op. cit.,* p. 50, and Hitti, *Heritage, op. cit.,* p. 9.

85. See Aziz Atiya, *The Crusade in the Later Middle Ages,* 2d ed. (New York: Kraus Reprint Co., 1970), pp. 87–88; and Hitti, *History, op. cit.,* pp. 245–246.

86. Atiya, *op. cit.,* p. 75, *n3.*

87. Grunebaum, *op. cit.,* p. 51.

88. *Ibid.,* p. 52.

89. Francesco Gabrieli, *Muhammad and the Conquests of Islam,* trans. Virginia Luling and Rosamund Linell (New York: World University Library, 1968), p. 194.

90. Reinhard Dozy, *Spanish Islam; A History of the Moslems in Spain* (London: Frank Cass, 1972), p. 268.

91. Philip K. Hitti, *Makers of Arab History* (New York: St. Martin's Press, 1968), p. 198.

92. Denis Mack Smith, *A History of Sicily; Medieval Sicily 800–1713* (New York: Viking Press, 1968), p. 7.

93. John Julius Norwich, *The Other Conquest* (New York: Harper & Row, 1961), p. 191.

94. Smith, *op. cit.,* p. 25.

95. Aziz Ahmad, *A History of Islamic Sicily* (Edinburgh: University of Edinburgh Press, 1975 [Islamic Surveys No. 10]), p. 65.

96. Lewis, *op. cit.,* p. 120.

97. Ahmad, *op. cit.,* pp. 90–91.

98. C.H. Haskins, *Studies in the History of Medieval Science* (Cambridge, Mass.: Harvard University Press, 1927), p. 202.

Chapter III

1. See Harold Nicolson, *The Evolution of Diplomatic Method* (London: Constable & Co., 1954), pp. 32–34.

2. See Appendix in John B. Allen, *Post and Courier Service in the Diplomacy of Early Modern Europe* (The Hague: Martinus Nijhoff, 1972).

3. *Ibid.,* pp. 32–33.

4. V. Wheeler-Holohan, *The History of the King's Messengers* (New York: n.p., n.d.), pp. 26, 34–35, 52–92, *passim.*

5. William James Roosen, *The Age of Louis XIV, the Rise of Modern Diplomacy* (Cambridge, Mass.: Schenkman Pub. Co., 1976), p. 65. They were Prussia, Poland, England, Spain, Portugal, the Netherlands, and the Holy Roman Empire.

6. 13th century: G.P. Cuttino, *English Diplomatic Administration 1259–1339,* 2d ed. (Oxford, Eng.: Clarendon Press, 1971), pp. 133, 139; Henry VIII: Nicolson, *loc. cit.*

7. Roosen, *loc. cit.*

8. Garrett Mattingly, *Renaissance Diplomacy* (Boston: Houghton Mifflin, 1955), p. 236.

9. François de Callières, *On the Manner of Negotiating with Princes,* trans. A.F. Shyte (Boston: Houghton Mifflin, 1919). Originally published in Paris by Michel Brunet at the Mercure Galant, 1716.

10. Mattingly, *op. cit.,* p. 217.

11. *Ibid.,* p. 237.

12. Mattingly, *loc. cit.* Quoting Arnold Oskar Meyer, *Die Englische Diplomatie in Deutschland zur Zeit Edwards VI und Mariens* (Breslau: Kommissions Verlag von M. & H. Marcus, 1900), pp. 6–8.

13. Phyllis S. Lachs, *The Diplomatic Corps Under Charles II and James II* (New Brunswick, N.J.: Rutgers University Press, 1965), p. 55.

14. This curious word derives, originally, from the Arabic *tirgiman.* Corrupted versions of the Turkish became the standard term for "interpreter" in a score of European tongues, among them the Bulgarian *tlumach,* Polish *tłumacz,* Hungarian *tolmacs,* Rumanian *talmaci,* Serbo-Croatian *tumac,* Slovakian *tlmocnik,* Slovenian *tolmac,* Czech *tlumocnik,* even the German *dolmetscher.*

15. Lachs, *op. cit.*

16. George Frederick Abbott, *Under the Turk in Constantinople* (London: Macmillan & Co., 1920), p. 149.

17. D.C.M. Platt, *The Cinderella Service, British Consuls Since 1825* (London: Longmans, 1971), p. 164.

18. Gordon A. Craig and Felix Gilbert, *The Diplomats 1919–1939* (Princeton, N.J.: Princeton University Press, 1953), p. 127.

19. Sir Vincent Corbett, K.C.V.O., *Reminiscences: An Autobiographical and Diplomatic of Sir Vincent Corbett* (London: Hodder & Stoughton, 1927), pp. 196–197.

20. Abbott, *op. cit.*, p. 50.

21. Corbett, *op. cit.*, p. 194.

22. See Article XIV of the French Capitulation, in "Capitulations françaises dans le proche-orient, sources et documents," *Europe Nouvelle* VII, 338 (1927), pp. 1028–1033.

23. Hereditary immunity: Nasim Sousa, *The Capitulatory Regime of Turkey: Its History, Origins and Nature* (Baltimore: Johns Hopkins Press, 1933), pp. 100–101; three dragomen: Abbott, *op. cit.*, p. 267.

24. Abbott, *op cit.*, p. 51, p. 95; p. 116.

25. Dorothy M. Vaughan, *Europe and the Turk, a Pattern of Alliances, 1350–1700* (Liverpool: University Press, 1954), p. 122.

26. Corbett, *op. cit.*, p. 197.

27. This story is found in Abbott, *op. cit.*, pp. 197–199.

28. "Memorandum Read by the Turkish Delegate at the Lausanne Conference at the Meeting of Dec. 2, 1922, of the Commission on the Regime of Foreigners," in Appendix V, Sousa, *op. cit.*, pp. 332–343.

29. For all of my information on the Crutta family, I am indebted to what appears to be the sole source, Jan Reychman, "Une Famille de drogmans orientaux en Pologne au XVIII siècle," *Rocznik Orientalistyczny* (Warsaw) XXV, 1 (1961), *passim*.

30. The Russian envoy, Boulhakoff, related this bit of gossip in a dispatch to Catherine II on September 22, 1786. See *ibid.*, p. 89.

31. Hilde Spiel (ed.), *The Congress of Vienna: An Eyewitness Account,* trans. Richard H. Weber (Philadelphia: Chilton Book Co., 1968), Introd., p. xvii.

32. As he was styled by J.G. Lockhart, *The Peacemakers, 1814–1815* (London: Duckworth, 1932), p. 35.

33. Le Comte A. de la Garde-Chambonas, *Anecdotal Recollections of the Congress of Vienna* (London: Chapman & Hall, 1902), p. 159.

34. Paul R. Sweet, *Friedrich von Gentz* (Madison: University of Wisconsin Press, 1941), p. 141.

35. Eva Paneth, "Friedrich von Gentz — A Patron of Translators?" *Babel* III, 2 (June 1957), p. 88; Sweet, *op. cit.*, p. 316.

36. Sir Charles Webster, *The Congress of Vienna, 1814–1815* (New York: Barnes & Noble, 1963), pp. 99–100.

37. Alexander Ostrower, *Language, Law and Diplomacy; A Study of Linguistic Diversity in Official International Relations and International Law,* Vol. I (Philadelphia: University of Pennsylvania Press, 1965), p. 288, quoting J.G. Meiern, *Acta Pacis Westphaliae Publica,* IV (Hannover and Tübingen, 1736), p. 916.

38. Rt. Hon. Sir Ernest Satow, *A Guide to Diplomatic Practice,* 3d ed. (London: Longmans, Green & Co., 1932), p. 292.

39. Prince Eugene: Ferdinand Brunot, "Les Debats du français dans la diplomatie," *Revue de Paris,* Dec. 15, 1913, in Henriette Roumigière, *Le Français dans les relations diplomatiques,* Vol. V (Berkeley: University of California Press, 1926), p. 421; Quadruple Alliance: Guillaume de Lamberty, *Memoires pour servir à l'histoire du XVIIIme siècle,* Vol. X (La Haye: H. Scheurleer, 1724–1731), pp. 50–51.

40. Satow, *op. cit.*, p. 54.

41. *Ibid.*, p. 55.

42. Ostrower, *op. cit.*, p. 356.

43. Alexander Lane, "La Question des languages et la fonction publique internationale," *Babel* XI, 4 (1965), p. 159.

44. Dr. Hans Wehberg, *The Problem of an International Court of Justice,* trans. Charles G. Fenwick (Oxford, England: Clarendon Press, 1918), p. 231.

45. Gordon A. Craig, "Techniques of Negotiation," in Ivo J. Lederer (ed.), *Russian Foreign Policy: Essays in Historical Perspective* (New Haven, Conn.: Yale University Press, 1962), p. 353.

46. D.B. Horn, *The British Diplomatic Service 1689-1789* (Oxford, England: Clarendon Press, 1961), p. 137.

47. Vladimir D. Pastuhov, *A Guide to the Practice of International Conferences* (Washington, D.C.: Carnegie Endowment for International Peace, 1945), p. 123, *n21.*

48. Edward Gaylord Bourne, *Spain in America 1450-1580* (New York: Barnes & Noble, 1962), p. 24, and Sir Arthur Helps, *The Spanish Conquest in America,* Vol. I (New York: AMS Press, 1966), p. 82.

49. F.A. Kirkpatrick, *The Spanish Conquistadores* (Cleveland: World Pub. Co., 1934), p. 21. The habit of capturing the local inhabitants and taking them back to the mother country to be trained as interpreters became commonplace among explorers of all nationalities, in various parts of the world. Probably the first to do so was Antonio Gonçalvez, "master of the robes" to Prince Henry of Portugal, who, in 1411, on a voyage to West Africa, seized some Africans and sent them back to Europe to learn Portuguese. See Helps, *op. cit.,* Vol. I, p. 19.

50. Bourne, *op. cit.,* p. 77.

51. Helps, *op. cit.,* Vol. IV, p. 293.

52. Pedro Castañeda, *The Journey of Coronado* (Ann Arbor: University of Michigan, University Microfilms, 1966), pp. 65, 168.

53. Alvar Núñez Cabeza de Vaca, *Relation of Núñez Cabeza de Vaca* (Ann Arbor: University of Michigan, University Microfilms, 1966), p. 29.

54. Helps, *loc. cit.*

55. On Ortíz: Theodore Maynard, *De Soto and the Conquistadores* (New York: AMS Press, 1969), pp. 152, 220-221, 252.

56. Salvador de Madariaga, *The Rise of the Spanish Empire* (New York: Free Press, 1947), p. 31.

57. Kirkpatrick, *op. cit.,* p. 66.

58. My chief source of information on Marina is W.H. Prescott, *The History of the Conquest of Mexico,* ed. C. Harvey Gardiner (Chicago: University of Chicago Press, 1966), pp. 71-72.

59. Salvador de Madariaga, *Hernán Cortés, Conqueror of Mexico* (Coral Gables, Fla: University of Miami Press, 1942), p. 153.

60. See Charles Braden, *Religious Aspects of the Conquest of Mexico* (New York: AMS Press, 1966), pp. 86-87; and Madariaga, *Hernán Cortés,* pp. 151-152, 240-246, *passim.*

61. Prescott, *op. cit.,* p. 128.

62. Martín and Felipillo: Helps, *op. cit.,* Vol. III, p. 312; Maynard, *op. cit.,* pp. 100-101; Don Hemming, *The Conquest of the Incas* (New York: Harcourt Brace Jovanovich, 1970), pp. 281-282.

63. Fate of Atahualpa: Helps, Vol. III, *op. cit.,* p. 368; Kirkpatrick, *op. cit.,* p. 159; Philip Ainsworth Means, *Fall of the Inca Empire and the Spanish Rule in Peru: 1530-1780* (New York: Gordian Press, 1964), p. 43.

64. Misinterpretation: Helps, *op. cit.,* Vol. III, p. 371n; Means, *loc. cit.;* Felipillo's fate: Maynard, *loc. cit.*

65. Huáman Poma (Don Felipe Huáman Poma de Ayala), *Letter to a King: A Peruvian Chief's Account of Life Under the Incas and Under Spanish Rule* (New York: E.P. Dutton, 1978), p. 113.

66. Means, *op. cit.,* p. 123.

67. Samuel Eliot Morison, *Samuel Champlain, Father of New France* (Boston: Little, Brown, 1972), p. 95.

68. Samuel Eliot Morison, *The Parkman Reader, From the Works of Francis Parkman* (Boston: Little, Brown, 1955), p. 122.

69. Benjamin Sulte, "Les Interprètes du temps de Champlain," *Royal Society of Canada, Proceedings and Transactions,* Vol. I, 1882–1883 (Montreal: Dawson Brothers, 1883), p. 47; Morison, *Samuel Champlain, op. cit.,* p. 29.

70. Brûlé and Marsolet: Sulte, *op. cit.,* p. 56; Morison, *Samuel Champlain, op. cit.,* p. 161; Sulte, *op. cit.,* p. 47.

71. N.E. Dionne, Champlain, *Founder of Quebec, Father of New France* (Toronto: University of Toronto Press, 1963), *passim,* and Sulte, *op. cit., passim.*

72. Dionne, *ibid.,* p. 208.

73. *Ibid.,* p. 143.

74. *Ibid.,* p. 87.

75. Jacques Marquette, *Voyages of Marquette in the Jesuit Relations,* 59 (Ann Arbor: University of Michigan, University of Microfilms, 1966), p. 89.

76. Henri Joutel, *The Last Voyages Performed by de la Sale* (Ann Arbor: University of Michigan, University Microfilms, 1955), Introd., p. xvii.

77. George W. Ellis and John E. Morris, *King Philip's War* (New York: Grafton Press, 1906), p. 23.

78. J. Evarts Greene, "Our Dealings with the Indians," *Proceedings of the American Antiquarian Society,* n.s. XI (April 1896–1897, 1898), p. 30.

79. Alexander Young (ed.), *Chronicles of the Pilgrim Fathers of the Colony of Plymouth from 1602 to 1625* (Boston: Charles C. Little and James Brown, 1841), p. 182.

80. *Ibid.,* p. 190, *n3.*

81. Samuel Eliot Morison, *The Story of "Old Colony" of New Plymouth (1620–1692)* (New York: Knopf, 1956), p. 70.

82. Young, *Chronicles, op. cit.,* p. 183, *n2.*

83. Louis B. Wright (ed.), *The Elizabethan's America* (Cambridge, Mass.: Harvard University Press, 1965), p. 143.

84. Morison, *Old Colony, op. cit.,* p. 217.

85. Rev. William Hubbard, *The History of the Indian Wars in New England; From the First Settlement to the Termination of the War with King Philip in 1677,* Vol. I (Roxbury, 1865; reprinted by Kraus Reprint Co., New York, 1969), p. 299.

86. Samuel Kercheval, *A History of the Valley of Virginia,* 4th ed. (Strasburg, Va.: Shenandoah Pub. House, 1925), pp. 24–25.

87. Ellis and Morris, *op. cit.,* pp. 28–*29, 31.*

88. Morison, *Old Colony, op. cit.,* p. 249.

89. John Fiske, *New France and New England* (Boston: Houghton Mifflin, 1902), p. 237.

90. Wilbur R. Jacobs, *Wilderness Politics and Indian Gifts: The Northern Colonial Frontier, 1748–1763* (Lincoln: University of Nebraska Press, 1966), p. 84.

91. *Ibid.,* p. 34.

92. New York State. *Documents Relating to the Colonial History of New York,* Vol. V, pp. 480–481.

93. Weiser and others: Jacobs, *op. cit.,* pp. 41, 42, 153–154, 183.

94. William C. Reichel (ed.), *Memorials of the Moravian Church,* Vol. I (Philadelphia: J.B. Lippincott, 1870), pp. 95–96.

95. George Washington, *The Writings of George Washington; From the Original Manuscript Sources, 1745–1799,* ed. John C. Fitzpatrick, Vol. I (Washington, D.C.: U.S. Gov. Printing Office, 1931), pp. 52–53.

96. *Ibid.,* pp. 197–198, 217–218.

97. *Ibid.,* p. 105, from *Pennsylvania Archives,* 1st ser. II, 12.

98. Lois Mulkearn, "Half King, Seneca Diplomat of the Ohio Valley," *Western Pennsylvania Historical Magazine* 37, 2 (1954), p. 76.

99. Fiske, *op. cit.,* p. 240.

100. *Ibid.,* p. 244.

101. *Ibid.,* p. 244.

102. *Ibid.,* pp. 79–80.

103. Reuben Gold Thwaites, *France in America, 1497–1763* (New York: Cooper

Square Publishers, 1968), pp. 161–163.

104. Mulkearn, *loc. cit.*

105. *Loc. cit.*

106. John Logan Allen, *Passage Through the Garden: Lewis and Clark and the Image of the American Northwest* (Urbana: University of Illinois, 1975), pp. 208–209.

107. *Ibid.,* pp. 211, 377.

108. Timothy Severin, *Explorers of the Mississippi* (New York: Knopf, 1968), p. 245.

109. Taylor, Pintard, Freneau: Lewis Leary, *That Rascal Freneau: A Study in Literary Failure* (New York: Octagon Books, 1964), notes to Chapt. 8, no. 160; Pinto: Gaillard Hunt, *The Department of State; Its History and Functions* (New Haven, Conn.: Yale University Press, 1914), pp. 96–97.

110. Mary Weatherspoon Bowden, *Philip Freneau* (Boston: Twayne Publishers, 1976), p. 44.

111. Leary, *op. cit.,* p. 233.

112. Mary S. Austin, *Philip Freneau, The Poet of the Revolution; A History of His Life and Times* (New York: A. Wessels & Co., 1901), pp. 232–233, 239.

113. Philip M. Marsh, *Philip Freneau, Poet and Journalist* (Minneapolis: Dillon Press, 1967), p. 368.

114. James B. Angell, *Reminiscences* (London: Longmans, Green & Co., 1912), p. 195.

115. Letter to Charles Eliot Norton, Oct. 23, 1877, in Houghton Library, Harvard, quoted in Lawrence H. Klibbe, *James Russell Lowell's Residence in Spain, 1877–1880* (Newark, N.J.: Washington Irving Pub. Co., 1964), p. 49.

116. Carlton J. Hayes, *Wartime Mission in Spain, 1942–1945* (New York: Da Capo Press, 1976), pp. 27–28.

117. Peter Lisagor and Marguerite Higgins, *Overtime in Heaven: Adventures in the Foreign Service* (New York: Doubleday, 1965), pp. 13, 25.

118. Bayard Taylor, *The Unpublished Letters of Bayard Taylor in the Huntington Library,* San Marino, Cal., 1937. (Letter to Edmond C. Stedman, Feb. 25, 1863.)

119. Elsie Porter Mende, *An American Soldier and Diplomat* (New York: Frederick A. Stokes Co., 1927), pp. 232–233.

120. Henry Lane Wilson, *Diplomatic Episodes in Mexico, Belgium and Chile* (Garden City, N.Y.: Doubleday, 1927), pp. 13 and 47.

121. Edward Younger, *John A. Kasson* (Iowa City: State Historical Society of Iowa, 1955), p. 284.

122. Joseph C. Grew, *Turbulent Era: A Diplomatic Record of Forty Years* (Boston: Houghton Mifflin, 1952), p. 89.

Chapter IV

1. Alexander Ostrower, *Language, Law and Diplomacy, A Study of Linguistic Diversity in Official International Relations and International Law,* Vol. I (Philadelphia: University of Pennsylvania Press, 1965), p. 234.

2. S.M. Meng, *The Tsungli Yamen: Its Origin and Functions* (Cambridge, Mass.: East Asian Research Center, Harvard University Press, 1962), p. 5.

3. Norman Wild, "Materials for the Study of the Ssui-kuan (Bureau of Translators)," *Bulletin* (School of Oriental and African Studies, University of London) XI, 3 (1945), p. 617.

4. *Ibid.,* p. 618.

5. *Ibid.,* p. 625.

6. Meng, *op. cit.,* p. 6.

7. J.J. Duyvendak, *China's Discovery of Africa,* Lectures at the University of London, Jan. 22–23 (London: Arthur Probsthain, 1948), p. 7.

8. Brig.-Gen. Sir Percy Sykes, *The Quest for Cathay* (London: A. & C. Black, 1936), p. 48. For the Roman side, see also C. Clayton Dove, *Marcus Aurelius Antoninus: His Life and Times* (London: Watts & Co., 1930), pp. 115–116.

9. Donald F. Lach, *Asia in the Making of Europe,* Vol. I, Bk. 1 (Chicago: University of Chicago Press, 1965), p. 36, *n107.*

10. Nigel Cameron, *Barbarians and Mandarins: Thirteen Centuries of Western Travel in China* (New York: Weatherhill Book, 1970), pp. 90–94. Toward the close of his career, John wrote, "I have a competent knowledge of the Tartar [Mongolian] language and write and preach openly and in public." See *ibid.,* pp. 98–99.

11. Duyvendak, *op. cit.,* p. 30.

12. Matteo Ricci, *China in the Sixteenth Century: The Journals of Matthew Ricci: 1583–1610,* trans. Louis J. Gallagher, S.J. (New York: Random House, 1953), p. 387.

13. Ssu-yu Teng and John K. Fairbank *et al., China's Response to the West; A Documentary Survey, 1839–1923* (New York: Atheneum, 1967), p. 51.

14. Ricci, *op. cit.,* p. 143.

15. William Alexander Martin, *A Cycle of Cathay; or, China South and North* (New York: Fleming H. Revell Co., 1896), pp. 20–21.

16. Ricci, *op. cit.,* pp. 162–165.

17. C.Y. Chao, *Foreign Advisors and the Diplomacy of the Manchu Empire* (Taipei: China Culture Pub. Found., 1954), pp. 2–3.

18. *Ibid.,* p. 5.

19. Cameron, *op. cit.,* p. 229.

20. Meng, *op. cit.,* pp. 6–7.

21. John E. Wills, Jr., "Ch'ing Relations with the Dutch, 1662–1690," in John King Fairbank (ed.), *The Chinese World Order, Traditional China's Foreign Relations* (Cambridge, Mass.: Harvard University Press, 1968), p. 247.

22. Wolfgang Franke, *China and the West,* trans. R.A. Wilson (Columbia: University of South Carolina Press, 1967), pp. 27–28.

23. Chester Holcombe, *The Real Chinese Question* (New York: Dodd, Mead & Co., 1900), pp. 199–200.

24. J. Dyer Ball, *Macao, The Holy City: The Gem of the Orient Earth* (London: China Baptist Publications Society, 1905), p. 57.

25. George W. Keeton, "The International Status of Macao Before 1887," *Chinese Social and Political Science Review,* Public Documents Suppl., XI (1927), p. 404.

26. Great Britain, Foreign Office, Historical Section. *Peace Handbooks,* Vol. XIII, no. 81, *Macao* (London: H.M. Stationery Office, 1920), pp. 8–9.

27. Ball, *op. cit.,* p. 55.

28. Hosea Ballou Morse, *The International Relations of the Chinese Empire; The Period of Conflict, 1834–1860* (London: Longmans, Green & Co., 1910), p. 49.

29. Gaston Cahen, *History of the Relations of Russia and China Under Peter the Great, 1689–1730* (Bangor, Me.: University Prints and Reprints, 1914), p. 1. See also Aitchen K. Wu, *China and the Soviet Union, A Study of Sino–Soviet Relations* (Port Washington, N.Y.: Kennikat Press, 1950), p. 5.

30. Cameron, *op. cit.,* p. 250, and Cahen, *op cit.,* p. 3.

31. Chao, *op. cit.,* p. 6.

32. Tien-fong Cheng, *A History of Sino–Russian Relations* (Washington, D.C.: Public Affairs Press, 1957), p. 23.

33. Morse, *op. cit.,* p. 60. As such, the procedure is of some interest. It is described as follows: "The Chinese plenipotentiaries appeared in state and signed and sealed the Manchu and Latin copies. The Russians handed one copy in Latin and one in Russian to the Chinese, and the Chinese handed one copy in Latin and one in Manchu to the Russians. The Latin copies were signed and officially sealed by both parties and therefore were regarded as authentic." See Vincent Chen, *Sino–Russian Relations in the Seventeenth Century* (The Hague: Martinus Nijhoff, 1966), pp. 98–99.

34. Until the Jesuits were ousted from China in 1773, in the so-called "Chinese rites controversy": see John K. Fairbank *et al., East Asia: Tradition and Transformation* (Cambridge, Mass.: Harvard University Press, 1978), pp. 244–251, *passim.*

35. Orthodox mission, wine and women, Rossokhin: Cahen, *op. cit.,* pp. 90–92, 120, 121; Treaty of Kiakhta: Morse, *op. cit.,* p. 61.

36. *The First Chinese Embassy to the West, The Journals of Kuo Sung-t'ao, Hsi-hung and Chang Te-yi,* trans. J.D. Frodsham (London: Clarendon Press, 1974), Introd., pp. xx, xxi, xxii.

37. Earl H. Pritchard, "Confusion About Portuguese and Other Europeans in Early Ch'ing China: A Case of Cultural Blindness," in *International Symposium on the History of Eastern and Western Cultural Contacts* (Tokyo: Japanese National Commission for UNESCO, 1959), pp. 117–120.

38. Frodsham, *op. cit.,* p. 140.

39. Pinghou C. Liu, *Chinese Foreign Affairs* — Organization and Control, Ph.D. dissertation (New York University, Graduate School, 1936), p. 5.

40. Teng and Fairbank, *op. cit.,* p. 41.

41. Cameron, *op cit.,* pp. 288, 310. This College is a story in itself. Father Matteo Ripa served as a missionary to China 1710–1723, ultimately falling into disfavor because of his objections to a fellow priest's constructing a fountain for a Taoist temple. Forced to return to his native Naples, Ripa took with him five Chinese students. Triumphing over the displeasure of his superiors who, at first, were annoyed at these extra mouths to feed, Ripa turned the group into a College (1732) for the preparation of missionaries to China. The College would also accept an occasional layman who wished to learn the Chinese language. In 1860, the translator of Ripa's *Memoirs* visited the still-existing College and found eight pupils there — six Chinese and two Greeks. See Matteo Ripa, *Memoirs of Father Ripa, During Thirteen Years' Residence at the Court of Peking in the Service of the Emperor of China,* trans. Fortunado Prandi (London: John Murray, 1861), *passim.*

42. Austin Coates, *Prelude to Hongkong* (London: Routledge & Kegan Paul, 1966), pp. 103, 114–115.

43. Morse, *op. cit.,* p. 127.

44. Meng, *op. cit.,* p. 8.

45. Martin, *op. cit.,* p. 295.

46. Frodsham, *op. cit.,* Introd., pp. xxvii.

47. Chang Hao, "The Anti-Foreignist Rôle of Wo-jen (1804–1871)," *Papers on China* I, 29 (Cambridge, Mass.: Harvard University Press, 1960 [Committee on Regional Studies, 14]), pp. 12–14.

48. Martin, *loc. cit.,* pp. 295, 296.

49. *Additonal Convention of Peace and Friendship Between France and China, Signed at Peking, 25th October, 1860,* in Geoffrey P. Hertslet, *China Treaties,* Vol. I (London: H.M. Stationery Office, 1908), pp. 287–291.

50. Liu, *op. cit.,* p. 5.

51. Meng, *op. cit.,* p. 64.

52. *Ibid.,* pp. 36, 67. Liang was a reforming journalist and scholar, leader of the Progressive Party, who for nearly 20 years after the overthrow of the Manchu Dynasty was the most widely read and respected thinker of the land, and the dominant voice in the May 4th Movement that began in 1919 and lasted well into the 1920s.

53. Martin, *op. cit.,* pp. 295–296, p. 311.

54. Teng and Fairbank, *op. cit.,* p. 75.

55. J. MacMurray, *Treaties and Agreements with and Concerning China,* Vol. I (New York: Oxford University Press, 1921), p. 284.

56. Liu, *op. cit.,* p. 11.

57. Richard Dean Burns and Edward M. Bennett, *Diplomats in Crisis, United States–Chinese-Japanese Relations, 1919–1941* (Santa Barbara, Calif.: American Bibliographic Center, 1974), pp. 8–9.

58. E.S. Bates, *Intertraffic: Studies in Translation* (London: Jonathan Cape, 1943), p. 50.

59. Arthur F. Wright, *Studies in Chinese Thought* (Chicago: University of Chicago Press, 1953), p. 279, quoting Edward Ernest Kellett.

60. Quoted from Eric Clark, *Corps Diplomatique* (London: Allen Lane, 1973), p. 224.

61. Robert T. Oliver, *Culture and Communication; The Problem of Penetrating*

National and Cultural Boundaries (Springfield, Ill.: Charles C. Thomas, 1962), pp. 57, 58.

62. George Steiner, *After Babel: Aspects of Language and Translation* (New York: Oxford University Press, 1975), p. 34.

63. Mario Pei, *One Language for the World* (New York: Devin-Adair, 1958), p. 341.

64. Robert B. Ekvall, *Faithful Echo* (New York: Twayne Publishers, 1960), *passim.* All of the material on Col. Ekvall's career is taken from this source.

65. *Ibid.,* pp. 88–90.

66. Oliver, *op. cit.,* p. 102.

67. Lu Tien-yang, "Translating from English into Chinese; Its Principles and Techniques," quoted in Wolfgang Bauer, *Western Literature and Translation Work in Communist China* (Hamburg: Institut für Asien Kunde, Alfred Metzner Verlag, 1964), p. 10.

68. Chester Holcombe, *The Real China* (New York: Dodd, Mead & Co., 1895), p. 66. Holcombe was, for many years, interpreter, secretary and, ultimately, acting minister of the United States legation in Peking.

69. *Ibid.,* p. 63.

70. Derk Bodde, *Peking Diary* (New York: Schuman Pub. Co., 1950), pp. 190–191.

71. Chiang Kai-shek, *Resisting External Aggression and Regenerating the Chinese Nation* (Hankow: China Information Committee, 1938), p. 15.

72. Morse, *op. cit.,* pp. 125–126, *n.*

73. Donald F. Lach, *Asia in the Making of Europe,* Vol. I, Bk. 2 (Chicago: University of Chicago Press, 1965), p. 655.

74. Donald F. Lach, *Japan in the Eyes of Europe: The Sixteenth Century* (Chicago: University of Chicago Press, 1968), pp. 679–680.

75. Michael Cooper, S.J., *Rodrigues the Interpreter, an Early Jesuit in Japan and China* (New York: Weatherhill, 1974), p. 24.

76. *Ibid.,* p. 105.

77. *Ibid.,* pp. 199, 218, 247.

78. *Ibid.,* pp. 267–268.

79. J.H. Gubbins, *The Making of Modern Japan* (Philadelphia: J.B. Lippincott, 1922), pp. 30–31. Gubbins was first secretary and Japanese secretary at the British embassy in Tokyo.

80. Mikiso Hane, *Japan; A Historical Survey* (New York: Charles Scribner's Sons, (1972), p. 237.

81. Donald Keene, *The Japanese Discovery of Europe, 1720–1830* (Stanford, Calif.: Stanford University Press, 1969), pp. 78–79.

82. Edwin O. Reischauer *et al., Japan, the Changing Tradition: A Study Guide* for the course "Japan" (Lincoln, Neb.: University of Mid-America, 1978), p. 41.

83. Francis L. Hawks, *Narrative of the Expedition of an American Squadron to the China Seas and Japan* (New York: Coward McCann, 1952), pp. 17, 48, 26.

84. Arthur Walworth, *Black Ships Off Japan; The Story of Commodore Perry's Expedition* (Hamden, Conn.: Archon Books, 1966), pp. 144, 174.

85. United States, House of Representatives, 33d Congress, 2d Session, *Narrative of the Expedition of an American Squadron to the China Seas and Japan, Performed in the Years 1852, 1853, and 1854, Under the Command of Commodore M.C. Perry,* Vol. I (Washington, D.C.: A.O.P. Nicholson, 1856), p. 269. Of particular interest in this volume are the tinted daguerrotypes of several of the Japanese interpreters who serviced the Perry expedition, including that of Moriyami Einosuke. See pages 318, 377–378.

86. Hawks, *op. cit.,* p. 73.

87. *Ibid.,* pp. 295–296.

88. "Diary of an Official of the Bakufu" (no author or translator given), *Transactions of the Asia Society of Japan,* 2d ser. VII, pp. 98–119, *passim.*

89. Gifts: Hawks, *op. cit.,* p. 218; knees: United States, *Narrative of the Expedition, op. cit.,* Vol. II, p. 209.

90. Western intepreters: Sir Ernest Satow, *A Diplomat in Japan* (London: Seeley, Service & Co., 1921), p. 58; Japanese interpeters: Henry Heusken, *Japan Journal 1855–1861,* trans. and ed. Jeanette C. van der Corput and Robert A. Wilson (New Bruns-

wick, N.J.: Rutgers University Press, 1964), p. 99. Except where otherwise specified, the details of Heusken's career are derived from this source.

91. William Elliot Griffis, *Townsend Harris, First American Envoy to Japan* (Boston: Houghton Mifflin, 1896), p. 19.

92. *Ibid.*, p. 20.

93. Griffis, *op. cit.*, pp. 151, 243.

94. Great Britain, Civil Service Examination, *Open Competition for the Situation of Student Interpreter in China, Japan or Siam* (London, July 1903).

95. Satow, *op. cit.*, p. 55. I am indebted to this volume for all of my material on Sir Ernest.

96. Certain powerful Japanese lords continued to resist Western encroachment upon their domains until the emperor laid down the law to them. See Gubbins, *op. cit.*, pp. 66–67.

97. Satow, *op. cit.*, p. 70.

98. Henry Norman, *The Real Japan, Studies of Contemporary Japanese Manners, Morals, Administration and Politics* (London: T. Fisher Unwin, 1891), p. 64.

99. Reischauer, *op. cit.*, pp. 145–146.

100. Norman, *op. cit.*, p. 102.

101. Frederick J. Pohl, *Amerigo Vespucci: Pilot Major* (New York: Octagon Books, 1966), p. 106. All material on Guaspare is taken from this source.

102. Tamil grammar: Donald F. Lach, *India in the Eyes of Europe—Sixteenth Century* (Chicago: University of Chicago Press, 1968), pp. 436–437; Akbar: *ibid.*, p. 462.

103. Sir Edward Blunt, *The I.C.S.; The Indian Civil Service* (London: Faber & Faber, 1937), p. 193.

104. L.S.S. O'Malley, *The Indian Civil Service 1601–1930* (London: John Murray, 1931), pp. 232–233.

105. Blunt, *op. cit.*, p. 196.

106. O'Malley, *loc. cit.*, pp. 232–233, 234.

107. M.A. Muttalib, *The Union Public Safety Commission* (New Delhi: Indian Institute of Public Administration, 1967), p. 29.

108. Great Britain, Civil Service Commission, *Open Competition for the Civil Service of India*, August 1903.

109. Great Britain, Civil Service Commission, *Examinations of Officers of the Army in Modern Foreign Languages* (London, October 1903).

110. "A Ballad," from James Hume (ed.), *A Selection from the Writings, Prose and Poetical, of the Late Henry W. Torrens, Esq.*, Vol. I (Calcutta: R.C. LePage & Co., 1854), p. 26.

111. Blunt, *op. cit.*, pp. 104–106.

112. O'Malley, *op. cit.*, p. 74, quoting Sir George Campbell in *Modern India*, 1853.

113. All of my information on the O.T. I owe to the only available source, Z.A. Barni, *Romance of the Oriental Translator's Office* (Karachi: T'Alimi Markaz, 1950), *passim*. Barni worked under seven different O.T.s from 1918 to 1945.

114. Blunt, *op. cit.*, p. 165.

115. Barni, *op. cit.*, p. 9.

116. *Ibid.*, pp. 10–11.

117. *Ibid.*, pp. 13–14.

118. Barni, *op. cit.*, pp. 30–34.

Chapter V

1. Sir Maurice Hankey, "Diplomacy in Conference," a paper read at a meeting of the Institute of the Royal Society of Arts, *Proceedings of the British Institute of International Affairs*, London, Nov. 2, 1920, p. 18.

2. Harold Nicolson, *Peacemaking 1919* (London: Constable & Co., 1934), p. 124.

3. Franklin Roudybush, *Diplomatic Language* (Basle: Satz & Repro Ag., 1972), p. 12.

4. See Nicolson, *Peacemaking,* p. 240 (Nicolson, a participant in the conference, noted in his diary covering Jan. 13–20, 1919, how "infuriated" the French were at this parity for the English language); and Vladimir D. Pastuhov, *A Guide to the Practice of International Conferences* (Washington, D.C.: Carnegie Endowment for International Peace, 1945), p. 123. For footnote, see Brian Weinstein, "Francophonie: A Language-Based Movement in World Politics," *International Organization* 30, 3 (1976), p. 494.

5. Pastuhov, *A Guide,* p. 123.

6. Statement from the League's Secretariat, Bibliothèque du Bureau International des Fédérations d'Enseignement Secondaire, Fasc. no. 5, p. 4, quoted in Shenton, *op. cit.,* pp. 382, 384.

7. Egon F. Ranshofen-Wertheimer, *The International Secretariat* (Washington, D.C.: Carnegie Endowment for International Peace, 1945), pp. 279, 282–283, and 143.

8. Judith Jackson and Stephen King-Hall (eds.), *The League Yearbook,* 3d ed. (London: Ivor Nicholson & Watson, 1934), pp. 458–460.

9. Manley O. Hudson, *International Legislation,* Vol. I, 1912–1921 (Washington, D.C.: Carnegie Endowment for International Peace, 1931), p. 265.

10. Jackson and King-Hall, *op. cit.,* p. 483.

11. Francis Graham Wilson, *Labor in the League System; A Study of the International Labor Organization in Relation to International Administration* (Stanford, Calif.: Stanford University Press, 1934), pp. 120–121.

12. Hudson, *International Legislation,* Vol. IX, p. 541; and Manley O. Hudson, *The Permanent Court of International Justice* (New York: Macmillan, 1934), p. 295, *n33.*

13. Jean Herbert, "How Conference Interpretation Grew," *Proceedings of the NATO Symposium on Language Interpretation and Communication,* San Giorgio Maggiore, Venice, Italy, Sept. 26–Oct. 1, 1977, eds. David Gerver and H. Wallace Sinaiko (New York: Plenum Press, 1978), p. 7.

14. *Annals of the American Academy of Political and Social Science* 234 (July 1944), p. 30.

15. Eugene P. Chase, *The United Nations in Action* (New York: McGraw-Hill, 1950), pp. 48–49.

16. Clyde Eagleton, "The Charter Adopted at San Francisco," *American Political Science Review* 39 (Oct. 1945), p. 935.

17. Alexander Ostrower, *Language, Law and Diplomacy; A Study of Linguistic Diversity in Official International Relations and International Law,* Vol. I (Philadelphia: University of Pennsylvania Press, 1965), p. 238.

18. Eleanor Roosevelt and William de Witt, *The UN: Today and Tomorrow* (New York: Harper & Bros., 1953), p. 43.

19. Report of the Secretary-General of the United Nations (A/624), August 27, 1948, *Yearbook of the United Nations,* p. 43ff.

20. Calculated as between 3.17 and 2.89 pages per day by Claude Piron and Humphrey Tonkin, "Translation in International Organizations," *Esperanto Documents,* n.s. 20A (1979), pp. 7–8.

21. *Ibid.,* pp. 8–9.

22. Ostrower, *op. cit.,* pp. 539, 541.

23. Theodore Meron, *The United Nations Secretariat: The Rules and the Practice* (Lexington, Mass.: D.C. Heath, 1977), p. 23.

24. Stephen S. Goodspeed, *The Nature and Function of International Organization* (New York: Oxford University Press, 1967), p. 378.

25. Herbert and Mary Stewart Krosney, *Careers and Opportunities in International Service* (New York: E.P. Dutton, 1965), p. 36.

26. June L. Sherif, *Careers in Foreign Languages; A Handbook* (New York: Regents Pub. Co., 1975), pp. 110–111. Except where otherwise indicated, material on this page concerning U.N. interpreters, translators and guides is derived largely from this source.

27. Hudson, *International Legislation, op. cit.,* Vol. IX, *Statute of the International Court of Justice,* Art. 39, p. 522.

28. *Encyclopaedia Britannica,* 15th ed., Vol. 9 (1975), p. 735.

29. Michel Doucet, "Le Service linguistique de la Cour de justice des Communautes européenes," *Babel* XV, 1 (1969), p. 27.

30. *Ibid.*, p. 30.

31. Thérèse Nilski, *Conference Interpreting in Canada* (Ottowa: Queen's Printer for Canada, 1969 [Documents of Royal Commission on Bilingualism and Biculturalism, no. 2]), p. 73, *Notes* to Chapt. III.

32. J. Goetschalckx, "Translation, Terminology and Documentation in International Organizations," *Babel* XX, 3 (1974), p. 186. The English, one notes, refer to lemon custard, of the sort used in lemon meringue pies, as "lemon cheese."

33. *The Statute of the Council of Europe,* Chapt. III, Art. 12, Rule 18, in A.H. Robertson, *The Council of Europe: Its Structure, Functions and Achievements* (New York: Praeger, 1956), Appendix I.

34. *Ibid.*, p. 56.

35. Shenton, *op. cit.*, p. 27, 248–249.

36. Ostrower, *op. cit.*, p. 525.

37. Paul Gordon Lauren, *Diplomats and Bureaucrats: The First Institutional Responses to Twentieth Century Diplomacy in France and Germany* (Stanford, Calif.: Hoover Institute Press, 1976), p. 10.

38. William James Roosen, *The Age of Louis XIV; The Rise of Modern Diplomacy* (Cambridge, Mass.: Schenkman Pub. Co., 1976), p. 74.

39. Edward A. Whitcomb, *Napoleon's Diplomatic Service* (Durham, N.C.: Duke University Press, 1979), pp. 47, 60.

40. Harold Nicolson, *Diplomacy,* 3d ed. (London: Oxford University Press, 1963), pp. 214–215.

41. Stephen Gaselee, *The Language of Diplomacy* (Cambridge, England: Bowes & Bowes, 1939), p. 74.

42. Bayard Taylor, letter to Alfred B. Street, March 31, 1863, in *The Unpublished Letters of Bayard Taylor in the Huntington Library,* San Marino, 1937, p. 65.

43. Stephen D. Kertesz and M.A. Fitzsimmons, *Diplomacy in a Changing World* (South Bend, Ind.: University of Notre Dame Press, 1959), p. 220.

44. Geoffrey Moorhouse, *The Diplomats; The Foreign Office Today* (London: Jonathan Cape, 1977), p. 62.

45. Lauren, *op. cit.*, pp. 16, 17.

46. *Ibid.*, p. 27.

47. Fritz Konrad Krüger, *Government and Politics of the German Empire* (World Book Co., 1915), pp. 257–258.

48. Gordon A. Craig, *From Bismarck to Adenauer; Aspects of German Statecraft* (New York: Harper & Row, 1965), p. 5.

49. Lamar Cecil, *The German Diplomatic Service, 1871-1914* (Princeton, N.J.: Princeton University Press, 1976), p. 34.

50. Lauren, *op. cit.*, p. 139.

51. Nicolson, *Diplomacy, op. cit.*, p. 214.

52. Henry Kittredge Norton, *Foreign Office Organization,* Suppl., v. CXLIII, *Annals of the American Academy of Political & Social Science* (Philadelphia, May 1920), p. 34.

53. Gaselee, *op. cit.*, p. 74.

54. Vasily Osipovich Kluchevsky, *A History of Russia,* Vol. III, trans. C.J. Hogarth (London: J.M. Dent & Sons, 1960), p. 288.

55. *An Introduction to Russian History,* eds. Robert Autry and Dimitri Obolensky (Cambridge, England: Cambridge University Press, 1976), p. 171.

56. S.V. Bakhrushin and S.D. Skazkin, "Diplomatic Institutions in Russia Under Peter I," in Alfred Erich Senn, *Readings in Russian Political and Diplomatic History,* Vol. I (Homewood, Ill.: Dorsey Press, 1966), p. 55.

57. Kluchevsky, *op. cit.*, Vol. IV, p. 252.

58. *Ibid.*, p. 175.

59. Grigory Bessedovsky, *Revelations of a Soviet Diplomat,* trans. Matthew Norgate (London: Williams and Norgate, 1931), p. 93.

60. Louise Bryant, *Mirrors of Moscow* (New York: Thomas Seltzer, 1923), pp. 123–124.

61. Vernon V. Aspaturian, *Process and Power in Soviet Foreign Policy* (Boston: Little, Brown, 1971), p. 631.

62. Philip W. Buck and Martin B. Travis, Jr., *Control of Foreign Relations in Modern Nations* (New York: W.W. Norton, 1957), p. 673.

63. Eric Clark, *Diplomat; The World of International Diplomacy* (New York: Taplinger Pub. Co., 1974), p. 224.

64. Aleksandr Kaznacheev, *Inside a Soviet Embassy,* ed. Simon Wolin (Philadelphia: J.B. Lippincott, 1962), p. 31.

65. *The Soviet Diplomatic Corps 1917–1967,* ed. Edward L. Crowley (Munich: Institute for the Study of the USSR; Metuchen, N.J.: Scarecrow Press, 1970), pp. 9–10.

66. Meron, *op. cit.,* p. 32.

67. Rt. Hon. Sir John Tilley, G.C.M.G., and Stephen Gaselee, *The Foreign Office* (London: G.P. Putnam's Sons, 1933), pp. 20, 73.

68. *Ibid.,* p. 236.

69. Chester Lloyd Jones, *The Consular Service of the United States; Its History and Activities* (Philadelphia: University of Pennsylvania, 1906 [Series in Political Economy and Public Law, no. 18]), pp. 90, 93.

70. Tilley, *op. cit.,* p. 81.

71. *Ibid.,* pp. 146–147.

72. Ray Jones, *The Nineteenth Century Foreign Office; An Administrative History* (London: London School of Economics and Political Science, 1971), pp. 52–53.

73. Tilley, *op. cit.,* p. 253.

74. Zara S. Steiner, *The Foreign Office and Foreign Policy 1898–1914* (Cambridge, England: Cambridge University Press, 1969), p. 17.

75. Henry Serrano Villard, *Affairs at State* (New York: Crowell, 1969), p. 35.

76. Kertesz and Fitzsimmons, *op. cit.,* p. 179.

77. Gaselee, *op. cit.,* pp. 72–73.

78. D.C.M. Platt, *The Cinderella Service, British Consuls Since 1825* (London: Longman, 1971), p. 231.

79. Moorhouse, *op. cit.,* pp. 45, 64, 78.

80. Graham H. Stuart, *The Department of State; A History of Its Organization, Procedure and Personnel* (New York: Macmillan, 1949), p. 83.

81. Gaillard Hunt, *The Department of State; Its History and Functions* (New Haven, Conn.: Yale University Press, 1914), p. 229.

82. Thomas, Stevens, Martin: Stuart, *op. cit.,* p. 290.

83. Hunt, *op. cit.,* pp. 425, 423.

84. Stuart, *loc. cit.*

85. Graham H. Stuart, *American Diplomats and Consular Practice* (New York: D. Appleton-Century, 1936), p. 143.

86. John P. Leacacos, *Fires in the In-Basket; The ABC's of the State Department* (New York: World Pub. Co., 1968), p. 427.

87. Rachel West, *The Department of State on the Eve of the First World War* (Athens: University of Georgia Press, 1978), pp. 115–116.

88. Spruille Braden, *Diplomats and Demagogues* (New Rochelle, N.Y.: Arlington House, 1971), p. 128.

89. U.S. Department of State, Director General of the Foreign Service, *Some Facts about the Foreign Service* (Washington, D.C.: U.S. Gov. Printing Office, 1950), p. 9.

90. *American Foreign Service Journal,* July 1926, p. 225.

91. Emmerson, *op. cit.,* p. 31.

92. George F. Kennan, *Memoirs 1925–1950* (London: Hutchinson, 1968), pp. 23–24, 33.

93. Executive Order April 18, 1940, No. 8396, in Green Haywood Hackworth, *Digest of International Law,* Vol. IV (Washington, D.C., 1942) pp. 408–409; *Foreign Service Regulations,* Jan. 1941.

94. *Prospectus,* Foreign Service Institute, March 23, 1951.

95. W. Wendell Blancké, *The Foreign Service of the United States* (New York: Frederick A. Praeger, 1969), Appendix II, p. 267.

96. Leacacos, *op. cit.,* p. 427.

97. Patrick E. Linehan, *The Foreign Service Personnel System; An Organizational Analysis* (Boulder, Colo.: Westview Press, 1976), pp. 86, 87.

98. Sherif, *op. cit.,* p. 106.

99. Douglas Busk, *The Craft of Diplomacy, Mechanics and Development of National Representation Overseas* (London: Pall Mall Press, 1967), p. 217.

100. J. William Fulbright, "My Turn," *Newsweek,* July 30, 1979.

101. Quoted in Carl Rowan, "Why U.S. Keeps Falling Behind in World Community," *Atlanta Constitution,* Jan. 14, 1981.

102. West, *op. cit.,* p. 117.

103. Rowan, *loc. cit.*

104. Barton Reppert, "Sorry, Buddy, No Spikka da Rooshian Lingo," *Atlanta Constitution,* Dec. 30, 1980.

105. Richard Reeves, "Wish I'd Written That," *Atlanta Constitution,* Dec. 30, 1980.

106. Sherif, *op. cit.,* p. 102.

107. *Ibid.,* pp. 79–108, *passim,* 116.

108. Nilski, *op. cit.,* p. 9. The data in this paragraph are paraphrased from this source.

109. Johan Kaufmann, *Conference Diplomacy; An Introductory Analysis* (Leyden: A.W. Sijthoff, 1970), p. 46.

110. Bill Richard, "Near the Pole, Eskimos Ponder Political Unity," *Washington Post,* June 14, 1975.

111. R.K. Lochner, "Conference Interpretation and the Modern World," *Babel* XXII, (1976), p. 103.

112. All statistics in this paragraph come from Denys-Ferrando-Durfort, "L'Enquête EPTI," *Babel* XX, 2 (1974), p. 72 (reprint from *Traduire* 76 [Automne, 1973]).

113. James Coveney, "Training Linguists for International Organizations," *Babel* XXII, 3 (1976), p. 121.

114. Goetschalckx, *loc. cit.*

115. Ferrando-Durfort, *op. cit.,* p. 78.

116. Jean Herbert, *The Interpreters' Handbook* (Geneva: Université de Genève, École d'Interprètes, 1952), Preface, *passim.*

117. A.H. Birse, *Memoirs of an Interpreter* (London: Michael Joseph, 1967), *passim.*

118. Alexander Barmine, *Memoirs of a Soviet Diplomat,* trans. Gerard Hopkins (London: Lovat Dickson, 1938), *passim.*

119. Kaznacheev, *op. cit., passim.*

120. Edouard Raditi, "Hans Jacob, 1896–1961," *Babel* II, 2 (1961), *passim.*

121. Eugen Dollmann, *The Interpreter; Memoirs of Doktor Eugen Dollmann,* trans. J. Maxwell Brown John (London: Hutchinson, 1967), *passim.*

122. *Ibid.,* p. 76.

123. Nils Brouwer, "Translators Are Servants, But They Need Not Be Servile," *Babel* XVIII, 2 (1972), p. 4.

124. *Babel* XVIII, 3 (1972), p. 6.

125. Chester Holcombe, *The Real Chinese Question* (New York: Dodd, Mead, 1900), p. 269.

126. Nigel Cameron, *Barbarians and Mandarins; Thirteen Centuries of Western Travellers in China* (New York: Weatherhill, 1970), p. 317.

127. Dr. Paul Schmidt, *Hitler's Interpreter,* ed. R.H. Steed (New York: Macmillan, 1951), pp. 10, 13.

128. Brouwer, *op. cit.,* p. 3.

129. Schmidt, *op. cit.,* pp. 17–18.

130. *Ibid.,* p. 11.

131. *Washington Post,* Dec. 15, 1977.

132. *Straits Times,* Singapore, Jan. 11, 1946.

133. Philip R. Piccigallo, *The Japanese on Trial: Allied War Crimes Operations in the East, 1945-1951* (Austin: University of Texas Press, 1979), p. 86.

134. Lord Russell of Liverpool, *The Knights of Bushido, A Short History of Japanese War Crimes* (London: Cassel, 1958), pp. 121-127, *passim.* My entire story of the *Lisbon Maru* is derived from this source.

135. Brouwer, *op. cit.,* p. 4.

136. Nilski, *op. cit.,* pp. 15-16. This is the source of my information on "active" and "passive" languages.

137. Lochner, *op. cit.,* p. 104.

138. Henry Fischbach, "The American Translators Association: A Brief History," *Babel* XXII, 4 (1976), pp. 149-151.

139. I am, once again, grateful to Dr. Andor C. Klay for permission to paraphrase this little gem from his "Interpretive Diplomacy," *U.S. Foreign Service Journal* 36, 11 (Nov. 1959).

Bibliography

Omitted are a large number of newspaper articles (the reader is directed to existing indexes), and government documents (largely U.S. Dept. of State, British Civil Service Commission and Foreign Office, League of Nations, and U.N.), suggested for in-depth research.

Abbott, George Frederick. *Under the Turk in Constantinople.* London: Macmillan, 1920.

Albin, Pierre (ed.). *Les Grandes Traités politiques; recueil des principaux textes diplomatiques de 1815 à 1914,* 3d ed. Paris: Librairie Félix Alcan, 1923.

Allen, John B. *Post and Courier Service in the Diplomacy of Early Modern Europe.* The Hague: Martinus Nijhoff, 1972.

Allen, John Logan. *Passage Through the Garden; Lewis and Clark and the Image of the American Northwest.* Urbana: University of Illinois Press, 1958.

Anderson, Matthew Smith. *Britain's Discovery of Russia.* New York: St. Martin's Press, 1958.

American Foreign Service Journal. (For example, July, 1926, and June, 1932.)

Angell, James B., *Reminiscences.* London: Longmans, Green, 1912.

Annals of the American Academy of Political and Social Science. (For example, Vol. 234, July, 1944.)

Arrian. *The Campaigns of Alexander,* trans. Aubrey de Selincourt. Harmondsworth, England: Penguin Books, 1971.

Aspaturian, Vernon. *Process and Power in Soviet Foreign Policy.* Boston: Little, Brown, 1971.

Auerbach, Hakon. "Professional Translators in Sweden." *Babel,* vol. xi, no. 4, 1965.

Austin, Mary S., *Philip Freneau, The Poet of the Revolution; A History of His Life and Times.* New York: A. Wessels, 1901.

Autry, Robert, and Obolensky, Dimitri (eds.). *An Introduction to Russian History,* Cambridge, England: Cambridge University Press, 1976.

Aylmer, G.E. *The States' Servants, The Civil Service of the English Republic 1649-1660.* London: Routledge & Kegan Paul, 1973.

Aziz, Ahmad. *A History of Islamic Sicily.* Edinburgh: University of Edinburgh Press, 1975 *(Islamic Surveys No. 10).*

Aziz Atiya. *The Crusade in the Late Middle Ages.* New York: Kraus Reprint Co., 1970.

Babel (the periodical).

Baikie, Rev. James. F.R.A.S., *The Amarna Age; A Study of the Crisis of the Ancient World.* London: A. & C. Black, 1926.

Ball, J. Dyer. *Macao, the Holy City: The Gem of the Orient Earth.* London: China Baptist Publications Society, 1905.

Barmine, Alexander. *Memoirs of a Soviet Diplomat,* trans. Gerard Hopkins. London: Lovat Dickson, 1938.

Barni, Z.A. *Romance of the Oriental Translator's Office.* Karachi: T'Alimi Markaz, 1950.

Barzun, Jacques. "In Favor of Particular Clichés." *Translation 73,* vol. I, no. 1, 1973.

Bates, E.S. *Intertraffic: Studies in Translation.* London: Jonathan Cape, 1943.

Bauer, Wolfgang. *Western Literature and Translation Work in Communist China.* Hamburg: Alfred Metzner Verlag, 1964.

Bessedovsky, Grigory. *Revelations of a Soviet Diplomat,* trans. Matthew Norgate. London: Williams and Norgate, 1931.

Birse, A.H. *Memoirs of an Interpreter.* London: Michael Joseph, 1967.

Blancké, W. Wendell. *The Foreign Service of the United States.* New York: Frederick A. Praeger, 1969.

Blunt, Edward. *The I.C.S., The Indian Civil Service.* London: Faber & Faber, 1937.

Bodde, Derk. *Peking Diary.* New York: Schuman Publishing Co., 1950.

Bourne, Edward Gaylord. *Spain in America, 1450-1580.* New York: Barnes & Noble, 1962.

Bowden, Mary Weatherspoon. *Philip Freneau.* Boston: Twayne Publishers, 1976.

Boxer, Charles R. *Fidalgos in the Far East, 1550-1770.* London: Oxford University Press, 1968.

Boyd, Andrew. *Fifteen Men on a Powder Keg; A History of the U.N. Security Council.* New York: Stein & Day, 1971.

Braden, Charles. *Religious Aspects of the Conquest of Mexico.* New York: AMS Press, 1966.

Braden, Spruille. *Diplomats and Demagogues.* New Rochelle, N.Y.: Arlington House, 1971.

Bradford, William. *Of Plymouth Plantation, 1620-1647,* ed. Samuel Eliot Morison. New York: Alfred A. Knopf, 1952.

Brand, Charles M. *Byzantium Confronts the West, 1180-1204.* Cambridge, Mass.: Harvard University Press, 1968.

Breasted, James. *A History of Egypt.* New York: C. Scribner's Sons, 1954.

Brislin, Richard W. *Translation: Applications and Research.* New York: Gardner Press, 1976.

Brouwer, Nils. "Translators are Servants, But They Need Not Be Servile." *Babel,* vol. XVIII, no. 2, 1972.

Brown, Peter. *The World of Late Antiquity: From Marcus Aurelius to Mohammed.* London: Thames & Hudson, 1971.

Brunot, Ferdinand. "Les Débats due français dans la diplomatie." *Revue de Paris,* Dec. 15, 1913.

Bryant, Louise. *Mirrors of Moscow.* New York: Thomas Seltzer, 1923.

Buck, Philip W., and Travis, Martin B., Jr. *Control of Foreign Relations in Modern Nations.* New York: W.W. Norton, 1957.

Burns, Richard Dean, and Bennett, Edward M. *Diplomats in Crisis, United States-Chinese-Japanese Relations, 1919-1941.* Santa Barbara, Calif.: American Bibliographical Center, 1974.

Busk, Douglas. *The Craft of Diplomacy, Mechanics and Development of National Representation Overseas.* London: Pall Mall Press, 1967.

Cabeza de Vaca, Alvar Nuñez. *Relation of Nuñez Cabeza de Vaca.* One good edition (1966) is that available from University Microfilms, Ann Arbor, Mich.

Caesar, Julius. *Caesar's Commentaries De Bello Gallico and De Bello Civili.*

Cahen, Gaston. *History of the Relations of Russia and China Under Peter the Great, 1689-1730.* Bangor, Me.: University Prints and Reprints, 1914.

Callières, François de. *On the Manner of Negotiating with Princes* (Paris, 1716), trans. A.F. Shyte. Boston: Houghton Mifflin, 1919.

Cameron, Nigel. *Barbarians and Mandarins; Thirteen Centuries of Western Travel in China.* New York: Weatherhill, 1970.

Canada. Royal Commission on Bilingualism and Biculturalism. Thérèse Nilski, *Conference Interpreting in Canada,* Documents of Royal Commission, no. 2. Ottawa: Queen's Press for Canada, 1969.

"Capitulations française dans le proche-orient; sources et documents." *Europe Nouvelle,* vol. VII, no. 338, 1927.

Castañeda, Pedro. *The Journey of Coronado.* One good edition (1966) is that available from University Microfilms, Ann Arbor, Mich.

Cecil, Lamar. *The German Diplomatic Service, 1871–1914.* Princeton, N.J.: Princeton University Press, 1976.

Chaigne, Louis. *Paul Claudel; The Man and the Mystic,* trans. Pierre de Fontnouvelle. Westport, Conn.: Greenwood Press, 1961.

Chakraborty, Ashit. "Translation in Medieval Bulgaria, Theory and Practice of Translation Throughout the Ages." *Subarnarekha 73* (New Delhi), vol. II, part 4, 1972.

Chang, Hao. "The Anti-Foreignist Role of Wo-jen (1804–1871)." Cambridge: Harvard University Press, 1960 (*Papers on China,* I, 29).

Chao, C.Y. *Chinese Diplomatic Practice and Treaty Relations 1842–1943.* Taipei: China Cultural Service, 1955.

_____. *Foreign Advisors and the Diplomacy of the Manchu Empire.* Taipei: China Culture Publishing Foundation, 1954.

Chao, Ming-kuo. *Essays on Chinese and Foreigners.* Mukden: Sin Hua Press, 1930.

Chase, Eugene P. *The United Nations in Action.* New York: McGraw-Hill Book Co., 1950.

Chen, Vincent. *Sino–Russian Relations in the Seventeenth Century.* The Hague: Martinus Nijhoff, 1966.

Cheng, Tien-fong. *A History of Sino–Russian Relations.* Washington, D.C.: Public Affairs Press, 1957.

Chiang, Kai-shek. *Resisting External Aggression and Regenerating the Chinese Nation.* Hankow: China Information Committee, 1938.

Church, Alfred J. *Carthage, or the Empire of Africa.* Freeport, N.Y.: Books for Libraries Press, 1981.

Cicero, Marcus Tullius. *The Letters of Marcus Tullius Cicero.*

_____. *Three Dialogues on the Orator.*

Citroen, I.J. (ed.). "Ten Years of Translation." In *Proceedings of the Fourth Congress of the International Federation of Translators,* Dubrovnik, 1963. London: Pergamon Press, 1964.

Clark, Eric. *Corps Diplomatique.* London: Allen Lane, 1973.

_____. *Diplomat, the World of International Diplomacy.* New York: Taplinger Pub. Co., 1974.

Coates, Austin. *Prelude to Hongkong.* London: Routledge & Kegan Paul, 1966.

Cohen, Warren I. *The Chinese Connection: Roger S. Greene, Thomas W. Lamont, George E. Sokolsky, and American–East Asian Relations.* New York: Columbia University Press, 1978.

Congrat-Butlar, Stefan (ed.), *Translation and Translators.* New York: R.R. Bowker, 1979.

Cooper, Michael. *Rodrigues the Interpreter; an Early Jesuit in Japan and China.* New York: Weatherhill, 1974.

Corbett, Vincent. *Reminiscences: An Autobiographical and Diplomatic of Sir Vincent Corbett.* London: Hodder & Stoughton, 1927.

Coveney, James. "Training Linguists for International Organizations." *Babel,* vol. XXII, no. 3, 1976.

Craig, Gordon A., and Felix, Gilbert. *The Diplomats 1919–1939.* Princeton, N.J.: Princeton University Press, 1953.

Craig, Gordon A. *From Bismarck to Adenauer; Aspects of German Statecraft.* New York: Harper & Row, 1965.

Cross, Samuel Hazzard, and Sherbowitz-Wetzor, Olgerd P. (trans. and eds.). *The Russian Primary Chronicle,* Laurentian text. Cambridge, Mass.: Crimson Pub. Co., 1953. (Medieval Academy of America, Publication no. 60).

Crowley, Edward L. (ed.). *The Soviet Diplomatic Corps 1917–1967.* Metuchen, N.J.: Scarecrow Press, 1970.

Cutting, G.P. *English Diplomatic Administration 1259–1339.* Oxford, England: Clarendon Press, 1971.

Daniel, Norman. *The Arabs and Medieval Europe.* London: Longman, 1975.

D'Auvergne, Edmund B. *Envoys Extraordinary.* London: Geo. B. Harrap & Co., 1937.

De Bary, William Theodore. "Translation: An Indispensable Art." *Translation 73,* vol. I, no. 1, Winter 1973.

Demosthenes. *De Corona* and *De Falso Legation.*

"Diary of an Official of the Bakufu." *Transactions of the Asia Society of Japan,* 2nd ser., vol. VII.

Diener, Bertha. *Imperial Byzantium,* trans. Eden and Cedar Paul. Boston: Little, Brown, 1938.

Dionne, N.E. *Champlain, Founder of Quebec, Father of New France.* Toronto: University of Toronto Press, 1963.

The Diplomat (the periodical).

Doder, Dusko. "Chinese Jail Term Ends for American." *Washington Post,* Dec. 17, 1977.

Dollmann, Eugen. *The Interpreter, Memoirs of Doktor Eugen Dollmann,* trans. J. Maxwell Brown John. London: Hutchinson & Co., 1967.

Doucet, Michel. "Le Service linguistique de la Cour de justice des Communautés européenes." *Babel,* vol. XV, no. 1, 1969.

Dove, C. Clayton. *Marcus Aurelius Antoninus: His Life and Times.* London: Watts, 1930.

Dozy, Reinhard. *Spanish Islam; A History of the Moslems in Spain.* London: Frank Cass, 1972.

Drake, Samuel G. *Indian Captivities, or Life in the Wigwam* (Auburn, 1851). Reprinted by AMS Press, New York, 1975.

Duggan, Alfred. *King of Pontus: The Life of Mithridates Eupator.* New York: Coward McCann, 1959.

Durant, Will. *The Story of Civilization: Caesar and Christ.* New York: Simon & Schuster, 1944.

Duyvendak, J.J. *China's Discovery of Africa.* London: Arthur Probsthain, 1948.

Dvornik, Francis. *Byzantine Missions Among the Slavs, Ss. Constantine-Cyril and Methodius.* New Brunswick, N.J.: Rutgers University Press, 1970.

Eagleton, Clyde. "The Charter Adopted at San Francisco." *American Political Science Review,* vol. 39, Oct. 1945.

Ekvall, Robert B. *Faithful Echo.* New York: Twayne Publishers, 1960.

Ellis, George W., and Morris, John E. *King Philip's War.* New York: Grafton Press, 1906.

Elmandjra, Mahdi. *The United Nations System; An Analysis.* London: Faber & Faber, 1973.

Emmerson, John K. *The Japanese Thread; A Life in the U.S. Foreign Service.* New York: Holt, Rinehart & Winston, 1978.

Eversley, Lord, and Chirol, Valentine. *The Turkish Empire from 1288 to 1914.* New York: Howard Fertig, 1969.

Fairbank, John K. (ed.). *The Chinese World Order, Traditional China's Foreign Relations.* Cambridge, Mass.: Harvard University Press, 1968.

————. *East Asia: Tradition and Transformation.* Cambridge, Mass.: Harvard University Press, 1978.

Ferrando-Durfort, Denys. "L'enquête EPTI." *Babel,* vol. XX, no. 2, 1974. (Reprinted from *Traduire,* no. 76, Automne, 1973.)

Fischbach, Henry. "The American Translators Association; A Brief History." *Babel,* vol. XXII, no. 4, 1976.

Fiske, John. *New France and New England.* Boston: Houghton Mifflin, 1902.

Flavius, Josephus. *The Jewish War.*

Fleming, Thomas. "Freedom to Write." *Translation 73,* vol. I, no. 1, Winter 1973.

Franke, Wolfgang. *China and the West,* trans. R.A. Wilson. Columbia: University of South Carolina Press, 1967.

Frerk, Charles. "The Organization of Translation Services for International Congresses." *Babel,* vol. VI, no. 2, June, 1960.

Fulbright, William J. "My Turn." *Newsweek,* July 30, 1979.

Fulcher of Chartres. *A History of the Expedition to Jerusalem 1095-1127,* trans. Frances Rita Ryan. Knoxville: University of Tennessee Press, 1969.

Gabrieli, Francesco. *Muhammad and the Conquests of Islam,* trans. Virginia Luling and Rosamund Linell. New York: World University Library, 1968.

Ganshof, François L. *The Middle Ages; A History of International Relations.* New York: Harper & Row, 1970.

Garde-Chambonas, le Comte A. de la. *Anecdotal Recollections of the Congress of Vienna.* London: Chapman & Hall, 1902.

Gaselee, Stephen. *The Language of Diplomacy.* London: Bowes & Bowes, 1939.

Geanokoplos, Deno John. *Byzantine East and Latin West: Two Worlds of Christendom in the Middle Ages and Renaissance.* Hamden, Conn.: Archon Books, 1976.

_____. *Interaction of the 'Sibling' Byzantine and Western Cultures in the Middle Ages and Italian Renaissance (330-1600).* New Haven, Conn.: Yale University Press, 1976.

Gehman, Henry Snyder. *The Interpreters of Foreign Languages Among the Ancients.* Ph.D. dissertation, University of Pennsylvania, 1914.

Gerver, D. "The Effects of Source Language Presentation Rate on the Performance of Simultaneous Conference Reporters." In E. Foulke (ed.), *Proceedings of the 2nd Louisville Conference on Rate and/or Frequency Controlled Speech.* Louisville, Ky.: University of Louisville Press, 1969.

Gibson, Hugh. *Extracts from His Letters and Anecdotes to His Friends.* New York: Belgian American Educational Foundation, 1956.

Goetschalckx, J. "Translation, Terminology and Documentation in International Organizations." *Babel,* vol. XX, no. 3, 1974.

Gold, David L. "On Quality in Interpreting." *Babel,* vol. XIX, no. 3, 1973.

Goodrich, Leland M. "Geographical Distribution of the Staff of the UN Secretariat." *International Organization,* vol. XVI, no. 3, 1962.

Goodspeed, Stephen S. *The Nature and Function of International Organization.* New York: Oxford University Press, 1967.

Great Britain. Civil Service Commission. *Examinations of Officers of the Army in Modern Foreign Languages.* London: 1903.

_____. _____. *Open Competition for the Civil Service of India.* London: Aug. 1903.

_____. _____. *Open Competition for the Situation of Student Interpreter in China, Japan or Siam.* London: July, 1903.

_____. Foreign Office. Historical Section. *Peace Handbook,* vol. XIII, no. 81, *Macao,* 1920.

Greene, J. Evarts. "Our Dealings with the Indians." In *Proceedings of the American Antiquarian Society,* n.s. vol. XI (April 1896-1897), 1898.

Grew, Joseph C. *Turbulent Era; A Diplomatic Record of Forty Years.* Boston: Houghton Mifflin, 1952.

Griffis, William Elliot. *Townsend Harris, First American Envoy to Japan.* Boston: Houghton Mifflin, 1896.

Grunebaum, Gustave E. von. *Medieval Islam, A Study in Cultural Orientation.* Chicago: University of Chicago Press, 1954.

Gubbins, J.H. *The Making of Modern Japan.* Philadelphia: J.B. Lippincott, 1922.

Hackworth, Green Haywood (ed.). *Digest of International Law,* vol. IV. Washington, D.C., 1941-1942.

Hane, Mikiso. *Japan, a Historical Survey.* New York: Charles Scribner's Sons, 1972.

Hankey, Maurice. "Diplomacy by Conference." In *Proceedings of the British Institute of International Affairs,* London, Nov. 2, 1920.

Harley, John Eugene. *Selected Documents and Material for the Study of International Law and Relations.* Los Angeles: Times-Mirror Press, 1926.

Harris, Whitney R. *Tyranny on Trial; The Evidence at Nuremburg.* Dallas: Southern Methodist University Press, 1954.

Haskins, C.H. *Studies in the History of Medieval Science.* Cambridge, Mass.: Harvard University Press, 1927.

Hawks, Francis L. *Narrative of the Expedition of an American Squadron to the China Seas and Japan.* New York: Coward McCann, 1952.

Hayes, Carlton J. *Wartime Mission in Spain, 1942–1945.* New York: Da Capo Press, 1976.

Heckewelder, John. *History, Manner and Customs of the Indian Nations.* Philadelphia: Historical Society of Pennsylvania, 1876.

Heeren, A.H.L. *Historical Researches into the Politics, Intercourse and Trade of the Carthaginians, Ethiopians and Egyptians* (Oxford, England, 1832). Reprinted by Negro Universities Press, New York, 1959.

Helps, Arthur. *The Spanish Conquest in America.* New York: AMS Press, 1966.

Hemming, Don. *The Conquest of the Incas.* New York: Harcourt Brace Jovanovich, 1970.

Henderson, John A. "Note-taking for Consecutive Interpreting." *Babel,* vol. XXII, no. 2, 1976.

Herbert, Jean. "How Conference Interpretation Grew." In *Proceedings of the Symposium on Language Interpretation and Communication.* San Giorgio Maggiore, Venice, Sept. 26–Oct. 1, 1977. David Gerver and H. Wallace Sinaiko (eds.), New York: Plenum Press, 1977.

_____. *The Interpreters' Handbook.* Geneva: University of Geneva, School of Interpreters, 1952.

Herodotus. *History of the Greek and Persian War.*

Hertslet, Geoffrey P. *China Treaties.* London: H.M. Stationery Office, 1908.

Heusken, Henry. *Japan Journal 1855–1861,* trans. and ed. Jeannette C. van der Corput and Robert A. Wilson. New Brunswick, N.J.: Rutgers University Press, 1964.

Hill, Norman L. *International Administration.* New York: McGraw-Hill, 1931.

_____. *International Relations, Documents and Readings.* New York: Oxford University Press, 1950.

Hitti, Philip K. *The Arab Heritage,* ed. Nabim Amin Faris. New York: Russell & Russell, Inc., 1963.

_____. *History of the Arabs from the Earliest Times to the Present.* New York: St. Martin's Press, 1967.

_____. *Makers of Arab History.* New York: St. Martin's Press, 1968.

Holcombe, Chester. *The Real China.* New York: Dodd, Mead, 1895.

_____. *The Real Chinese Question.* New York: Dodd, Mead, 1900.

Holmes, T. Rice. *The Roman Republic and the Founder of the Empire.* Oxford, England: Clarendon Press, 1923.

Horgan, Paul. *Conquistadores in North American History.* New York: Farrar, Straus, 1963.

Horn, D.B. *The British Diplomatic Service 1689–1789.* Oxford, England: Clarendon Press, 1961.

Horwitz, Solis. "The Tokyo Trial." *International Conciliation,* no. 465, Nov. 1950.

Huáman Poma (Don Felipe Huáman Poma de Ayala). *Letter to a King: A Peruvian Chief's Account of Life Under the Incas and Under Spanish Rule.* New York: E.P. Dutton, 1978.

Hubbard, William. *The History of the Indian Wars in New England; From the First Settlement to the Termination of the War with King Philip in 1677* (Roxbury, 1865). Reprinted by Kraus Reprint Co., New York, 1969.

Hudson, Geoffrey F. *Europe and China; A Survey of Their Relations From the Earliest Times to 1800.* London: Edward Arnold & Co., 1931.

Hudson, Manley O. *International Legislation,* vol. I, 1912–1921. Washington, D.C.: Carnegie Endowment for International Peace, 1931.

_____. *The Permanent Court of International Justice.* New York: Macmillan, 1934.

Hunt, Gaillard. *The Department of State; Its History and Functions.* New Haven, Conn.: Yale University Press, 1914.

Ingram, Harold. *Arabia and the Isles.* New York: Frederick A. Praeger, 1966.

Iorga, N. *The Byzantine Empire,* trans. Allen H. Powles. London: Colston, 1927.

Jacobs, Wilbur R. *Wilderness Politics and Indian Gifts: The Northern Colonial Frontier, 1748–1763.* Lincoln: University of Nebraska Press, 1966.

Jones, Chester Lloyd. *The Consular Service of the United States, Its History and Activities.* Philadelphia: 1906 (University of Pennsylvania Series in Political Economy and Public Law, no. 18).

Jones, Ray. *The Nineteenth Century Foreign Office, an Administrative History.* London: London School of Economics and Political Science, 1971.

Joutel, Henri. *The Last Voyages Performed by de la Sale.* One edition (1955) is that available from University Microfilms, Ann Arbor, Mich.

Judd, Gerrit P. *A History of Civilization.* New York: Macmillan, 1966.

Kaufmann, Johan. *Conference Diplomacy; An Introductory Analysis.* Leyden: A.W. Sijthoff, 1970.

Kaznacheev, Aleksandr. *Inside a Soviet Embassy,* Simon Wolin, ed. Philadelphia: J.B. Lippincott, 1962.

Keene, Donald. *The Japanese Discovery of Europe, 1720–1830.* Stanford, Calif.: Stanford University Press, 1969.

Keeton, George W. "The International Status of Macao Before 1887." *Chinese Social and Political Science Review,* Public Documents Suppl., vol. XI, no. 1, 1927.

Kennan, George F. *Memoirs 1925–1950.* London: Hutchinson, 1968.

Kercheval, Samuel. *A History of the Valley of Virginia.* Strasburg, Va.: Shenandoah Pub. House, 1925.

Kertesz, Stephen D., and Fitsimmons, M.A. *Diplomacy in a Changing World.* South Bend, Ind.: University of Notre Dame Press, 1959.

Kirkpatrick, F.A. *The Spanish Conquistadores.* Cleveland: World Pub. Co., 1934.

Kitab, Futûh al Buldân. *The Origin of the Islamic State,* trans. Philip K. Hitti. New York: Columbia University (*Studies in History, Economics and Public Law,* vol. LXVIII, no. 163); reprinted by AMS Press, 1969.

Klay, Andor C. "Interpretive Diplomacy." *U.S. Foreign Service Journal,* vol. 36, no. 11, Nov. 1959.

Klibbe, Lawrence H. *James Russell Lowell's Residence in Spain, 1877–1880.* Newark, N.J.: Washington Irving Pub. Co., 1964.

Kluchevsky, Vasily Osipovich. *A History of Russia,* trans. C.J. Hogarth. London: J.M. Dent & Sons, 1960. 4 vols.

Kopczynski, Andrzej. "Conference Interpreting in Poland: An Overview of the Problems." *Babel,* vol. XXII, no. 3, 1976.

Kratchovil, Paul. *The Chinese Language Today.* London: Hutchinson, 1968.

Krosney, Herbert, and Mary Stewart. *Careers and Opportunities in International Service.* New York: E.P. Dutton, 1965.

Krüger, Fritz Konrad. *Government and Politics of the German Empire.* New York: World Book Co., 1915.

Kuo Sung T'ao, Hsi Hung, and Chang Te-yi. *The First Chinese Embassy to the West; The Journals of Kuo Sung T'ao, Hsi Hung and Chang Te-hi,* J.D. Frodsham, trans. London: Clarendon Press, 1974.

Labaree, Benjamin. *Colonial Massachusetts; A History.* Millwood: KTO Press, 1979.

Lach, Donald F. *Asia in the Making of Europe.* Chicago: Univ. of Chicago Press, 1965.

————. *India in the Eyes of Europe; The Sixteenth Century.* Chicago: University of Chicago Press, 1968.

————. *Japan in the Eyes of Europe; The Sixteenth Century.* Chicago: University of Chicago Press, 1968.

Lachs, Phyllis S. *The Diplomatic Corps Under Charles II and James II.* New Brunswick, N.J.: Rutgers University Press, 1965.

Lamberty, Guillaume de. *Memoires pour servir à l'histoire du XVIIIme siècle.*

Lane, Alexander. "Quelques Aspects de la terminologie juridique et administrative." *Babel,* vol. XV, no. 1, 1969.

————. "La Question des languages et la fonction publique internationale." *Babel,* vol. XI, no. 4, 1965.

Lauren, Paul Gordon. *Diplomats and Bureaucrats; The First Institutional Responses to Twentieth Century Diplomacy in France and Germany.* Stanford, Calif.: Hoover Institute Press, 1976.

Leacacos, John P. *Fires in the In-Basket; The ABC's of the State Department.* New York: World Pub. Co., 1968.

League of Nations. *The League Yearbook,* 3rd ed. (Judith Jackson and Stephen King-Hall, eds.). London: Ivor Nicholson & Watson, 1934.

Leary, Lewis. *That Rascal Freneau; A Study in Literary Failure.* New York: Octagon Books, 1964.

Lederer, Ivo J. (ed.). *Russian Foreign Policy, Essays in Historical Perspective.* New Haven, Conn.: Yale University Press, 1962.

Lewis, Bernard. *The Arabs in History.* London: Hutchinson, 1966.

Lewis, Naphtali, and Meyer, Reinhold, eds. *Roman Civilization; Selected Readings.* New York: Columbia University Press, 1951.

Linehan, Patrick E. *The Foreign Service Personnel System; An Organizational Analysis.* Boulder, Colo.: Westview Press, 1976.

Lisagor, Peter, and Higgins, Marguerite. *Overtime in Heaven: Adventures in the Foreign Service.* New York: Doubleday, 1965.

Liu, Pinghou C. *Chinese Foreign Affairs — Organization and Control.* Ph.D. dissertation, New York University, 1936.

Lochner, R.K. "Conference Interpretation and the Modern World." *Babel,* vol. XXII, no. 2, 1976.

Locke, William Nash, and Booth, A. Donald. *Machine Translation of Languages.* Cambridge, Mass.: MIT Press, 1955.

Lockhart, J.G. *The Peacemakers, 1814–1815.* London: Duckworth, 1932.

Longley, Patricia E. *Conference Interpreting.* London: Sir Isaac Pitman & Sons, 1968.

Loveday, A. *Reflections on International Administration.* Oxford: Clarendon Press, 1956.

McCarthy, Dennis J. *Treaty and Covenant, Analecta Biblica 21.* Rome: Pontifical Bible Institute, 1963.

Macmullen, Ramsay. *Constantine.* New York: Dial Press, 1969.

MacMurray, J. *Treaties and Agreements with and Concerning China.* New York: Oxford University Press, 1921.

Madariaga, Salvador de. *Hernán Cortés, Conqueror of Mexico.* Coral Gables, Fla.: University of Miami Press, 1942.

————. *The Rise of the Spanish Empire.* New York: Free Press, 1947.

Manchester, William. *American Caesar: Douglas Macarthur 1880–1864.* New York: Dell Pub. Co., 1978.

Marquette, Jacques. *Voyages of Marquette* in the Jesuit Relations 59. Available from University Microfilms, Ann Arbor, Mich.

Marsh, Philip M. *Philip Freneau, Poet and Journalist.* Minneapolis: Dillon Press, 1967.

Martin, William Alexander. *A Cycle of Cathay; or, China South and North.* New York: Fleming H. Revell, 1896.

Mathieu, George J. "Words Before Peace." *United Nations World,* Jan., 1949.

Mattingly, Garrett. *Renaissance Diplomacy.* Boston: Houghton Mifflin, 1955.

Maynard, Theodore. *De Soto and the Conquistadores.* New York: AMS Press, 1969.

Means, Philip Ainsworth. *Fall of the Inca Empire and the Spanish Rule in Peru: 1530–1780.* New York: Gordian Press, 1964.

Meiern, J.G. *Acta Pacis Westphaliae Publica.* Hannover and Tübingen, 1736.

Mende, Elsie Porter. *An American Soldier and Diplomat.* New York: Frederick A. Stokes, 1927.

Meng, S.M. *The Tsungli Yamen: Its Origin and Functions.* Cambridge, Mass.: Harvard University Press, 1962.

Meron, Theodore. *The United Nations Secretariat; The Rules and Practices.* Lexington, Mass.: D.C. Heath, 1977.

Meyer, Arnold Oskar. *Die Englische Diplomatie in Deutschland zur Zeit Edwards VI und Mariens.* Breslau: Kommissions Verlag von M. & H. Marcus, 1900.

Miller, Dean A. *Imperial Constantinople.* New York: John A. Wiley Sons, 1969.
Moorhouse, Geoffrey. *The Diplomats: The Foreign Office Today.* London: Jonathan Cape, 1977.
Morison, Samuel Eliot. *The Parkman Reader; From the Works of Francis Parkman.* Boston: Little, Brown, 1955.
_____. *Samuel Champlain, Father of New France.* Boston: Little, Brown, 1972.
_____. *The Story of 'Old Colony' of New Plymouth (1620–1692).* New York: Alfred A. Knopf, 1956.
Morse, Hosea Ballou. *The International Relations of the Chinese Empire, The Period of Conflict, 1834–1860.* London: Longmans, Green, 1910.
Mosley, D.J. *Envoys and Diplomacy in Ancient Greece.* Wiesbaden: Franz Steiner Verlag, 1973.
Mulkearn, Lois. "Half King, Seneca Diplomat of the Ohio Valley." *Western Pennsylvanian Historical Magazine,* vol. 37, no. 2, 1954.
Muttalib, M.A. *The Union Public Safety Commission.* New Delhi: Indian Institute of Public Administration, 1967.
National Academy of Sciences. Division of Behavioral Sciences. *Language and Machines: Computers in Translation and Linguistics.* A Report by the Automatic Language Processing Advisory Committee, National Research Council, 1966.
Nicolson, Harold. *Diplomacy.* London: Oxford University Press, 1963.
_____. *The Evolution of Diplomatic Method.* London: Constable, 1954.
_____. *Peacemaking 1919.* London: Constable, 1934.
Nilsson, Martin P. *Imperial Rome,* trans. Rev. G.C. Richards, D.D. New York: Harcourt, Brace, n.d.
Norman, Henry. *The Real Japan; Studies of Contemporary Japanese Manners, Morals, Administration and Politics.* London: Fisher Unwin, 1891.
Norton, Henry Kittredge. *Foreign Office Organization.* Suppl. to vol. CXLIII of *Annals of the American Academy of Political and Social Science,* May, 1920.
Norwich, John Julius. *The Other Conquest.* New York: Harper & Row, 1961.
Numelin, Ragnar. *The Beginnings of Diplomacy; A Sociological Study of Intertribal and International Relations.* New York: Philosophical Library, 1950.
Obolenski, Dimitri. *The Byzantium Commonwealth: Eastern Europe 500–1453.* New York: Praeger Publishers, 1971.
Oldenbourg, Zoé. *The Crusades,* trans. Anne Carter. New York: Pantheon Books, 1966.
Oliva, L. Jay. *Russia and the West from Peter to Khrushchev.* Boston: D.C. Heath, 1965.
Oliver, Robert T. *Culture and Communication: The Problem of Penetrating National and Cultural Boundaries.* Springfield, Ill.: Charles C. Thomas, 1962.
Olmstead, A.T. *History of the Persian Empire, Achaeminid Period.* Chicago: University of Chicago Press, 1948.
O'Malley, L.S.S. *The Indian Civil Service 1601–1930.* London: John Murray, 1931.
Ostrogorsky, George. *History of the Byzantine State,* trans. Joan Hussey. New Brunswick, N.J.: Rutgers University Press, 1969.
Ostrower, Alexander. *Language, Law and Diplomacy; A Study of Linguistic Diversity in International Relations and International Law.* Philadelphia: University of Pennsylvania Press, 1965.
Paneth, Eva. "Friedrich von Gentz—A Patron of Translators?" *Babel,* vol. III, no. 2, June, 1957.
Pares, Bernard. *A History of Russia.* New York: Alfred A. Knopf, 1968.
Pastuhov, Vladimir, D. *A Guide to the Practice of International Conferences.* Washington, D.C.: Carnegie Endowment for International Peace, 1945.
Payne, Robert. "The Possibility of Translation." *Translation 73,* vol. I, no. 1, Winter 1973.
Pears, Edwin. *The Destruction of the Greek Empire and the Story of the Capture of Constantinople by the Turks.* London: Longmans, Green, 1903.
Pei, Mario. *One Language for the World.* New York: Devin-Adair, 1958.
_____. *The Story of Language.* Philadelphia: J.B. Lippincott, 1965.

Perez-Peix, Alvaro D'ors. "Estudios sobre la Constitutio Antoniniana." *Emerita* (Madrid), vol. XI, 1943.

Perkins, Dexter. *A History of the Monroe Doctrine.* Boston: Little, Brown, 1963.

Philipson, Coleman. *The International Law and Customs of Ancient Greece and Rome.* London: Macmillan, 1931.

Picard, Gilbert Charles. *The Life and Death of Carthage,* trans. Dominique Collon. New York: Taplinger Pub. Co., 1969.

Piccigallo, Philip R. *The Japanese on Trial: Allied War Crimes Operations in the East, 1945-1951.* Austin: University of Texas Press, 1979.

Pilley, A.T. "The Multilingual Parliaments of Asia." *Babel,* vol. VIII, no. 1, 1962.

Piron, Claude, and Tonkin, Humphrey. *Translation in International Organizations.* Rotterdam: Universal Esperanto Association, 1979 (*Esperanto Documents,* n.s., no. 20A).

Platt, D.C.M. *The Cinderella Service, British Consuls Since 1825.* London: Longman, 1971.

Plischke, Elmer. *Conduct of American Diplomacy,* 3d ed. Princeton, N.J.: D. Van Nostrand Co., 1967.

Plutarch. *Lives.*

_____. *Plutarchus.*

Pohl, Frederick J. *Amerigo Vespucci: Pilot Major.* New York: Octagon Books, 1966.

Prescott, W.H. *The History of the Conquest of Mexico,* ed. C. Harvey Gardiner. Chicago: University of Chicago Press, 1966.

Pritchard, Earl H. "Confusion About Portuguese and Other Europeans in Early Ch'ing China: A Case of Cultural Blindness." *International Symposium on the History of Eastern and Western Cultural Contacts.* Tokyo: Japanese National Commission for UNESCO, 1959.

Pritchard, John. "The Nature and Significance of British Postwar Trials of Japanese War Criminals, 1945-1948." *Proceedings of the British Association for Japanese Studies.* Sheffield, England: University Centre of Japanese Studies, 1976.

Proceedings of the Council of Four, Paris Peace Conference, 1919. Paris: L'Institut Universitaire de Hautes Études Internationales, Publication no. 43.

Purves, Chester. *The Internal Administration of an International Secretariat.* London: Royal Institute of International Affairs, 1945.

Quinn, Eileen Moore. "Bloody Banners of the Buccaneers." *Key West Classic,* vol. 2, no. 1, 1981.

Raditi, Edouard. "Hans Jacob, 1896-1961." *Babel,* vol. II, no. 2, 1961.

Ranshofen-Wertheimer, Egon F. *The International Secretariat.* Washington, D.C.: Carnegie Endowment for International Peace, 1925.

Read, Jan. *The Moors in Spain and Portugal.* London: Faber & Faber, 1974.

Reichel, William C. (ed.). *Memorials of the Moravian Church.* Philadelphia: J.B. Lippincott, 1870.

Reischauer, Edwin O. et al. *Japan, the Changing Tradition: A Study Guide* for the course "Japan." Lincoln: University of Mid-America, 1978.

Reychman, Jan. "Une Famille de drogmans orientaux en Pologne au XVIII siècle." *Rocznik Orientalistyczny* (Warsaw), vol. XXV, no. 1, 1961.

Ricci, Matteo. *China in the Sixteenth Century: the Journals of Matteo Ricci 1583-1610,* trans. Louis J. Gallagher, S.J. New York: Random House, 1953.

Richard, Bill. "Near the Pole, Eskimos Ponder Political Unity." *Washington Post,* June 14, 1975.

Richardson, Linda. "Translating Your Language Skills into $35,000 a Year." *Ms.,* Nov., 1979.

Rigby, T.H. *Lenin's Government: Sovnarkom, 1917-1922.* Cambridge, England: Cambridge University Press, 1979.

Ripa, Matteo. *Memoirs of Father Ripa, During Thirteen Years Residence at the Court of Peking in the Service of the Emperor of China,* trans. Fortunato Prandi. London: John Murray, 1861.

Robertson, A.H. *The Council of Europe: Its Structure, Functions and Achievements.* New York: Frederick A. Praeger, 1956.

Roetter, Charles. *The Diplomatic Art; An Informal History of World Diplomacy.* Philadelphia: Macrae Smith, 1963.

Roosen, William James. *The Age of Louis XIV, The Rise of Modern Diplomacy.* Cambridge: Schenkman Pub. Co., 1976.

Roosevelt, Eleanor and DeWitt, William. *UN: Today and Tomorrow.* New York: Harper & Bros., 1953.

Rossi, Salvatore. "Quando Cattone il Censore Apprese la lingua Greca." Messina: Atti della R. Accademia Peloritana, Tipografia D'Amico, Anno XVI, 1902-03.

Rosten, Leo. "Diversions." *Saturday Review World.* April 6, 1974.

Roudybush, Franklin. *Diplomatic Language.* Basle: SATZ + Repro AG, 1972.

Roumigière, Henriette. *Le Français dans les relations diplomatiques.* Berkeley: University of California Press, 1926.

Russell, Bertrand. "Logical Positivism." *Revue Internationale de Philosophie,* vol. IV, 1950.

Russell, of Liverpool, Lord. *The Knights of Bushido; A Short History of Japanese War Crimes.* London: Cassell, 1958.

Sallustius, Crispus C. *The Conspiracy of Catiline and the War of Jugurtha.*

Satow, Ernest. *A Diplomat in Japan.* London: Seeley, Service, 1921.

_____. *A Guide to Diplomatic Practice.* London: Longmans, Green, 1932.

_____. *International Congresses.* London: H.M. Stationery Office, 1920.

Saunders, J.J. *A History of Medieval Islam.* London: Routledge & Kegan Paul, 1966.

Savory, Theodore (ed.). *The Art of Translation.* Boston: "The Writer," 1968.

Schmidt, Dr. Paul. *Hitler's Interpreter,* ed. R.H. Steed. New York: Macmillan, 1951.

Schwartz, Hans. "Legal and Administrative Language." *Babel,* vol. XXIII, 1977.

Scott-Kilvert, Ian (trans.). *The Rise and Fall of Athens: Nine Greek Lives.* Harmondsworth, England: Penguin Classics, 1960.

Senn, Alfred Erich. *Readings in Russian Political and Diplomatic History.* Homewood, Ill.: Dorsey Press, 1966.

Severin, Timothy. *Explorers of the Mississippi.* New York: Alfred A. Knopf, 1968.

Sheean, Vincent. "An Error in Translation." *United Nations World,* Sept. 1947.

Shenton, Herbert Newhard. *Cosmopolitan Conversation, the Language Problems of International Conferences.* New York: Columbia University Press, 1933.

Sherif, June L. *Careers in Foreign Languages; A Handbook.* New York: Regents Pub. Co., 1975.

Signoret, Simone. *Nostalgia Isn't What It Used to Be.* New York: Harper & Row, 1978.

Smith, Denis Mack. *A History of Sicily, Medieval Sicily 806-1713.* New York: Viking Press, 1968.

Smith, Walter Bedell. *My Three Years in Moscow.* Philadelphia: J.B. Lippincott, 1950.

"Some Earlier Embassies to China." Peking: *The Peiping Chronicle,* no. 14, July, 1935.

Sousa, Nasim. *The Capitulatory Regime of Turkey: Its History, Origins and Nature.* Baltimore: Johns Hopkins Press, 1933.

Spaulding, Robert M., Jr. *Imperial Japan's Higher Civil Service Examinations.* Princeton, N.J.: Princeton University Press, 1967.

Speer, Percival. *India; A Modern History.* Ann Arbor: University of Michigan Press, 1961.

Spiel, Hilde (ed.). *The Congress of Vienna, An Eyewitness Account,* trans. Richard H. Weber. Philadelphia: Chilton Book Co., 1966.

Steiner, George. *After Babel: Aspects of Language and Translation.* London: Oxford University Press, 1975.

Steiner, T.R. *English Translation Theory 1650-1800.* Amsterdam: Van Gorcum Press, 1975.

Steiner, Zara. *The Foreign Office and Foreign Policy 1898-1914.* Cambridge, England: Cambridge University Press, 1969.

Stockton, Charles H. *Outlines of International Law.* New York: Scribner's, 1914.

Strabo. *The Geography.*

Strang, Lord. *The Foreign Office.* London: George Allen & Unwin, 1957.

Stuart, Graham H. *American Diplomatic and Consular Practice.* New York: D. Appleton-Century, 1936.

_____. *The Department of State; A History of Its Organization, Procedure and Personnel.* New York: Macmillan, 1949.

Suetonius Tranquillus, C. *The Lives of the Twelve Caesars.*

Sulte, Benjamin. "Les Interprètes du temps de Champlain." *Royal Society of Canada, Proceedings and Transactions,* vol. I (1882–1883). Montreal: Dawson Bros., 1883.

Sweet, Paul R. *Friedrich von Gentz.* Madison: University of Wisconsin Press, 1941.

Swift, Richard W. "Personnel Problems and the United Nations Secretariat." *International Organization,* vol. XI, no. 2, 1957.

Sykes, Percy. *The Quest for Cathay.* London: A. & C. Black, 1936.

Taylor, Bayard. *The Unpublished Letters of Bayard Taylor in the Huntington Library.* San Marino, Calif., 1937.

Teng, Ssu-yu, and Fairbank, John K. et al. *China's Response to the West; A Documentary Survey, 1839–1923.* New York: Atheneum, 1967.

Thass-Thienemann, Theodore. *The Interpretation of Language.* New York: Jason Aronson, 1973.

Thayer, Charles Wheeler. *Diplomat.* New York: Harper & Row, 1959.

Thomas, Bertram. *The Arabs.* London: Thornton Butterworth, 1966.

Thwaites, Reuben Gold. *France in America, 1497–1763.* New York: Cooper Square Publishers, 1968.

Tilley, John, and Gaselee, Stephen. *The Foreign Office.* London: G.P. Putnam's Sons, 1933.

Torrens, Henry W. *A Selection from the Writings, Prose and Poetical, of the Late Henry W. Torrens, Esq.,* James Hume, ed. Calcutta: R.C. LePage, 1854.

Toynbee, Arnold. *Constantine Porphyrogenitus and His World.* London: Oxford University Press, 1973.

Trevelyan, Humphrey. *Diplomatic Channels.* London: Macmillan, 1973. United Nations. *Yearbook.*

U.S. Department of State. *Agreement for the Establishment of an International Military Tribunal, Charter of the International Military Tribunal.* Washington, D.C.: U.S. Gov. Printing Office, 1945 (Dept. of State Publication 2420).

_____. _____. *Trial of Japanese War Criminals.* Washington, D.C.: U.S. Gov. Printing Office, 1946 (Dept. of State Publication no. 3613).

_____. House of Representatives, 33d Congress, 2nd Session. *Narrative of the Expedition of an American Squadron to the China Seas and Japan, Performed in the Years 1852, 1853 and 1854, Under the Command of Commodore M.C. Perry.* Washington, D.C.: A.O.P. Nicholson, 1856.

Vacalopoulos, Apostolos E. *The Greek Nation, 1453–1669.* New Brunswick, N.J.: Rutgers University Press, 1976.

Vaughan, Dorothy M. *Europe and the Turk; A Pattern of Alliances, 1350–1700.* Liverpool: University of Liverpool Press, 1954.

Villard, Henry Serrano. *Affairs at State.* New York: Thos. Y. Crowell, 1969.

Villehardouin and de Joinville. *Memoires of the Crusades,* trans. Sir Frank T. Marzials. New York: E.P. Dutton, 1958.

Vryonis, Speros, Jr. "The Byzantine Legacy and Ottoman Forms." Washington: Center for Byzantine Studies, 1969–1970 (*Dumbarton Oaks* Paper nos. 23–24).

Walworth, Arthur. *Black Ships Off Japan; The Story of Commodore Perry's Expedition.* Hamden: Archon Books, 1966.

Warmington, B.H. *Carthage.* London: Robert Hale, 1960.

Washington, George. *The Writings of George Washington; From the Original Manuscript Sources, 1745–1799,* John C. Fitzpatrick, ed. Washington, D.C.: U.S. Gov. Printing Office, 1931. 14 vol.

Webster, Charles. *The Congress of Vienna, 1814–1815.* New York: Barnes & Noble, 1963.

Wehberg, Dr. Hans (trans. Charles C. Fenwick). *The Problem of an International Court of Justice.* Oxford: Clarendon Press, 1918.

Weinstein, Brian. "Francophonie: A Language-based Movement in World Politics." *International Organization,* vol. 30, no. 3, 1976.

West, Rachel. *The Department of State on the Eve of the First World War.* Athens: University of Georgia Press, 1978.

Wheeler-Holohan, V. *The History of the King's Messengers.* New York: n.p., n.d.

Whitcomb, Edward A. *Napoleon's Diplomatic Service.* Durham, N.C.: Duke University Press, 1979.

Whitley, A.F. *The Tremulous Hero: The Age and Life of Cicero.* London: Pallas Pub. Co., 1939.

Wieruszowski, Helene. *Politics and Culture in Medieval Spain and Italy.* Rome: Edizioni di Storia e Letteratura, 1971.

Wild, Norman. "Materials for the Study of the Ssui-kuan (Bureau of Translators)." London: University of London, School of Oriental and African Studies, 1945 (*Bulletin,* vol. XI, part 3).

Wilson, Francis Graham. *Labor in the League System; A Study of the International Labor Organization in Relation to International Administration.* Stanford, Calif.: Stanford University Press, 1934.

Wilson, Henry Lane. *Diplomatic Episodes in Mexico, Belgium and Chile.* Garden City, N.Y.: Doubleday, 1927.

Wolff, Helen. "Translator and Publisher." *Translation 73,* 1973.

Wolkomir, Richard. "A Manic Professor Tries to Close the Language Gap." *Smithsonian,* May, 1980.

Wright, Arthur F. *Studies in Chinese Thought.* Chicago: University of Chicago Press, 1953.

Wright, Louis B. (ed.). *The Elizabethan's America.* Cambridge, Mass.: Harvard University Press, 1965.

Wu, Aitchen K. *China and the Soviet Union; A Study of Sino–Soviet Relations.* Port Washington, N.Y.: Kennikat Press, 1950.

Xenophon. *The Whole Works.*

Yngve, Victor. "Implications of Mechanical Translation Research." *Proceedings of the American Philosophical Society,* no. 108, 1964.

Young, Alexander (ed.). *Chronicles of the Pilgrim Fathers of the Colony of Plymouth From 1602 to 1625.* Boston: Charles C. Little and James Brown, 1841.

Younger, Edward. *John A. Kasson.* Iowa City: State Historical Society of Iowa, 1955.

Index

175